FIRM FOUNDATIONS

A Chronicle of Toronto's
Metropolitan United Church
and Her Methodist Origins
1795 - 1984

Judith St. John

Metropolitan United Church
1988

Canadian Cataloguing in Publication Data
St. John, Judith
  Firm Foundations

  Includes index.
  ISBN 0-919599-55-9

  1. Metropolitan United Church (Toronto,
Ont.) - History. I. Title.
BX9882.8.T674S24 1988   287'.92'09713541
                          C88-091099-2

Cover design and page makeup: James Taylor
Cover photo: Harriet Smith
Other photographs: listed and acknowledged on pages 204-206

produced by
Wood Lake Books Inc.,
Box 700,
Winfield, B.C., Canada V0H 2C0

for the
Metropolitan United Church
51 Bond St.,
Toronto, Canada M5B 1X1

Printed in Canada by
Friesen Printers,
Altona, Man. R0G 0B0

CONTENTS

ACKNOWLEDGEMENTS

Although I am grateful to all writers of the books, pamphlets, articles, reports, newsletters, and minutes, who provided the source material for this book, I am especially grateful to the Reverend Dr. C. Glenn Lucas for access to his unpublished manuscript, and to Edith G. Firth, the editor and compiler of *The Town of York*, published in two volumes by the University of Toronto Press. These works not only supplied information, they directed me to some quotations and sources which I should not have otherwise located.

I should like to thank the members and friends of the Metropolitan who answered my questions and willingly placed their memories at my disposal. I am grateful to the members of the Committee for their patient support and to the staff of the United Church Archives for kind and efficient service.

Judith St. John

FOREWORD

Approximately ten years ago, the late Dr. John McIntosh initiated and launched a project for the publication of a history of this congregation, and contacted the United Church's Archivist-Historian, the Reverend Glenn Lucas, for his counsel and assistance. We are indebted to Dr. Lucas for his knowledge and advice through the years, although we accept full responsibility for this history, which is inevitably an interpretation of what happened in the past.

We hope that you will find this book not only informative, which it is, but also a stimulating story of men and women, old and young, who found in this church, or its earlier places of worship, spiritual and moral guidance as well as human fellowship. For serious students of our history, a Bibliography is available from the Church Office.

Our deep gratitude is owed to several people—to Mrs. Mary Jackman, who contributed the funds necessary to finance the project and assisted with her knowledge and support through the years, to Miss Judith St. John who, as a labour of love, worked for months researching and writing this volume, bringing to it the care of a historian and the enthusiasm of a warmly stimulating Christian, and to Mrs. Marion Moore, who contributed many hours of her time and ability with her word processor to facilitate the production of the final manuscript.

The members of the Committee through the ten years were John and Molly Bryce, Joyce Anne Cumings, Mary Jackman, Anne Litherland, Dr. John McIntosh (deceased), Ruth Peckover, Fred Stinson, Dr. Bascom St. John (deceased), Judith St. John, Austin Thompson (deceased), and Isabel Uren. My thanks are recorded for their individual and invaluable help.

There is no list of Ministers or other officials and leaders, whether staff or volunteer, who moulded the life of this church, since such lists would be longer than the book itself. To all such unnamed persons of past years we to-day record our thanks.

Frank Brisbin
Chairperson
History Book Committee
1983-1987

❁

In 1979, the Official Board of the Metropolitan Church warmly endorsed a proposal that the Historical Book, when published, be dedicated to the memory of the late Dr. John McIntosh, who provided such initial impetus and inspiration for the project. The present committee members fully agree, and wish to so dedicate this book in grateful appreciation.

Dr. John McIntosh

INTRODUCTION

The Metropolitan, before entering the United Church of Canada on 10 June 1925, was a Methodist Church, the successor of the first Methodist Chapel in the town of York, as Toronto was called before 1834.

John Wesley, with his brother Charles, was the acknowledged leader of the first Methodist Societies of England. These brothers were the sons of the Reverend Samuel Wesley, the faithful Anglican rector of Epworth parish in Lincolnshire. Their paternal grandfather was a Nonconformist preacher who had been imprisoned for refusing to use *The Book of Common Prayer*. Their maternal grandfather, the respected Dr. Samuel Annesley, was known as the St. Paul of Nonconformists. In 1689, his daughter, Susannah Annesley, became the wife of the Reverend Samuel Wesley. They had nineteen children, eight of whom died in infancy.

John Wesley, the fifteenth child, was born in 1703. When he was five years old, the Epworth rectory was destroyed by fire. John, asleep in the attic, had been forgotten until he appeared at a window and was, he often said, 'a brand plucked from the burning'. His devout and devoted mother wrote: 'I do intend to be particularly careful of the soul of this child, that Thou hast so mercifully provided for.'

Robert Southey referred to Susannah Wesley as 'the Mother of Methodism'. She presided over a well-ordered household, managed by rules to prevent 'hurry and worry'. She found time to teach her own children and to give instruction, as well, to the children of their rough parishioners.

John Wesley was sent to Charterhouse School in London, and from there was admitted to Christ Church, Oxford, as an 'exhibitioner from

Charterhouse'. He was ordained in 1725. His scholastic studies were so successful that he became a member of the faculty and a Lincoln College Fellow in 1726, at the age of twenty-three. He became active as the Leader of the Holy Club, founded by his brother, Charles, in 1729. This group of young men studied the New Testament, observed rules of prayer and fasting, visited the needy and the imprisoned, and attended weekly Communion services. Their lives were so methodical, with time-tables for each day of the week, that the Holy Club members were derisively named 'Methodists' by their worldly associates.

After his father's death, and after fifteen years as an Oxford Scholar, John Wesley, who was discouraged in his faith, volunteered to go, with his brother Charles, on a Mission to Georgia, under the auspices of the Society for the Propagation of the Gospel. During the stormy crossing of the Atlantic, John Wesley was impressed with the conduct of a group of Moravians who cheerfully sang during the hurricane. Wesley envied their faith which cast out fear.

The expedition to Georgia was unsuccessful. Charles Wesley returned to England the next year because of ill health. John formed, in 1736, a Society of about thirty or forty people which met once a week. It is claimed as the second Methodist Society to be formed.

Wesley returned to England in 1738 disturbed and disappointed. His faith was strengthened by a visit to his Moravian friends. On 24 May 1738, at a small gathering in Aldersgate Street, London, he felt 'his heart strangely warmed'. He wrote:

> I feel I did, at that moment, trust in Christ, and in Christ alone, for my salvation. . . . I then testified openly to all there what I now first felt in my heart.

His brother, Charles, had undergone conversion the day before. They set out to tell of the transforming power of Christ to the millions of people who were outside the Church.

The Church of England had been severely weakened during the 'Age of Reason' of the eighteenth century. Although some clergymen, like the Reverend Samuel Wesley, were devout and compassionate, many were indifferent and often neither lived in nor visited their parishes. John and Charles Wesley preached in the pulpits that were open to them but many of the clergy refused them this privilege after their conversion.

George Whitefield, an eloquent preacher who had been a member of the Holy Club, went to Bristol in February 1739. When he found the churches closed to him, he began to preach in the open air. He urged John Wesley to come to work with him. It was difficult for Wesley to decide to

John Wesley

preach outside a church, but on 2 April 1739 he 'proclaimed in the hedgeways the glad tidings of salvation' to about three thousand people. He realized that this was the only way to meet the multitudes.

That year, John Wesley began to record the events of his busy life in his *Journal* which the historian, Augustine Birrell, described as 'the most amazing record of human exertion every penned by man'. During his long life, Wesley rose every morning at four o'clock, preached an average of sixteen times a week and annually rode on horseback about eight thousand miles.

The foundation stone of the first Methodist 'preaching house' was laid on 12 May 1739. Because nonconformists were forbidden to erect churches, Wesley's 'preaching houses' were all equipped with fireplaces to make them 'houses', legally. John Wesley organized weekly class meetings made up of about twelve people, with Leaders to look after their spiritual welfare. He instituted Love Feasts, modelled on the agape of the early Church. He realized that the fellowship of the Last Supper in the Upper Room had not been retained in services of Holy Communion. Love Feasts were held quarterly with admission by Society tickets issued to class members in good standing. With his brother, Charles, John Wesley introduced testimonies given in public and in private; they encouraged prayer meetings and watchnights. Stewards were appointed to look after finances.

John and Charles Wesley drew up *Rules of the Society of the People Called Methodists* in 1743. The sixty rules were divided into three sections. The first had rules against such evils as profaning the Lord's Day, drunkenness, fighting, quarrelling, brawling, brother going to law with brother, returning evil for evil, unprofitable conversation, particularly speaking evil of ministers, laying up treasures upon earth and borrowing without a probability of paying. Each rule was accompanied by the biblical authority. John Wesley in a Letter succinctly summed up the nineteen positive rules of conduct set forth in the second part:

> Do all the good you can
> By all the means you can
> In all the ways you can
> In all the places you can
> At all the times you can
> As long as ever you can.

The rules of the third section were 'expected of all who desire to continue in these Societies': they should attend public worship, partake of Holy Communion, engage in family and private prayer, in 'searching the scriptures' and in fasting and abstinence.

Wesley had compassion for the bodily comfort of the poor of England, as well as concern for their souls. He established a school, an orphanage, a Loan Society, a Labour Bureau, a Strangers' Friend Society and a Methodist Book Room to provide suitable reading material. He protested against war and the liquor traffic and supported Wilberforce in his efforts to stop the slave trade.

Charles Wesley became the outstanding Christian hymn-writer, expressing Christian convictions in hymns that made Methodists a 'singing people'. He gave to Christendom such hymns as 'Christ the Lord is Risen Today', 'Jesu, Lover of my Soul', and 'Hark the Herald Angels Sing'. John Wesley translated hymns from the German and Latin and adapted some of Isaac Watts' hymns, such as 'I'll Praise my Maker, While I've Breath' and 'Before Jehovah's Awful Throne'.

John Wesley travelled all over England, Wales, and Cornwall. He made the first of forty-two trips to Ireland in 1749 and the first of twenty-two visits to Scotland in 1752. When he was in Ireland he visited a colony of German Protestants who had fled from the Palatinate in 1709 and had been placed on the Southwell Estate near Limerick. Philip Embury and his cousin Barbara Ruckle, who later married Paul Heck, were converted. In 1760 they, with other members of that community, immigrated to New York. It has been recorded that Philip Embury encouraged Barbara Heck to form the first Methodist Society in the Northern United States. A Methodist Chapel was opened in 1768. A request was sent to John Wesley for missionaries. Two arrived in 1768 and, in 1771, Francis Asbury arrived. He was the only one to remain during and after the Revolutionary War when most Anglican clergymen returned to England. Again John Wesley was appealed to for advice and assistance. Because he realized that the American Societies would disintegrate without clergy, he decided to ordain Thomas Coke as Superintendent, sending him to America with instructions to ordain Francis Asbury as his assistant.

On 24 December 1784, near Baltimore, Maryland, the Methodist Episcopal Church was organized to be administered by Bishops, Presiding Elders and Deacons. Coke and Asbury were elected as Bishops. Presiding Elders conducted Official Board meetings, examined Exhorters (laymen who assisted in the conduct of services), licensed Local Preachers, authorized the building of chapels and recommended candidates for the itinerant ministry. The Methodist Episcopal Church assumed charge of missions to New Brunswick, Nova Scotia and Upper and Lower Canada.

Barbara and Paul Heck and other families of their community came to Canada during the American Revolution and settled in the Bay of Quinte area as United Empire Loyalists. Mrs. Heck established the first Methodist Society in Upper Canada. She also has been called the 'Mother of Methodism'. Bishop Asbury sent the first missionary to Upper Canada in 1791. Two Methodist chapels were built in 1792, the year that the Lord's Supper was celebrated for the first time in Upper Canada. Three years later, a missionary reached the settlement at York.

In the early days of the Methodist Revival, Wesley was stoned, beaten and reviled. He lived to know honour and esteem throughout the English-speaking world. He continued to preach the Christian faith until the last week of his long life, which ended in 1791. 'Our main doctrines,' he wrote, 'which include all the rest, are repentance, faith and holiness. The first of these we account, as it were, the porch of religion; the next, the door; the third, religion itself.' Authorities claim that because he converted the masses to a desire to worship God and aspire to holiness, England was spared the horrors of a revolution.

John Wesley regarded the whole world as his parish. The Methodist leaders of Toronto who were responsible for building the Metropolitan Church, shared some of his vision for they coveted the Dominion of Canada as their parish. A pamphlet prepared for the opening of the Church in 1872, written by the Secretary of the Board of Trustees, William T. Mason, reads:

The new church was not built, moreover, merely to supply the needs of a particular congregation which would have been amply satisfied by the creation of a smaller, less costly building. It was intended to provide a Representative Wesleyan Methodist Church in the Chief City of the Province of Ontario, where not only might a large congregation find a spiritual home but 'whither', at times of special gathering or festival, the Public might 'go up, the tribes of the Lord, unto the testimony of Israel, to give thanks unto the name of the Lord'. (Psalm 122)

On three occasions the people of Canada contributed to the building, the rebuilding and the debt reduction of the Metropolitan. Without this assistance, the Church could not have survived. The unofficial status as the 'Cathedral of Methodism' has carried over into the United Church. This role was dramatically exemplified during the pastorate of the Very Reverend Dr. N. Bruce McLeod which began in October 1984. The United Church of Canada celebrated her sixtieth anniversary on 9 June 1985 with a National Celebration and Communion Service. People from far and near gathered for a brief service at the Mutual Street Arena where the inaugural ceremonies had taken place. They formed a procession to the Metropolitan Church, led by the Metropolitan Silver Band. After a memorable service of dignity, ceremony and thanksgiving, a birthday party, complete with cake and candles and a carillon recital, took place in the Metropolitan Park.

The current members of the Metropolitan are deeply aware of their debt to generations of generous, dedicated people who have enabled the Church to carry out her Mission: 'to maintain in the heart of downtown Toronto, a church, rich in tradition, warm in fellowship, powerful in Christian witness, relevant in its ministries to a rapidly changing society.'

CHAPTER 1
The First Methodists
of Muddy York

1795 - 1818

In 1795, when the town of York boasted fewer than twenty log huts, 'it is a moral certainty' that the Reverend Elijah Woolsey conducted Methodist services in this frontier settlement. Two years earlier the Lieutenant-Governor, John Graves Simcoe, had moved his military headquarters across Lake Ontario from Newark (Niagara-on-the-Lake) to the site of the old French Fort Rouillé, known also as Fort Toronto, which had been destroyed in 1759. In keeping with Simcoe's policy of changing Indian names to English ones, he insisted that the new town be called York in honour of the 'grand old Duke of York', the youngest son of King George III. The government officials and employees were not moved from Newark until York was named the capital of Upper Canada in 1796. The Reverend Elijah Woolsey preached again that year for he was attached to the Bay of Quinte circuit and York was its most westerly point. Woolsey, who was born in 1771 in the State of New York, had volunteered as a missionary to Upper Canada in 1794. He spent two years as a circuit-rider in the rugged primeval wilds of the province before returning to the United States.

Late in 1796, the Church of England's first missionary to the settlement, the Reverend Thomas Raddish, arrived in York. He left the following summer and although he did not return, he did not resign until 1799. His successor, the Reverend George Okill Stuart was appointed in September 1800. In his report to the Society for the Propagation of the Gospel in November 1802, he stated that 'Methodists were numerous.' As an Anglican clergyman he had respect for these good people and an understanding of the Methodist movement. He was a supporter of the Wesleyan

Missionary Society and during his incumbency the Methodist community worshipped amicably with the Anglican congregation.

During his first year, the Reverend Nathan Bangs visited York. He recorded:

> I believe I was the first Methodist preacher that ever attempted to preach in Little York—as Toronto was then called—and I preached in a miserable, half-finished house on a week-evening, to a few people and slept on the floor under a blanket. This was in 1801. I was then attempting to form a circuit on Yonge Street—and I was induced to make a trial in this little village, the settlers of which were as thoughtless and wicked as the Canaanites of old.

Bangs was born in New England in 1778. At the age of twenty-one he migrated to the Niagara area where he taught school. He was converted to Methodism at a meeting in St. David's and became an itinerant preacher in 1801. The next year he established regular Methodist preaching in York and continued his exhausting ministry until 1808 when he returned to the United States. Ely Playter who later became a Methodist local preacher recorded in his diary a visit by the Reverend Nathan Bangs:

> Fryday, York 10th September 1802. . . . While at Tea A Miles & Phillip Cody came in, and when they had suped we all went up to Methodist Meeting at Mr. Hales. . . . The man gave us good Doctrin, took his Text the 46 Psalm & 4 verse, the same I had heard him Discourse upon near a year before at the same house, but I conceited he had improved in his explanation. We got home before 10 O'clock and went to bed.

Eliphalet Hales, according to records of 1799, was a bricklayer. Another Methodist, Dr. Thomas Stoyell, was also listed as a householder and a land assessor. Although he had trained as a doctor in the United States, he never practised medicine in Canada. In 1806 he became the proprietor of Stoyell's Tavern which he operated until the War of 1812. Later, he established a brewery and became the first President of the York Temperance Society. In 1817 he was the foreman of the jury for the Jarvis-Ridout duel. When he died in 1832 he was described as a Christian gentleman of great integrity. His home had always been a meeting place for Methodists.

The hospitable home of John Detlor also became a chief centre for the Methodists after his arrival in 1802. He was the son of Valentine Detlor, one of the group of Palatines who emigrated from Ireland to the American colonies and from there, in 1784, to the Bay of Quinte area as United Empire Loyalists. John's brother, Samuel, was a founder of the Hay Bay Church in 1792.

The Home District, which included York, was founded in 1804 and renamed the next year as the Yonge Street Circuit. The Methodist historian, the Reverend John Carroll, wrote:

> Let the respectable Methodists of Toronto and its neighbourhood remember that eighteen hundred and four was the date of their becoming a distinct pastoral charge by themselves, and that William Anson was the pastor.

By 1810 the Methodist Episcopal Church in Upper Canada had twelve church buildings in ten circuits under the supervision of the Reverend Henry Ryan, the Presiding Elder. The parish of York was under the care of well-organized circuit-riders who regularly visited the town.

The first Anglican church was opened in March 1807. Before their church was built, the Anglicans had held services in Government Buildings. The Methodists made no attempt to have services in competition with the Anglican Church. The first recorded Methodist Sunday services were held in 1808 at the Detlor home. The Reverend William Case, who had been ordained a deacon the previous year, recorded in his diary that two meetings were held on Sunday 28 August of that year. One had been scheduled for five o'clock but when a group arrived from a settlement twelve miles away, expecting that a meeting would be held, he preached at a one o'clock service as well, to a 'considerable congregation'.

The sympathetic Reverend George Okill Stuart contributed money towards the construction of Methodist chapels in the Kingston area. His father, the Reverend John Stuart, was the rector of St. George's Church in Kingston until his death in 1811. The Reverend G. O. Stuart succeeded his father and served in that church until his death forty years later.

The Methodists of York had good reason to know dismay and disappointment when the kindly Reverend George Okill Stuart moved away for he was succeeded by the Reverend John Strachan who had no understanding of Methodism because of his Calvinist Scottish background. He was born in Aberdeen, Scotland, in 1778, the son of dissenters from the Church of Scotland. After graduating from King's College with a Master of Arts degree, he joined the Church of Scotland and enrolled as a part-time divinity student at the University of St. Andrews. Knowing that he lacked the social prestige necessary for a good appointment, he immigrated to Canada in 1799. After applying unsuccessfully for the pulpit of St. Gabriel Street Presbyterian Church in Montreal, he joined the Church of England and was ordained in 1803. He was appointed to the parish at Cornwall, Ontario, where he also conducted a successful school. He considered Methodism to be a radical, sectarian movement, interpreting religious enthusiasm as fanaticism. His hostility continued unabated until his death in 1867.

Strachan had wanted to succeed the Reverend John Stuart and he refused the Bishop's proposal that he should go to York until General, Sir Isaac Brock wrote to offer him the chaplaincy of the York Garrison, in addition to the duties of rector of the Anglican Church. He arrived with his wife and three children in July 1812, the month that American forces crossed from Detroit to invade Upper Canada in the War of 1812. The Reverend John Strachan immediately took action to organize patriotic endeavours and he became an active director of the Loyal and Patriotic Society of Upper Canada which was formed in December 1812. When the town was invaded and occupied in April 1813, he turned the church into a hospital by removing the pews. He tended the wounded, encouraged the terrified, and took part in the negotiations for capitulation. From that time he was the acknowledged leader in the religious, educational, and governmental activities of the Province of Upper Canada, as well as the town of York.

When hostilities began, many American citizens and the American Methodist preachers who were serving in Upper Canada returned to the United States. The Methodist Episcopal Church was considered by many to be an enemy institution. Times were exceptionally difficult for those of American birth who remained. On the day of the invasion, 27 April 1813, Dr. Thomas Stoyell refused to bear arms against the American soldiers. From that day and for the next twenty years, Strachan derisively labelled the Methodists in York as Yankee republicans. The godly John Detlor was a casualty of the invasion. He died on 27 April following the amputation of his leg. The Methodists of York held no meetings from 1813 until the end of the war in 1815. The Methodist churches in other parts of the province were kept alive through the efforts of the Presiding Elder, the Reverend Henry Ryan, and the local preachers who assisted him. Ryan had come to Canada in 1805 and had been appointed Presiding Elder in 1810. Before his conversion he was said to be a pugilist. John Carroll, in his book *Past and Present*, describes him as muscular, plump and compact. 'His complexion was dark, head massive, forehead rather projecting, his nose curved a little downward, and his chin, which was a double one with a dimple in the centre, curved upwards. His face was large.'

Methodist preachers came again to York in the spring of 1815. Ely Playter recorded a meeting conducted by a Mr. Smith, on Friday 25 May. Two weeks later he recorded a second service:

> The house was crowded. Went to Stoyell's to dinner & to meeting again at 3 o'clock. The house more full than before—the People were pleased with the ministers. The same was here two weeks before.

After the close of the Napoleonic Wars, emigrants from the British Isles began to settle in Upper Canada. Statistics show that the adult population of York in 1814 had doubled by 1816. Two years later, it reached 1,058, three times greater than it had been at the end of the war. Many of the newcomers were devout Methodists. William Poyntz Patrick, a watchmaker, who was reputed to be the cousin of the Earl of March and the Earl of Spencer, immigrated to Kingston in 1800. He married in 1803 and was the father of six sons and six daughters. After serving in the War of 1812, he was appointed a senior clerk in the office of the House of Assembly. James Lever, who had heard John Wesley preach, arrived with his wife in 1818. He found that his old employee, James Hunter, had already established himself as a tailor in Little York. They began to hold weekly prayer meetings. The Reverend David Culp was appointed to the Yonge Street circuit and the Reverend James Jackson to the Duffin's Creek circuit, with instructions to conduct services on two Sundays a month in the town of York. The meetings were held in the large home of Dr. Thomas Stoyell at 204 King Street East, in the Court House, or in the ballroom of the Mansion House Hotel.

In May 1818, the Reverend Henry Pope, an English missionary who had come to Upper Canada in 1816, visited York and reported to the Wesleyan Methodist Missionary Society:

> . . . I found it pretty well supplied with spiritual instruction. An Episcopal minister preached there once and a Presbyterian, twice every Sabbath day. It is also supplied once a fortnight by Methodist ministers from the United States.

Although Pope had been appointed by the British Wesleyan Conference to the town of York, he decided to centre his activities in the Niagara and Fort George area.

Shortly after Pope's visit, the Methodist Episcopal Conference of New York and Genesee created the new circuit of York, separating it from the Yonge Street circuit. The Reverend David Culp was appointed as the first preacher. The Presiding Elder, the Reverend Henry Ryan, decided that the time had come for the Methodists of York to have their own chapel.

Above, the first chapel built on King Street, from an early watercolour. Right, the harbour of Muddy York, as drawn by James Gray in 1828.

CHAPTER 2

The King Street
Methodist Episcopal Chapel

1818 - 1833

Elder Ryan proceeded with plans to build the chapel. He mortgaged his own farm near Beamsville and bought a site on the south side of King Street, one block west of Yonge Street, from Jordan Post, a clock and watchmaker who conducted his business in a log house at the corner of King and Yonge Streets. At the time there were no sidewalks west of Yonge Street in what was called the New Town, a scantily populated area stretching from Jarvis to Peter Street, south of Queen. Ryan employed the joiner, Alexander Hemphill, 'a demonstrative Methodist', and the carpenter, Robert Petch, to build a plain, one-storied clapboarded structure, thirty by forty feet, and with a pointed roof. The raising of the frame on the posts that supported it was a noteworthy affair. According to John Carroll, neither whisky nor rum was served to the volunteers on that joyful occasion.

The Methodist people of Little York were so eager to worship in their new chapel that they could not wait for the building to be completed. With tools leaning against the walls, they held their first service at eleven o'clock on Sunday 8 November 1818. On the day before, Mr. Hemphill had swept up the shavings to make the chapel ready, assisted by Richard Coates (who became the grandfather of Dr. J.B. Willmott). Rough benches were placed on either side of the narrow aisle which led to a high, square pulpit. Two double doors, facing King Street, admitted the worshippers. The men sat on the right-hand side, the women on the left, a practice that continued as long as the chapel was in use. Barn-like rafters were above them. A gable window under the roof and three windows along each side gave light. A sheet-iron stove provided heat.

In the front pews sat the members of the first class that had been organized early in November. These six people were considered to be the first members for there was no formal ceremony for joining a Methodist Society. People who attended weekly class meetings and who were 'justified' in their faith and accepted the Methodist *Rules* were received into the fellowship. William Poyntz Patrick was the first class leader of the group that consisted of his wife, Elizabeth, Dr. Thomas Stoyell, who had waited twenty years for a Methodist Meeting House, James Lever and his wife, and James Hunter. The arrival of John Doel and his wife later that month increased the membership to eight. John Doel was a brewer who had come from Philadelphia to enter into partnership with Dr. Stoyell.

The preacher, the Reverend David Culp, has been described as a handsome young man of fair education, rather pompous in manner. He had an exceptionally beautiful voice and often sang a hymn before the sermon, or sometimes at the end, a solo of his own composition for he was a versifier. No remaining record gives the text or the topic of his sermon that first Sunday morning but it is known that the congregation joined in that triumphant hymn, 'How Firm a Foundation'. The second verse,

> Fear not, I am with thee; O be not dismayed!
> For I am thy God, I will still give thee aid;
> I'll strengthen thee, help thee,
> and cause thee to stand
> Upheld by my gracious, omnipotent hand.

must have been of special assurance to the congregation who knew privation, pestilence, danger, isolation, and loneliness, and who had been led from war and invasion to days of peace.

The Reverend James Jackson preached at the evening service when the chapel was lighted by candles in their sconces attached to the walls on either side and in sconces placed at each side of the pulpit. A short intermission was necessary to snuff and re-light the flickering candles. The Reverend John Carroll later described the American-born Jackson as 'tall and handsome, with dark hair and florid complexion; graceful, with an air of assumed dignity'. He is known, at some time, to have preached on the text, 'There are threescore queens, and fourscore concubines, and virgins without number' but the text that first Sunday evening is not recorded.

A Sunday School was organized on the second Sunday of that November by the Reverend Thaddeus Osgood who had come to Upper and Lower Canada in 1809 as a 'distributor of tracts'. In 1810 he had inserted a 'Note of thanks' in the *York Gazette*:

> to all those Gentlemen and Ladies who have repeatedly aided him in his humble attempt to do good, by Printing and disseminating useful books.
> Public notice is hereby given, that a variety of small books and entertaining pieces for children are left in the care of Mr. Adams, at his Book-Store in York. The terms are good. The poor may have them gratis and the rich may cast into the Charity Box whatever they please which shall be faithfully applied to printing more. The poor are however invited to bring what Rags they can spare towards making paper cheaper.

It must have given Mr. Osgood tremendous satisfaction to establish the first Sunday School in York, where children were taught reading, writing, spelling and simple arithmetic, as well as religious doctrine and instruction. The school was held from two to four o'clock on Sunday afternoons. The first Superintendents were William P. Patrick and Jesse Ketchum, a tanner who had come to York in 1799. He became a leading landowner, noted for his philanthropy. Thomas David Morrison, Patrick's brother-in-law, was the librarian, presumably to look after the tracts provided by the Reverend Thaddeus Osgood. John Carroll, one of the first scholars, described the school in *My Boy Life*:

> In the autumn of 1818, my dear mother returned one day from a visit to Mr. Ketchum's, and told us at home that Mr. Osgood had been in town, and that Messrs. Ketchum, Patrick, Carfra and Morrison were going to teach a school every Sunday afternoon in the new Methodist meetinghouse on King Street and it was decided that we, the three youngest boys, should attend. . . There were few books of any kind in that early day, and not enough Bibles and Testaments. My first lesson was the fragment of a Bible, a psalm, pasted on a shingle, which I read and committed to memory.

The York Methodist Episcopal Chapel flourished during the year of the Reverend David Culp's ministry. Soon three more classes were formed, led by Dr. Stoyell, James Hunter, and T.D. Morrison who was dismissed from his position of Chief Clerk of the Surveyor-General's office when he joined the Methodists. He took up the practice of medicine in 1824. With the exception of James Hunter's class which was held immediately after morning worship on Sundays, class meetings took place in the homes of the leaders on Tuesday and Thursday evenings. By August 1819, when Mr. Culp was replaced by Samuel Belton, the membership had increased to sixty-five with as many as two hundred 'hearers' crowding the chapel on Sunday evenings.

Unfortunately, discord and discontent soon shattered the King Street congregation. Samuel Belton, 'clean-shaven, plump, and comely' was an emotional and enthusiastic preacher. He was not ordained until 1821. The members, newly arrived from Britain, viewed him with suspicion. Many were deeply shocked when it became known that a young Irish girl who had returned home to pray after one of Belton's evening meetings had fallen into a trance. She remained unconscious for nearly a week while a succession of curious onlookers visited the home to view her in this unusual state.

John Laidlaw expressed his view in an unsympathetic letter written from York on 9 September 1819:

> I don't think the Methidests is very Sound in their Doctrine. They Save all infants and saposes a man may be Justified to day, and fall from it tomorrow; and the English Minister reads all he Says, unless it be his clark Craying at the end of Every peorid: "Good Lord Deliver us." . . . the Minister prays as loud as ever he can and the people all down on their knees keep crying Amen so that you can scarce hear him, and I have seen some of them jumping as if they would have gone to heaven soul and body through the loft, but their body was a filthy clog to them for they always fell down again.

The newly arrived English immigrants were deeply offended by the display of emotionalism, remembering that in 1812 the British Wesleyans had expelled the Primitive Methodists and Bible Christians from their Society because of excessive emotion. When the Reverend James Booth, a British Wesleyan minister from Kingston, paid a private visit to York, the discontented Methodists invited him to hold a service in a private home.

Samuel Belton was replaced by the local preacher, David Youmans of the Yonge Street circuit. Of Dutch descent, he had been a blacksmith before becoming a circuit rider who served the backwoods of Upper Canada during the War of 1812. He was a kindly, devout man, beloved by children, but he was an inveterate smoker. Preaching in an urban chapel was probably a difficult ordeal, for when he sat down behind the pulpit at the end of his sermon, he pulled a plug of tobacco and a jack-knife from his pocket and proceeded to fill his pipe. He puffed on it as he walked down the aisle to the door at the conclusion of the service to shake the hands of his departing parishioners. Although his appointment was only as a temporary supply, it proved to have disastrous consequences.

A group of British Methodists, unhappy in the 'Yankee chapel' as Strachan persisted in calling it, decided to hold their own services. They wrote to James Booth in Kingston, seeking his assistance in finding a minister. He arranged for John Fenton, a local preacher who had attended Kingswood, the school founded by John Wesley, to go to York to assess the situation and to see if a missionary's services were required. Fenton immediately organized a British Wesleyan congregation that met first in the homes and then in the Masonic Hall. He initiated a petition to go to the Society in London requesting the appointment of a missionary. Seventy-one householders, with Richard Coates and the carpenter, Robert Petch, leading the list, signed it on 12 October 1819. The Reverend Henry Ryan, the Presiding Elder of the Methodist Episcopal Church, attended one of their services and denounced them all as 'schismatics'.

In April 1820, the Reverend Henry Pope was ordered by the British Wesleyan Missionary Society to York. He attracted a substantial congregation. About ten families defected from the King Street chapel, including James Lever who was appointed Sunday School Superintendent. John Fenton was a class leader. Because the ties between the British Wesleyans and the Church of England had not yet been broken, Pope was able to cement relationships with the Anglican church for he had known Strachan in Cornwall where Mrs. Strachan had attended one of his services. In a letter to the Secretary of the Wesleyan Missionary Society, Pope wrote:

> . . . The American brethren have a small society here but their cause does not seem to prosper. As a British missionary is for various reasons, better received here than an American, it would, I think, be more for the Glory of God if existing differences were amiably adjusted by the two Conferences and the American Missionaries withdrawn; as the two interests would then become one and thereby render material pecuniary support to the Mission; the American Missionary might dispose of his labours to much greater advantage in some of those country places which are yet destitute of spiritual instruction; and (I might add) for which places the American Missionaries generally are much better adapted than for respectable towns. I have many pressing calls from 6 to 36 miles from town but I have to preach here twice every Sabbath to an intelligent congregation and to lead the classes, attend the prayer meetings, visit the sick etc. in the week. I have not been able to extend my labours very far. But if another were sent to labour with me, we could work the Town and Country alternately and form an excellent Circuit. . . .

After waiting twenty years for an organized Methodist Society, the little town of York now had two. The Methodist Episcopals believed that they belonged to a fully constituted denomination with episcopal structure and ordination of their clergy. The British Wesleyans, on the other hand, were Societies using John Wesley's version of the Church of England liturgy but only as a branch of Anglicanism with no separate ordination. They did not become a distinct denomination in England until 1836.

Meanwhile in 1820, the congregation of the King Street chapel was reduced to forty-three. In November of that year, Jesse Ketchum resigned as Sunday School Superintendent to join the Secessionist Presbyterians, giving them property on which to build their church. Because of the sadly depleted numbers and the debt on the Methodist chapel, an application was forwarded to the newly formed American Methodist Episcopal Missionary Society for a missionary to serve the parish. They appointed Fitch Reed, a highly intelligent, handsome young man who had almost completed his medical training when he answered his call to the Methodist ministry. He volunteered for service in Canada in 1819 and had gained experience in dealing with British Wesleyan missionaries in the St. Armand Mission of Lower Canada. During his first year in York he stayed in the hospitable home of W. P. Patrick and during the next year at the home of John Doel. Reed was well aware of the hostility in the town to Americans. He tried to overcome the prejudice by praying for the Royal Family every Sunday. He succeeded and was well received by the chapel members for he was a most accomplished preacher. It was recorded that at the class meetings, still held in the homes on Tuesdays and Thursdays, prayers were always offered for the young minister who did not miss a prayer meeting during his two-year stay.

During these troubled years the Bishops of the Methodist Episcopal Church and the British Wesleyan Conference entered into discussion by correspondence about Methodism in Upper Canada. Despite the letter from Henry Pope, it was finally agreed that the Wesleyan Conference would have jurisdiction over Lower Canada and the area around Kingston, while the rest of Upper Canada would be the responsibility of the American Methodist Episcopal Church. The Reverend William Case, who later became noted for his missionary work among the Indians, was assigned the task of reading to the Wesleyan congregation the agreement which dissolved their Society. He informed them that they must attend the York Methodist Episcopal Chapel and submit to its ministers. Mr. Pope was recalled in October 1821 and was stationed in the Eastern Townships. This solution did not completely resolve the problem. Several families, including the Coates and the Fentons, disobeyed the edict and continued to hold meetings in their homes. Some people joined the Church of England. John Fenton was appointed Parish Clerk of the Anglican church in 1822. He continued to be an irritant in the Methodist community until he eventually went to the United States.

The Reverend Fitch Reed returned to the United States in 1822. His successor was Kenneth McKendree Smith who had been converted by the Reverend David Culp. He had been appointed as Reed's assistant the year before so that the work of the circuit could be extended to the west by thirty miles. He was a zealous, industrious young man and an excellent preacher. During the year of his ministry the membership at class meetings increased to one hundred and four. The King Street chapel was extended to the south by an addition of twenty feet.

❂

From 1823 to 1827 the chapel was once again attached to the Yonge Street circuit which stretched from York to Lake Simcoe. It was served by two ministers assisted by local preachers and 'located' or inactive clergy, with the senior minister living in York. The bigotry of John Strachan continued unabated, even though the clergy, with one exception, were sons of Loyalists who had fought in the Revolutionary War. The Reverend John Ryerson was appointed in 1823. His father, Colonel Joseph Ryerson, who had taken up lands in New Brunswick after the Revolution, moved about 1799 to a large tract of land on the shores of Lake Erie in Norfolk County. Three of his six sons served with him in the War of 1812. He was a staunch member of the Church of England and was so infuriated when his son, William, was converted to Methodism by David Youmans, that he ordered him out of his house. The godly Mrs. Ryerson was sympathetic to the Methodists and with her encouragement, five sons entered the itineracy. John was the first to begin his ministry as a probationer in 1820 when he was twenty-one years of age. Three years later he was ordained and took up his duties as the senior minister at York. He has been described as 'genteel and intellectual in appearance, quiet and grave with sound judgement and resolute will'. His assistant, William Slater, was an Englishman who had been a farmhand before the Reverend Henry Pope persuaded him to become a preacher. He died suddenly in 1829, the year after he had been one of the delegates sent to the Pittsburg Conference to secure independence for Canadian Methodists.

On 29 December 1823, Henry Ryan conveyed the property of the King Street chapel to the Trustees: Thomas Stoyell, gentleman; Hugh Carfrae, gentleman; John Doel, maltster; James Hunter, tailor; and William Poyntz Patrick, watchmaker. The transaction was witnessed by David Culp and William Clark, the Clerk of the Town of York. Hugh Carfrae, who lived next door to W.P. Patrick, continued as a Trustee until 1830 when St. Andrew's Presbyterian Church was built.

The chapel now seemed to have recovered from the defection of the British Wesleyans four years earlier. Newcomers, such as Joshua Van Allen who led a young men's class, and the Willmott family, whose connection with the church was to last more than a century, lent strong support to the struggling congregation. Hoodlums in the town found sport in interrupting the evening services. One Sunday they burst into the service wheeling a drunken man up the aisle in a wheel-barrow. It is recorded that Joshua Van Allen evicted the interlopers single-handed. Pranksters also plagued the congregation by throwing cackling geese into the chapel or by managing to blow out all the candles during an evening service. The Methodists were beset by the rampages of the ignorant and the prejudices of the élite.

In an attempt to put an end to the chapel's reputation as a Yankee Meeting House, the Canada Conference was formed in 1824 at the General Conference of the American Methodist Episcopal Church held in Baltimore as a first step in granting complete independence. Up to this time, the circuits of Upper Canada had been under the jurisdiction of the New York and Genesee Conference. The Reverend Henry Ryan had agitated for an independent church but he was not elected as a delegate to the Baltimore meetings. Deeply hurt by this rebuff, he eventually withdrew from the Methodist Episcopals in 1827. According to the *Dictionary of Canadian Biography*, he was expelled because of his 'divisive activities'.

From September 1824 to July 1827, the year that York became a separate charge, the Presiding Elder was the Reverend Thomas Madden, a Loyalist who had been ordained by Bishop Asbury. He officially visited every circuit under his supervision every three months to conduct quarterly Board meetings. They commenced on a Saturday afternoon with a devotional period preceding a business meeting. On Saturday evening, the congregation met for prayer and testimony. At 8:30 on Sunday morning they gathered for a Love Feast, followed at 10:30 by a worship service with preaching and the celebration of the Lord's Supper. A Sunday afternoon meeting was followed by the regular evening service. The members of a circuit, covering a wide area, were brought together every three months for spiritual enrichment and renewal.

The Reverend John Ryerson was succeeded in 1824 by the American-born William H. Williams who was described by his assistant, James Richardson, as 'bland and generous . . . and an excellent colleague'. Richardson was appointed as a Probationer in October 1824. He had been converted at a Methodist meeting in a barn near Colborne, Ontario, and in 1818 began to serve as a Local Preacher. During the War of 1812, he had accepted a commission in the Provincial Marines and during a naval battle near Oswego, he lost his left arm. After the war he was a customs officer at Presqu'ile Harbour. Although he had moved in the social circles of his day, he too was ostracized after joining the Methodists. In a manuscript book of reminiscences he described his arrival in York:

> It was dark and raining, plenty of mud but no carriage in waiting. I went ahead to the residence of my wife's father, on the corner of King and Yonge Streets. Mr. Dennis taking a lantern, immediately went before me. We met my wife and children trudging through the mud and rain . . . Sarah Jane minus a shoe which had come off in the mud while crossing Wellington Street . . . (there was) no parsonage nor other house available for our residence . . . we were homeless except sheltered for the time by my wife's parents. Mr. Dennis having a small dilapidated house that had been once a dwelling but was now used as a joiner's shop, generously offered the use of it rent free, while I served on the circuit, if I could fit it up as to live in it. Seeing no alternative, I went to work assisted by my wife, and after two or three weeks hard labour, and an expenditure of about twenty dollars, succeeded in rendering the old house a tolerably comfortable dwelling for our stay on the Yonge Street circuit.

For his labours, Richardson received an annual salary of one hundred dollars, paid quarterly.

During the winter of 1824-25, the work of the King Street Chapel was extended by the formation of the East York Sunday School in a building on Market Lane. Joshua Van Allen was appointed the Superintendent. He had joined a Methodist class meeting soon after his arrival in York in 1822. John Carroll described him as 'conspicuous among the powerful singers who gave character to the wondrous singing for which the worship in that church was distinguished'.

In June 1825, Mr. Madden, the Presiding Elder, with the assistance of the two ministers, Williams and Richardson, decided to hold a camp meeting at Cummer's Mills, two miles east of Yonge Street and accessible by a road (now known as Cummer Avenue) which had been cut through the forest to the Middle Don River in 1819. John Cummer, who operated a sawmill there, set aside by the river a site of about two acres to be used for camp meetings. The property eventually became known as Scripture Town and later, Angel Valley. A fence, eight to ten feet high, enclosed the area. It was made of slabs from the mill with pointed ends to keep out intruders. Four gates, one wide enough for wagons, admitted the people. Although the area was cleared of scrub and underbrush, towering trees had been left to provide shade.

For weeks before the camp meeting, daily prayers were offered in York, asking God's blessing on the venture which began on a Thursday and ended on Monday. Early in the week, young men were sent to prepare the grounds, erecting wooden tents for the use of families and constructing a large wooden tent, fifty feet in length, 'with every convenience'. Benches made of boards from the mill were placed on a gentle slope so that a large congregation could look down on the preacher's stand by the river.

At sunrise on that Thursday morning, worshippers gathered at the King Street Chapel for prayer before starting out on the twelve-mile trek to the campsite. Some went on horseback or in wagons but most of them formed a procession to walk the distance, taking a road that skirted around Hogg's Hollow.

The meetings were in the charge of the Reverend Thomas Madden. Special preachers included William Ryerson and his younger brother, Egerton, assisted by the local preachers, David Youmans and Cornelius Flumerfelt. The Reverend John Carroll, who had been converted the year before at the age of fifteen, attended the camp meeting. He wrote a description of it in *Past and Present*, published in 1860:

> . . . I would not like to attempt estimating the numbers, but the ground was alive with people from early the first day to the last . . . The work of conversion began in the first prayer meeting held after the preaching the first night. The spirit of conviction seemed to rest on all the unconverted within the enclosure. They might be seen in little groups all over the ground,

pleading with God till near the morning light. It progressed with increasing interest and power through the several stages of the meeting to its close, . . . on which day no less than one hundred and forty persons came forward as the subjects of converting grace. The sacramental and farewell services at the close were the most exciting and intensely affecting that I ever witnessed. And I should think that such times are not often seen. The valedictory charge was delivered, at the request of the presiding elder, by the Rev. William Ryerson, whose preaching at that time was characterized by a pathos and persuasiveness that seemed to bear down all before it. There was much powerful preaching at that meeting.

Two of the converts who went forward to the penitents' bench were Margaret Marshall, who later married Thomas Vaux, and Margaret Bowes, who soon after converted and married Samuel Edward Taylor. Both women made significant contributions to the church for years to come.

Following the camp meeting, where close friendships were formed and religious zeal was inflamed, the King Street Chapel entered into a period of comparative peace and prosperity. At the Conference in September, the Reverend James Richardson was appointed senior minister of the Yonge Street Mission with the young Egerton Ryerson as his assistant. Egerton was the fifth son of Colonel Joseph Ryerson and the third to enter the Methodist ministry. When he became a member of the Methodist Society in 1821 at the age of eighteen, his father ordered him, too, to leave home. For two years he assisted his brother, George, who conducted a grammar school in Norwich. This gave Egerton an opportunity for study and in 1824 he went to Hamilton to attend the Gore District Grammar School with the intention of studying law. He was stricken, however, with a serious illness. After his recovery, and on his twenty-second birthday in March 1825, he accepted God's calling to enter the Methodist ministry. He was received on probation at the September Conference. James Richardson recorded:

A more agreeable and useful colleague I could not have desired. We laboured together with one heart and mind, and God was graciously pleased to crown our united efforts with success - we doubled the members in society, both in town and country, and all was harmony and love.

On Monday, 7 November 1825, Egerton wrote to his father with whom he had become reconciled:

. . . I am very well pleased with my appointment. I travel with a person, who is deeply pious, a true and disinterested friend, and a very respectable preacher. I travel about 200 Miles in four weeks, & preach 25 times, besides funerals. I spend two sabbaths in York, and two in the country. Our prospects on the circuit are encouraging. In York we have the most flattering prospects. We have some increase almost every week. Our Morning congregations fill the chapel, which was never the case before; and in the evening, the chapel will not contain but little more than three quarters of the people. Last evening several of the members of Parliament were present. I never addressed so large assemblies before, and I never was so much assisted from heaven in preaching as at this place. I have spent the two last Sabbaths in York. I go today in the country. I was requested yesterday in the afternoon to address the Union Sunday School, which contains about 150, or 200 children. It was a publick examination of the School. I never heard children recite so correctly and so perfectly as they did. There was quite a large congregation present as it was designed to make a contribution for the support of the school. I first delivered a short discourse to the children and then addressed the assembly. It was the most precious season that I ever experienced. It is my dear Father, the most delightful employment I ever was engaged in, to proclaim the (tear in ms) Jesus to lost Sinners . . .

Although he was not ordained until 1827, Egerton Ryerson was invited to become a spokesman for the Methodist Episcopal Church to challenge the unjust statements made by Dr. Strachan in his sermon preached at the funeral of Bishop Mountain and later published. In a long letter printed in William Lyon Mackenzie's *Colonial Advocate* in May 1826, Ryerson vehemently defended the Methodist clergy whom Strachan had denounced as disloyal Americans, ignorant and unsound in religion.

❂

During the summer of 1826, the chapel was again extended southward by about thirty feet, and a parsonage, at the corner of Jordan and Adelaide Streets, was acquired for the senior minister. William Ryerson, who was considered to be the most eloquent preacher in Upper Canada, was appointed in September 1826. His assistant, John Beatty, known as 'the Squire', entered the itineracy that year at the age of forty-four, 'to spend the evening of his years in usefulness'. Ryerson's fine preaching attracted many Anglicans, especially Irish immigrants who were opposed to a State Church. The Reverend John Harris of the Secessionist Presbyterian Church proved to be a dull preacher and some who had left the Methodist chapel returned. In 1827 the King Street Chapel separated from the Yonge Street Mission and became a self-supporting circuit with one hundred and seventy-three members and an estimated parish population of from four to six hundred.

The members of the York Methodist Episcopal Chapel must have felt that God's promise to 'strengthen them, help them and cause them to stand' had been miraculously fulfilled. The congregation, though largely from the lower classes, attracted some who were associated with the government élite. James Scott Howard, who had come to York in 1820, was a close friend of the aristocratic Baldwin family in spite of his Methodist activities. In 1828 he was appointed Postmaster of York although Dr. Strachan wrote to a colleague that he found it inconvenient to have a Methodist in a position where he could ascertain the identity of his correspondents.

Because the reputation of Methodists as disloyal Yankees persisted, it became apparent that the Canadian Conference should be severed from the American Methodist Episcopal Church. At their Conference in 1828, the Methodist Episcopal Church in Canada was granted complete independence. The following year, a law was passed to give Methodist clergy the right to perform marriages in Upper Canada.

When the American-born Reverend Franklin Metcalf began his two-year pastorate in September 1828, he found a growing and enthusiastic membership that was convinced that they had outgrown the old framed meeting house and that a new, larger church should be built. In October, the York Female Branch of the Missionary Society was organized with Mrs. Thomas Stoyell as President. Her husband was a generous supporter of the Methodist Episcopal Missionary Society which had been organized in 1824 to establish Christian missions among the Indians of Upper Canada. James Roger Armstrong had been the treasurer of this organization since its inception. He came to York in 1828, opened a dry-goods business, and became immediately active in the Methodist chapel. His daughter became Egerton Ryerson's second wife.

When the Leaders' and Stewards' monthly meetings were organized in January 1829, Armstrong was appointed Treasurer. The minute book of this committee, which met from 1829 to 1834, is extant. At the meetings, all expenditures were authorized, including the quarterly stipends of the preacher and the Presiding Elder. Class books were presented by the class leaders for examination along with the 'quarterage' or collections. At the

February meeting, Brothers Patrick and Vaux were appointed to draft a petition to the House of Assembly for power to sell the chapel and the ground around it. Thomas Vaux had arrived in York in 1827 to open a 'select school' with evening classes for workers. He soon became a class leader.

The April meeting of the committee was largely devoted to the preparation of a job description for a sexton. It was agreed that for five shillings a week he should keep the chapel clean and in proper order, attending to the fire, sawing the wood, cleaning and lighting lamps.

> The House should be swept twice a week and scrubbed once a month, the windows cleaned when wanted and the Seats dusted after sweeping and the person undertaking these Duties to furnish himself with brooms, sand, water, etc., and the person performing the above duties should not purchase anything without the consent of one of the Stewards.

The committee was concerned with the upkeep of the chapel: the repairing of the fence, the installation of ventilators, shutters and blinds. A committee was appointed to sell the old lamps and purchase two new ones. Brother Doel was authorized to obtain subscriptions for the purpose of providing a lamp or lantern for the front of the Meeting House. The debt on the old parsonage was discharged and new quarters for the preacher were rented.

In July 1829, the Leaders were directed to propose to their respective classes this question to each member:

> What do you feel able and willing to give per week towards the support of the Preacher?

with the understanding that the respective sum be paid regularly, weekly, monthly or at any convenient time.

The Sunday School continued to flourish; limited space was a problem. To ease the crowded situation the Leaders and Stewards in June 1829 appointed Thomas Vaux, Dr. Morrison, J.S. Howard, and W.P. Patrick to draft a petition to His Excellency, the Lieutenant-Governor, 'praying him to grant to the Methodist Episcopal Chapel a portion of the School Reserves for the purpose of erecting a School House thereon for the use of the said church'. This petition was ignored. In April 1830, the rules and regulations of the York Methodist Sunday School were published in the

Christian Guardian which had commenced the year before with young Egerton Ryerson as the first editor:

1st. That no class shall consist of more than eight scholars.

2nd. That the greatest number of verses from either the Scriptures or Hymns best learned and best recited, shall entitle the Scholar so learning and so reciting to stand at the head of his or her Class, and so on in succession according to the verses or hymns learned.

3rd. Unless the Scholars first recite the lesson of the day correctly, they shall not be allowed to recite any other verses.

4th. Every six verses well learned and well recited shall entitle any Scholar to a white ticket, and every ten white tickets so gained to a red one, and this red ticket shall entitle such Scholar to a book from the library for perusal, to be kept for the space of one or two weeks but not longer than two.

5th. It shall be the duty of the Teacher to return all books brought in by the Scholars to the Secretary when called on by him.

6th. In giving out books, the Teachers shall see that the children under their care do not stir from their seats until their class is called up by the Secretary, when the books will be given without that confusion which otherwise arises.

7th. It shall be the duty of every Teacher to take care that every book taken from the library by one of his or her Scholars, be duly restored to the Secretary at the proper time.

8th. It shall be the duty of every Teacher immediately on entrance into the School to proceed to, and remain at the head or in front of his or her class, and diligently endeavour to keep the class employed until the School be closed.

9th. It shall be the duty of every Teacher, upon absence of any one of his or her Scholars, for the space of two Sundays, to go and enquire of the parents or guardians of said child the reason for his or her absence, and report the same to the President for consideration.

10th. It shall be the duty of the Teachers to attend when possible, the Teacher's Meeting held on Wednesday evenings, for the purpose of studying the lesson for the next Sabbath with greater advantage.

11th. It shall be the duty not only of the Officers and Managers, but of the

Teachers to endeavour to get subscriptions and donations in aid of the funds of the society, at the same time giving in to the Secretary the names of the subscribers or donors with the amount paid, to be handed by him to the Treasurer, that he may enter their names in his book of subscriptions and donations.

12th. If any Teacher absent him or herself unnecessarily from the School without being able to render to the Officers and Managers a satisfactory excuse, the same shall for the first absence be fined one shilling and three pence, for the second two shillings and six pence, and for the third shall be expelled.

13th. It shall be the duty of the Secretary to keep a book with the Teachers names in it, to note down each Sunday whether they are absent or present.

14th. The fines shall be put to the same use as subscriptions or donations.

15th. If any Teacher shall at any time be reported to be guilty of immoral conduct, such as drunkenness, gaming, profane swearing, Sabbath breaking, &c., and shall by the Officers and Managers be found so, the same shall be immediately expelled.

16th. The School shall be opened precisely at two o'clock P.M. and shall be closed when practicable at four.

A strict attention to the foregoing rules is expected from every person who has taken or may hereafter take upon him or herself the important duties of a Teacher in this school.

The pastorate of the Reverend Franklin Metcalf came to an end at the Conference in August 1830, at which time he informed this body of ministers that the Trustees of the York station, with the consent of the Society, were willing to dispose of the chapel. According to John Carroll, Metcalf's ministry was 'one of the happiest the Methodist church in the Capital ever saw'.

❁

Metcalf was succeeded by the Reverend William Smith. In November 1830, he was largely responsible for the founding of the Temperance Society with Dr. Thomas Stoyell as President, William P. Patrick as Treasurer, and Egerton Ryerson as Secretary. By the end of its first year, it boasted two hundred and fifty-two members. Smith, who was born in Niagara in 1802 and converted at the age of twenty, was described as 'plain and affable . . . pleasant but grave, not narrow-minded but conscientious'. At the close of his year's ministry, he held a revival in conjunction with the annual Conference of the Methodist Episcopal Church in Canada which met in York for the first time. The congregation was strengthened with the conversion of thirty souls. The Conference meetings lasted for nine days and commenced with a prayer meeting held at five o'clock every morning. Business sessions took place from eight until five, preaching services began every evening at seven o'clock.

Discussions centred around the disquieting knowledge that the British Wesleyan Missionary Society had declared null and void the agreement made with the American Methodist Episcopal Church in 1820 to withdraw their missionaries from all parts of Upper Canada with the exception of the Kingston area. They had decided to build a chapel on George Street in 1832 with services conducted by John Fenton until the arrival of a missionary. The Reverend George Ryerson was commissioned to go to England to suggest that the British Wesleyans should send an observer to Upper Canada to determine the necessity of missionaries from England.

The members of the King Street chapel continued with their plan for a new church. At the Quarterly Board meeting on 5 December 1831, a building committee was appointed. It included J.R. Armstrong, John Doel, J.S. Howard, and W.P. Patrick. At the end of February the Methodist community was saddened by the death of Dr. Thomas Stoyell, a founding member, 'respected by all for his integrity as a man and his piety as a Christian'. His generous bequest to the Methodist Episcopal Church assured the committee that their plans for a large church seating one thousand people was financially possible.

The town of York was growing rapidly. In 1832 the population was 5,505, three thousand more than the number of men, women, and children recorded in 1829. The King Street Chapel had the largest congregation in the largest denomination in Canada. Two hundred and sixty-four people were attending thirty class meetings. Four of the Leaders were local preachers: Cornelius Flumerfelt who, from 1828 to 1834, 'ceased to travel' as an itinerant; Richard Woodsworth, a builder from Yorkshire who had come to York in 1829 (he became the grandfather of James Shaver Woodsworth, the founder of the Cooperative Commonwealth Federation); Mathias Holeby who had arrived from England in 1830; and

Joseph Easton who conducted a class for the military. Margaret Bowes Taylor, who had been converted at Cummer's Mills in 1825, conducted Class Number 11; Alexander Hamilton, a leading painter and paperhanger of York, led Class Number 12 and, as well, acted as Superintendent of the Sunday School. W.P. Patrick and Robert Petch were licensed Exhorters.

The Leaders and Stewards had hired a Singing Master, Mr. Baxter, as well as a sexton. They commended his work and influence by adopting a Resolution at their meeting in February 1832 which praised him for his 'prompt attention and diligence in the discharge of his duty'. A visiting preacher described the King Street singing, writing in the *Christian Advocate* in June 1832,

> in my whole life I have not known but two other congregations who seemed to profit so well by the Divine ordinance of singing. It was at once skilful, devotional and popular. They sung as if they believed it to be an experience worthy of heaven and were perfecting it to take part in it there.

In spite of these complimentary comments, Mr. Baxter fell into disfavour, for the motion to retain his services in the new Meeting House was defeated. A committee waited on Mr. Baxter to settle whatever might be owing to him. Another committee including Brothers Patrick, Doel, and Easton, was appointed to lead the singing.

At the April meeting of the Leaders and Stewards, it was moved by Thomas Vaux and seconded by W. P. Patrick that the internal arrangements of the new House be left to the male members of the Society to be approved at a meeting to be called at an early opportunity. A petition was sent from the officials of York Methodist Meeting House to the secretaries of the Wesleyan Missionary Society of London, England, protesting the appointment of a British missionary to York, stating that it would be as appropriate for Canadian Methodists to send missionaries to Great Britain. In spite of this letter, a representative of the British Conference arrived in York in July 1832 to inform the Canadian Methodist Episcopal Society that it was the intention of the British Wesleyans to form rival churches and that they had the support of the Canadian Colonial Office which had been disturbed by rumours of disloyalty and republicanism among Canadian Methodists.

When the Conference of the Methodist Episcopals met in August 1832, the three Ryerson brothers, John, William and Egerton, fearing a 'war on the circuits' proposed a union with the British Wesleyans. They realized that this Society would be in Canada permanently with almost unlimited financial resources. The Ryersons were also disturbed by the presence of the Primitive Methodists in the province and by the Canadian Wesleyan Methodist Church or Ryanites, established by Henry Ryan after his expulsion from the Methodist Episcopals in 1828. Dr. Strachan had personally donated to this cause, rejoicing in the evidence of a schism among the Methodists. George Ryerson opposed his brothers' recommendation. The decision was not unanimous but the Conference authorized Egerton Ryerson to go to Britain to make the necessary arrangements for church union which was considered the best solution for Canadian Methodism.

Meanwhile plans for the new large church to replace the King Street Chapel continued to be made in spite of the fact that St. Andrew's Church of Scotland at the corner of Church and Newgate Streets had been opened on 19 June 1831 and that the British Wesleyans had dedicated their new framed building on George Street on 14 July 1832. Under the guidance of the Reverend Alexander Irvine, who was appointed to the King Street Chapel at the 1832 Conference, final arrangements were made for the new church to be built at the southwest corner of Newgate Street (changed to Adelaide Street in 1844) and Toronto Street. The final services in the old Meeting House took place on 9 June 1833.

The King Street chapel had been rented since July 1832 for the afternoon services of a group of Congregationalists on the understanding that they would purchase the building. When this offer failed to materialize, the Trustees, William Poyntz Patrick, John Doel, and J.S. Howard, sold the chapel for five hundred and seventy-five pounds. The new owner soon rented it. A notice appeared in William Lyon Mackenzie's *Patriot* on 2 August 1833:

> **New Source of Entertainment and Instruction.**
> The public will rejoice to hear, that the large building in King Street, lately occupied as an American Brimstone dispensary is about to be converted into a Theatre, Messrs. Vaughan and Co. having taken it on a lease for that purpose.

It was given the name, Theatre Royal. This was the first of a succession of embarrassments for the new Newgate Street congregation.

The Adelaide Street Wes-
leyan Methodist Church,
pre-dating the present
Metropolitan Church. The
young Egerton Ryerson
(below) was a minister of the
King St. Chapel and the
Newgate St. Church. He
returned to the latter as a
member in 1844, and was a
trustee of the Metropolitan
from 1870 to 1882 (below,
right).

Adelaide-Street Methodist Church, erected in 1833.

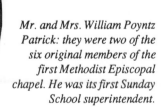

Mr. and Mrs. William Poyntz
Patrick: they were two of the
six original members of the
first Methodist Episcopal
chapel. He was its first Sunday
School superintendent.

CHAPTER 3
The Newgate Street/ Adelaide Street Wesleyan Methodist Church

1833 - 1867

The Newgate Street Methodist Episcopal Church was 'solemnly dedicated to the sacred worship of Almighty God' on 16 June 1833. The Reverend William Ryerson, the silver-tongued orator, preached at the morning and evening services. The Reverend Alexander Irvine took charge of the afternoon service. The church, described by the *Christian Guardian* as 'well-proportioned, neat and substantial' was filled to overflowing for all services. Built at a cost of fifteen hundred pounds, the building, of simple Georgian architecture, seventy-four feet in length and fifty-four in width, had a seating capacity for one thousand people. The pulpit was at the south. Two aisles separated three sections of pews; each pew was equipped with a small door. The men continued to sit on the left and the women on the right in the nave and in the spacious galleries around three sides of the sanctuary. The basement was finished to provide meeting rooms, an 'infant room', a kitchen, and adequate accommodation for the large Sunday School.

When the Canada Conference met in the Newgate Street Church in October 1833, Egerton Ryerson presented the terms of the union with the British Wesleyan Missionary Society. It was agreed that the new Wesleyan Methodist Church in Canada should retain the liturgy of the Methodist Episcopals and adopt the British Wesleyan form of government. The conference closed after eight days when, according to the *Christian Guardian*, 'harmony and a high tone of religious feeling prevailed throughout the whole deliberation.' The members of the Societies were informed of the Union and the impending changes and were directed to submit to the decision in accordance with the Methodist *Discipline*.

Not everyone, however, agreed that church union was advisable or desirable. Many Methodist Episcopals deplored the fact that their well-constituted church should amalgamate with a Society that had no form of ordination. The British Wesleyan Societies, which did not separate from the Church of England until 1836, were constituted to have a President, elected annually, instead of government through bishops, presbyters, deacons, and presiding elders. The British Wesleyans were vehemently opposed to camp meetings. The minister of the George Street Chapel, John Barry, continued to attack the Canadian ministers as 'uncouth ignoramuses and traitorous republicans'. He was so opposed to the union that later in 1833 he asked to be transferred to Montreal. John Fenton was so bitterly against the union that he was asked to leave the George Street Chapel. He soon after fled to the United States because of a large accumulation of debts. He eventually became an Episcopalian minister.

Although the Newgate Street Church and the George Street Chapel were integrated into one circuit, the congregations continued to worship in their own churches and they had separate Sunday Schools. Alexander Irvine served until June 1834 when the Reverend Thomas Turner was appointed. The Newgate Street 'Leaders and Stewards', which met until the end of the year, adopted innovations that have remained in effect for one hundred and fifty years. They recommended that the singers practise on Wednesday or Thursday evenings after prayer meeting. They agreed to have a special collection at every Sacramental service to be used for the relief of the poor. They decided to have a Fellowship Hour after the evening service once a month.

The Town of York was incorporated as the City of Toronto in March 1834. At the end of that year, the Newgate Street Church had lost about forty members. Mr. and Mrs. J.S. Howard and Mrs. T.D. Morrison became occasional communicants in the newly organized Congregational Church. Several leading members had been among the six hundred victims of the cholera epidemic that raged in Toronto in 1832. The congregation was shocked to hear that the Leaders and Stewards, at their meeting on 22 December 1834, had expelled the highly respected Class Leaders, William Poyntz Patrick and Thomas Vaux, and the Local Preachers, William Warren and Joseph Easton, from their offices. The four men had previously been examined by the Local Preachers of the Conference who had determined that these men held views that were contrary to Methodism. After the Reverend Thomas Turner had asked them to deliver up their class books, a resolution was passed expressing the deep regret of the meeting 'especially because of their long-standing in the church' and 'the blamelessness of their conduct and the piety of their lives'. The resolution assured them of the tenderest affection held for them and the earnest hope that they might pledge within a week not to disseminate any other but Methodist doctrine. The four brethren held firmly to their newly acquired convictions.

W.P. Patrick had been converted by George Ryerson who, during his sojourn in England, had come under the influence of Edward Irving, the originator of the Irvingite Movement, officially known as the Catholic Apostolic Church. It was based on belief in the unity of all Christians and emphasized prophecy, the Second Coming, and the speaking in tongues. Patrick began to hold meetings for prayer and Bible study in his home on Bay Street. In 1834 the hospitable Patrick entertained two missionaries of the sect. He persuaded the officials to allow them to preach in the Newgate Street Church. Several people were converted and Patrick and his three associates were tried for heresy. Not only were they among the most dedicated members but Patrick had been the largest contributor. He donated a site and gave five hundred pounds towards the building of the Catholic Apostolic Church. The Reverend George Ryerson became its minister in 1837. Thomas Vaux later returned to Methodism when he moved to Quebec City. Patrick worshipped occasionally in the Newgate Street Church. Egerton Ryerson ruefully observed that the Catholic Apostolic Church converted 'unsuspecting persons of strong imagination and ardent temperament, especially when in a low state of religious enjoyment'.

In 1835 a new form of church government, following the British Wesleyan traditions, was introduced. The Leaders' and Stewards' meetings were abolished and the Missionary Society of the Methodist Episcopals became an auxiliary of the British Wesleyan Missionary Society. The Female Branch ceased to exist. The office of Presiding Elder was eliminated and the Quarterly Board meetings took on a different character. A self-perpetuating Trustee Board was established. The members were nominated by the Superintendent of the Circuit and approved by Board members. The business of the church was now discussed and decided in secret, for the Trustees were not responsible to the congregation. The Reverend Matthew Lang persuaded the Trustees to permit pew rents although many in the congregation had been bitterly opposed to this practice. Lang dismissed their dismay and wrote to the Reverend Robert Alder:

> A few left the Society but we had no cause to regret their leaving as they were very violent in their opposition of everything British and they kept the Church in a constant state of excitement for two or three years.

By 1835, Richard Woodsworth was the only local preacher attached to the Newgate Street Church.

The following June of 1836, John Doel, one of the six original members of the King Street Chapel, withdrew to organize a continuing Methodist Episcopal Church. Although there were only twenty-one members, they bought a lot on Richmond Street and a small frame chapel was opened in July 1837. The Reverend James Richardson, who had left the Wesleyan Methodist ministry, was appointed to the charge.

Joseph Smith and Brigham Young of the Mormons or Latter-Day Saints, visited Upper Canada in 1836. One of their converts was the class leader, John Taylor, who had come from England in 1832. He persuaded several members to leave the Methodists and to attend meetings in his home. At a special conference of leading clergy held to discuss with these members their reasons for adhering to Mormon teachings, the President of the Conference concluded:

> Brethren, we esteem you as brethren and gentlemen; we believe you are sincere, but we cannot fellowship your doctrine. Wishing, however, to concede all we can, we would say: 'You may believe your doctrines if you will not teach them, and we will still retain you in fellowship as members, leaders and preachers.'

Because Taylor and his followers would not comply with this conciliatory statement, they were deprived of their church offices. In the summer of 1837, Joseph Smith ordained Taylor as a high priest in charge of Mormon endeavour in Upper Canada. Later that year, he was made an Apostle and in 1877 he succeeded Brigham Young as the third President of the Church of Jesus Christ of Latter-Day Saints.

The loss of class leaders was somewhat relieved by the saintly Margaret Bowes Taylor who assumed responsibility for four classes. In 1836, the George Street Sunday School was closed. It met with the Sunday School of Newgate Street Church in its commodious basement. The officials merged in September of that year and in 1837, the George Street chapel was closed and rented to the Zion Congregationalist Church. William

Ryerson, the first Canadian-born minister since the union of 1833, was appointed to Newgate Street in September 1837. Joseph Stinson, the popular General Superintendent of Missions, served as an assistant preacher. T.E. Champion, in *The Methodist Churches of Toronto*, describes him as 'remarkably comely and handsome . . . as lovely in mind as in person'.

Political tensions were high in the autumn of 1837. Many Methodists were Reformers but some, like Richard Woodsworth, were staunch Conservatives. Egerton Ryerson had disassociated himself from the Reformers in 1833 because he believed that injustices could be rectified by existing constitutional means. Most Methodists were vehemently opposed to the use of force but they were strongly opposed to the way in which Crown lands had been designated by the Family Compact, as the governing circle was called. Egerton Ryerson maintained a constant battle of words about the disposition of all Clergy Reserves to the Church of England which could only claim ten percent of the population as members. The insurrection known as the Rebellion of Upper Canada began on 4 December 1837. Insurgents arrived at Montgomery's Tavern on Yonge Street where a skirmish took place on 7 December. The rebellion ended on 13 December when an uprising in the London area was put down by the militia. The Reverend William Ryerson, who had strong sympathy for the Reformers, was infuriated when, without his knowledge, Samuel Edwin Taylor, the husband of the godly Margaret Bowes Taylor, invited one hundred and fifty militia men to quarter in the basement of the Newgate Street church from Sunday, 10 December until Wednesday morning, 13 December. An anonymous pencilled account, written on the back page of the Leaders' and Stewards' Minute Book, records that several members, including Richard Woodsworth, 'assisted us to make them comfortable by cooking victuals, making tea, soup, coffee etc. for them'.

The authorities in government meted out prompt reprisals to the people involved in the Rebellion. J.S. Howard was removed from his post as Postmaster because of his sympathy with the Reformers. Although the godly Dr. T.D. Morrison had been a member of the Legislative Assembly in 1834 and Toronto's third mayor in 1836, he was arrested and tried for High Treason in 1838 because it was known that he had conferred with William Lyon Mackenzie. He was acquitted, but he fled to Rochester, New York, and did not return until the amnesty of 1843. The young Irish immigrant, James Austin, who had been employed by Mackenzie, also escaped to the United States remaining there until the furor died down. He became a successful businessman, building his mansion, *Spadina*, in 1866. He was the father of Albert William Austin, and the great-grandfather of the late Austin Thompson.

The year of 1838 was filled with apprehension about the future of the Province because many citizens were fleeing the country. William Ryerson wrote to his brother, Egerton, in April about his own despair:

> The very painful excitement caused by the execution of Lount and Matthews has in some degree subsided but dissatisfaction with the state of things is, I fear, increasing from day to day. Emigration to the States is the fear of the hour. It is indeed going on to an extent truly alarming and astonishing. . . . An emigration society has been formed, embracing some of the leading citizens. . . . My own spirit is almost broken down. I feel, I assure you, like leaving Canada, too, and I am not alone in those feelings; some of our friends whom you would not suspect, often feel quite as much down in the throat as I do. If ever I felt the need of faith, and wisdom, and patience, it is at the present. I have just returned from visiting the prisoners. After all, we know but little of the calamities and miseries with which our once happy land is now afflicted, and yet Sir Frances (Bond Head), the most guilty author of this misery, escapes without punishment; yes, with honour and praise! How mysterious are the ways of Providence, how dark, crooked, and perverse, the ways of man.

During this troubled time, many former Methodist Episcopals were becoming increasingly unhappy with the changes brought about by the union with the British Wesleyans. William Ryerson, regretting his support of the union, wrote to his brother, Egerton, in May 1837:

> It is my deliberate opinion, confirmed by painfull experience, that the less we have to do with the English Conference, and their Preachers, the better it would be for our Conference and the Church.

William Ryerson's successor at the Newgate Street Meeting House was the Reverend Matthew Richey who, in 1836, had been appointed the first Principal of the Upper Canada Academy at Cobourg, which became Victoria College in 1841. Richey had emigrated at the age of sixteen from County Donegal to Nova Scotia. In 1825 he was admitted to the British Wesleyan Conference. He became a noted preacher and his eloquence was 'equally admired by the most cultivated and intelligent and by the simple and unlettered.' He and his assistant, Joseph Stinson, were loyal Conservatives. In January 1840, they wrote to the newly appointed Governor-General, C.E.P. Thomson (created Lord Sydenham in 1841 after the union of Upper and Lower Canada), advising him that 'the Church of England being in our estimation *The Established Church* of all the British Colonies, *we* entertain no objection to the distinct recognition of her as such.' The Canadian Methodists were filled with indignation and exasperation. At the Conference in Belleville in June 1840, stormy sessions, with charges and counter-charges, resulted in the dissolution of the Union of 1833. Egerton Ryerson, who had promoted the idea of union, led the Canadian Methodists out of it. Richey and Stinson, along with William and Egerton Ryerson, attended the British Conference in England where the union was nullified.

The Reverend Matthew Richey and the Reverend Joseph Stinson returned from England to lead forty members of the Newgate Street Meeting House back to the George Street Chapel which was vacated by the Congregationalists. These people, referred to as 'the forty thieves' by the Newgate Street congregation, included Thomas Storm, the builder, Richard Woodsworth, Mr. Baxter, John George Bowes (Mrs. Margaret Taylor's brother), twice mayor of Toronto, Thomas Clarke, the hatter, and Robert Petch, the carpenter who had worked on both the King Street and the Newgate Street churches. It was the third time he had left the congregation to worship with the British Wesleyans.

In the autumn of 1840, Egerton Ryerson was appointed the minister of the depleted Newgate Street Church. He wrote later in his *Story of My Life*:

> Dr. Richey had carried off the greater part of the private and official members of the church and I was left with but a skeleton of each. When I ascended the pulpit for the first time, the pews in the body of the church, which had been occupied by those who seceded, were empty, and there were but scattered hearers, here and there, in the other pews and in the gallery.

In the winter of 1841, when the Province of Upper Canada became Canada West, Ryerson attempted to revitalize the congregation through an active Sunday School, a revival, and political preaching. The Sunday School had special programmes which were open to the public. Two converted Indians from the Credit River were the speakers at one gathering. For several weeks, beginning in March, revival services or 'a series of Protracted Meetings' were conducted by Egerton Ryerson, James

Richardson, and Anson Green, an outstanding preacher of the Methodist connexion. The *Christian Guardian* reported these meetings. On the first night there were twelve penitents, on the second night forty, and afterwards as many as fifty people came to the communion rail. Many families who had left the church returned at this time.

In October 1841, Ryerson was invited to become the principal of the newly constituted Victoria College in Cobourg. He carried, as well, the responsibility of the Newgate Street Church until the following June when he was succeeded by the Reverend Alexander McNab who had little interest in political affairs. His sermons and those of his assistant, the Reverend Lachlin Taylor (the great grand-uncle of Mrs. Joyce Anne Cumings), were strict interpretations of the Scriptures. In 1844, when the name of Newgate Street was changed to Adelaide Street, the congregation was able to start a new era under the new name of Adelaide Street Wesleyan Methodist Church.

○

Meanwhile, the George Street Chapel prospered. Increasing numbers were attracted by the preaching of the Reverend Matthew Richey and his assistant. The congregation outgrew the chapel even though it was extended by about thirty-four feet. In 1844, the wealthy hatter, Thomas Clarke, died leaving his entire estate to the George Street Chapel on the condition that the church would furnish his widow with an adequate annuity. The chapel was sold and in 1845 a large church was built on Richmond Street where Simpson's parking garage now stands.

The following year, Matthew Richey, who had moved to Montreal, attended the Conference of the British Wesleyan Missionary Society and was directed to suggest a possible reunion with the Canadian Wesleyans. Although Richey confessed that his efforts toward reunion were 'at the sacrifice of the finest feelings of his heart', the union was ratified at the Canadian Conference of 1847. It was recorded that Richey 'imbued with the spirit of a seraph carried the audience with him in his feelings of charity and love while delivering his impromptu but unequalled address'.

At this conference, Yorkville Chapel was added to the circuit of the Adelaide Street Church. The following year, the modest, kindly John Ryerson was appointed to the charge for a three-year pastorate. The *Christian Guardian* of 30 May 1849 commented editorially on the growing strength of this church:

> For several years the cause has been here maintained in the face of most formidable difficulties. And when we look back upon the serious disadvantages under which the Church laboured here, for years, we wonder that even a fragment should have been left to indicate a previous existence ... But Methodism is only in the morning of its power in this City . . . Difficulties have been removed. Prejudices have given way. Asperities have been softened down. Opponents feel their impotence. Methodists feel their power.

From November 1851 until the end of June 1852, an extended revival took place in Toronto when the evangelist, Dr. James Caughey, a leader in the Holiness Movement in the Methodist Episcopal Church, preached seven evenings and five afternoons a week in the new Richmond Street Church. He was a powerful preacher, believing in a 'material hell'. Hundreds were converted at these meetings and the Adelaide Street Church was strengthened by them. The membership rose from 212 to 497 while that of Richmond Street increased from 602 to 1,046. Because this number could not be accommodated, a church was built on Elm Street as a direct result of the revival. Richard Woodsworth became one of its founding members.

The next year, the Reverend Wellington Jeffers, the strong-minded son of a Methodist preacher, was appointed to the Adelaide Street Church. He was determined to follow the rules of the Methodist *Discipline* which insisted that members must attend weekly class meetings to receive the ticket of admission to the Quarterly Love Feast and the monthly Sacraments of the Lord's Supper. A prominent member, John George Hodgins, was astonished when Jeffers refused to issue him his ticket. He was also disqualified from holding his official positions in the church. Hodgins had come to Toronto after graduating from Victoria College in 1844 to become a clerk in the Department of Education of Canada West. He was made both a Trustee and a Steward of Adelaide Street Church. Egerton Ryerson sprang to the defence of his friend and colleague although the minister had every right to refuse the ticket. The disagreement came before the Conference of 1854. Jeffers' decision was upheld and compulsory class attendance was affirmed. He was moved, however, to another charge. John G. Hodgins joined St. James' Cathedral and Egerton Ryerson resigned from the Methodist ministry. His resignation was accepted but he was reinstated the following year. Hodgins edited Ryerson's incomplete autobiography which was published in 1883.

As well as insisting on compulsory attendance at class meetings, the Methodist Church remained strict in prohibiting theatre-going, dancing, and card-playing. These worldly pleasures were renounced by Methodists in accordance with John Wesley's rule to abjure from 'such diversions as cannot be used in the name of the Lord Jesus' based on the text from Colossians: 'Whatsoever ye do in word or deed, do all in the name of the Lord Jesus.' The Methodist community enjoyed 'social means of grace': sacred concerts, lectures, tea-meetings and rallies. By attending weekly class meetings and prayer meetings, morning and evening worship services on Sundays, afternoon Sunday School and the Tuesday midweek worship service, Methodists had no time or inclination for 'trivial pursuits'.

The congregational fellowship was strengthened by the presence of Methodist ministers who worshipped at Adelaide Street. Egerton Ryerson attended it after his return to Toronto as Superintendent of Public Instruction for Canada West in 1844. The next year the Reverend Anson Green, the newly appointed Book Steward, began his long association with this struggling church. From 1851, the Reverend Lachlin Taylor lent his support when he was agent for the Upper Canada Bible Society and later as the Secretary of the Missionary Society. These men played a large part in the founding of the Metropolitan Church in 1868.

A new organ was installed in the gallery over the narthex of the church in April 1857. T. P. Norton of Toronto, who had received his training in both England and the United States, built it in four months. The *Christian Guardian* commented:

> The organ at present promises to be, both for strength and beauty of workmanship and quality of tone, equal if not superior to the very best that have been constructed either in the Province or in the United States.

Daily prayer meetings, similar to those in New York City, were instituted in 1858. They were held in the Lecture Room from twelve to one o'clock and were open to members of any church. The *Christian Guardian* in April 1858 reported that the meetings were largely attended by ministers and members of several denominations and concluded:

> One good thing which will inevitably result from the association of the various churches, is the promotion of union of spirit and effort amongst the

members of several denominations for the revival of the work of God in this city.

The Methodists of Toronto were saddened by the death of the godly Mrs. Margaret Bowes Taylor (the aunt of Mrs. J.B. Willmott) in March 1859. Since her conversion at the camp meeting of 1825, she had lived a blameless life and had attained a state of 'Christian Perfection' with a purity of mind so cleansed by God's grace that it was impossible for her to entertain an evil or unworthy thought or desire. She was known as a 'Methodist Saint', sharing this uncommon distinction with Holy Ann Preston of Thornhill, Ontario. W.H. Pearson described Mrs. Taylor and her funeral in *Recollections and Records of Toronto of Old*, published by William Briggs in 1914:

> She resided on the north side of Richmond Street, a little east of Victoria, and was noted for her piety and benevolence and had an almost seraphic appearance and a remarkable gift of prayer. Looking upon her death as a gateway to a brighter and a better world, she requested that there should be no mourning for her when she died, but that instead, hymns of rejoicing should be sung by those who followed her to her burial. This request was complied with and a large number (of whom I was one) followed in the funeral cortege from the house to Adelaide Street Methodist Church, singing hymns all the way. Possibly no other such funeral has taken place in Canada.

Mrs. Taylor's tombstone now rests in the vault of the Metropolitan Church.

The newly built Berkeley Street Church was added to the circuit of Adelaide Street and Yorkville Churches in 1858. It had evolved from the Sunday School established in 1824 by Joshua Van Allen of the King Street Chapel. In 1840 it was reopened by Thomas Storm and others who had moved to the George Street chapel. Mr. and Mrs. Storm were among the first class leaders of the church. In order to provide Sunday services in the Berkeley Street Church, a third minister was added to the charge under the superintendency of the Reverend John Borland. They rotated around this triangular circuit. The Quarterly Board included representation from the three congregations. By 1862, the circuit was declared free of debt. The scale of the ministers' salaries was set at $1,200 per annum for the Superintendent, $700 for the married assistant, and $440 for the third unmarried cleric. When the Board made plans for a circuit tea-meeting in November

1864, eight brethren formed a committee to arrange for this gathering 'held for the purpose of bringing members of the Society together' with the proceeds for circuit funds. The following May, the members of the Yorkville chapel felt it 'conducive to the word of God' to separate from the circuit. The Conference gave its approval in June and formed the Toronto City East Circuit made up of the Adelaide Street and Berkeley Street Churches. At the first meeting of the new Quarterly Board, the ladies of the Adelaide Street Church served tea to the officials. The minutes of the meeting concluded:

> After one of the most pleasant, harmonious and quiet Quarterly meetings which it ever fell to the lot of the Recording Steward to attend, the Board dispersed mutually well-pleased with each other on the benediction having been pronounced by the Chairman.

In spite of tea-meetings and a campaign for subscriptions, deficiencies were reported for the third year in February 1867. The Board decided to reduce the ministers' stipends, allowing $1,000 per annum for the Superintendent, $440 if the junior minister were married, or $400 if unmarried. It was agreed that the appointed ministers should have small families to excuse the circuit from the grant for children, and that for 'proper walking of the circuit' it would be desirable to have men 'in full vigour of life'. A new parsonage was rented for the senior minister at 239 Jarvis Street. The Reverend William Stephenson was appointed at the Conference in June 1867.

Because Adelaide Street was becoming a downtown church with many of its members moving to newer sections of the city, the Quarterly Board decided in August 1867 to insert paid notices of church services in the *Globe* and the *Leader* in their effort to attract worshippers. The next month it was moved and seconded that collection plates should be procured and used instead of bags for taking up collections.

The advertisements must have brought newcomers to the congregation because the Board discussed the courtesies due to strangers in meeting them at the door and escorting them to their seats. It was suggested that the minister should preach on this subject. Deficits, however, persisted. The building, after thirty-five years of use, was in need of many repairs. The future of Adelaide Street Church seemed gloomy.

The Rev. Anson Green (left), and the Rev. Dr. Morley Punshon (right), two of the prime movers in the purchase and development of McGill Square as the site of the Metropolitan Church.

M.W.M.C.
AUGUST 24
1870

The original cornerstone of the Metropolitan Wesleyan Methodist Church, 1870, and a portion of the programme invitation. Admission to the grounds cost 20 cents; with refreshments, 50 cents.

CORNER-STONE
LAYING.

METROPOLITAN CHURCH,
McGILL SQUARE,

On WEDNESDAY, the 24th day of AUGUST, 1870,
AT 3:30 O'CLOCK, P.M.

ADMISSION TICKET TO GROUND AND COLLATION, 50 CENTS.

An architect's sketch of the building planned to be a 'cathedral of Methodism'; left, the temporary 'tabernacle' on the grounds, used while the large church was being built.

CHAPTER 4
McGill Square

1868 - 1871

The course of events was abruptly changed because the Reverend Anson Green, who had retired from his post of Book Steward, went walking along Queen Street one day. Between Church and Bond Streets he met a builder, Benjamin Walton, who was a prominent member of Richmond Street Church. Dr. Green recorded this encounter in his autobiography, *The Life and Times of Anson Green*:

> As I was walking by McGill Square on the 8 September and reflecting upon the manner in which the negotiations between the city and the Montreal Bank, for the Square, had fallen through, a builder of the city came to me saying: 'Doctor, you should now step in and buy this block for a church. You can sell old Adelaide for $10,000, and I will give you $1000 towards a new church. "Thank you," said I, "that is worth thinking about". Before I reached home, another gentleman David Thurston offered me $500 for the same object. I immediately went to Dr. Ryerson, my co-Trustee, and reported these facts. "First rate," said he, "let us call a committee and see what can be done." I then went to Morley Punshon, who agreed with us, and seventeen persons met and agreed to purchase the square.

This meeting, which occurred on 10 September 1868 with the Reverend William Stephenson in the chair, was composed of prominent clergy and a representation from neighbouring Methodist churches. The Reverend Lachlin Taylor informed the gathering that the Bank of Montreal, which had foreclosed the mortgage on McGill Square bounded by Queen, Shuter, Church, and Bond Streets, had unsuccessfully offered the site to the City of Toronto for a proposed City Hall. The Bank was willing to sell it for $25,000, with a down payment of $5,000, if a definite answer could be given the next day. The proposal was viewed with favour and a committee was set up consisting of Dr. Taylor; Benjamin Walton; David Thurston, the American Consul and a member of Adelaide Street Church; George Rowell and Dr. W.T. Aikins of the Berkeley Street congregation; and the Reverend William Stephenson. The Bank agreed to a short delay. A second meeting was called for Monday 14 September, with additional members, including Egerton Ryerson; A.W. Lauder, M.P.P., of Richmond Street Church; John Macdonald of Yorkville; and the Reverend Enoch Wood, Superintendent of Missions for the Wesleyan Methodist Church in Canada. It was decided to have a circular printed inviting all interested people to attend a meeting in the Adelaide Street Church on the following Wednesday. At that third meeting, Mr. Lauder reported that the City of Toronto had reconsidered its decision and was willing to buy the property for $25,000. The Bank of Montreal had informed him that $26,000 must now be paid and that the five thousand dollar deposit would be forfeited if this purchase were not completed by one o'clock on the following Saturday. The Reverend Egerton Ryerson moved 'that it is desirable to purchase McGill Square for connexional purposes including a representative church'. The motion was carried with only one dissenting vote. It was agreed that a Board of Trustees should be appointed with the responsibility of selecting

> a suitable site on the Square for the erection of a spacious and commodious Church, thereon, to take the place of the Adelaide Street Wesleyan Church of this city . . . Keeping in view the accommodation of that congregation and their funds as well as the credit of Methodism in general.

The Committee set up a subscription list and the sum of $5,700 was immediately promised.

The Trustees of the Adelaide Street Church were requested to sell their property as soon as possible, with the proceeds of the sale reverting to the fund for the new church. Ways and means of financing the project were discussed. John Macdonald, Toronto's 'Merchant Prince', and Abram W. Lauder were asked to solicit donations from the business area south of King Street. The Reverend Dr. Lachlin Taylor and the Reverend William Stephenson were put in charge of a financial campaign for the rest of the city, with a special city-wide canvass of all Methodists. A mammoth bazaar was suggested. The Missionary Society of the Wesleyan Methodist Church agreed to buy a lot on the southeast or southwest corner of the

Square for a new headquarters. It was suggested that the proposed theological college might be located on the north side of the property.

On Saturday morning, 16 September, the Reverend Morley Punshon and Abram W. Lauder went to the bank to ask for an extension. When they found it was impossible, they each gave a personal cheque for $2,500 as the down payment. The Reverend Anson Green recorded:

> They purchased the entire square, 3¼ acres for $26,000, but as the Mayor and the Roman Bishop were both anxious to get the property, a much larger sum than the one we gave was at once offered—but offered a few minutes too late!

The prompt action for this momentous venture could not have been undertaken without the enthusiasm, vision, and administrative skills of the Reverend William Morley Punshon, the President of the Wesleyan Methodist Church in Canada. He had arrived in Toronto at the beginning of May 1868 to begin his five-year term of office. The British Conference made the appointment in accordance with the regulations drawn up at the time of the reunion of 1847, but this body usually acted on the recommendation of the Canadian Church. Egerton Ryerson made the initial enquiries concerning the possibility of the appointment of Morley Punshon, one of Britain's most distinguished Methodists, an eloquent orator, an expert administrator, and a devout man of God. In 1861, he had been one of the founders of the *Methodist Recorder*, still the official organ of British Methodists. From 1862 to 1867 he had personally raised $10,000 through public lectures for the construction of chapels in England's seaside resorts. During his sojourn in Canada, he revitalized the denomination, travelling widely in his capacity of President. From his lecture tours in Canada, the United States, and Great Britain, he was able to contribute so generously to the 'Cathedral of Methodism' in McGill Square that it became known as 'Punshon's Church'.

A Committee of Management was appointed on 15 October 1868 with Mr. Punshon as Chairman and W.T. Mason as Secretary. It was made up of Dr. Egerton Ryerson, Dr. Anson Green, Dr. Lachlin Taylor, William Stephenson, Dr. Enoch Wood, and prominent laymen, including A.W. Lauder, John Macdonald and Dr. W.T. Aikins. It was agreed that the cost of the building should not exceed $40,000, that the church, seating two thousand people, should be Gothic in style, that a lecture room, classrooms for the Sunday School, and committee rooms should be attached to the church. By 31 October, they had announced a competition for the design of the building with a first prize of two hundred dollars and a second prize of one hundred dollars. Architects were invited to submit plans under a pseudonym by the first of February 1869. On 19 February, the first prize was awarded to William George Storm who had designed the Church of St. Andrew and Victoria College. Second prize went to Henry Langley. An altercation arose with Storm when he refused to hand over his plans until the prize money had been paid. The impasse was eventually resolved in January 1870 when the Committee decided to have the plans of Storm and Langley examined by reputable builders to confirm that they came within the $40,000 limit. When it was reported that the plans of W.G. Storm would cost $74,000, the competition was declared invalid and Henry Langley was commissioned to provide plans for a church seating 1,600 at a cost of $40,000.

The newly constituted Board of Trustees, made up of six clergymen and fifteen laymen, met officially for the first time on 11 April 1870, with Mr. Punshon in the chair. The clergy included all the senior officials of the denomination. The laymen were selected from Adelaide Street, Queen Street, Elm Street, Yorkville, and Richmond Street Churches, even though some had no intention of joining the new church. It was mandatory that all trustees contribute generously to the building fund. At this meeting, Henry Langley submitted his plans. As the interior bore a resemblance to St. George's Parish Church in Doncaster, England, where Morley Punshon had worshipped as a boy, it was obvious that he had had considerable influence in the design of the new church.

When tenders were called in May, the Trustees were consternated to discover that the costs, not including the furnishings, organ, lighting, and architect's fees, were estimated at from $85,000 to $115,000. The architect met with the contractor who had submitted the lowest bid, Joseph Gearing. Their alterations reduced the cost to $61,000. A second subscription from the generous Trustees resulted in an additional $10,000.

The Reverend Morley Punshon organized the Young Men's McGill Square Association in January 1870 to raise funds for the new church. He became the President. William T. Mason was the Secretary. The membership fee was twenty dollars per annum. Quarterly meetings were held in April, July, October, and December. That year, they sponsored two lectures by the Reverend Gervase Smith, a friend of Mr. Punshon's who came from England to address the Conference held in the Adelaide Street

Church in June. Their Annual Report described his lectures on 'The Spanish Armada' and 'The Siege of Derry' as 'abundantly successful'. His third lecture on 'Wycliffe, the Star of the Reformation' was sponsored by the McGill Square Ladies' Association. This group was organized when the wives of the Trustees were asked to convene the mammoth bazaar which raised four thousand dollars for the Building Fund. The popular Mrs. Punshon was elected President. The Young Men's Association eventually raised enough money to purchase the organ for the new church.

Meanwhile, the Adelaide Street Church attempted to gain strength so that it would be better fitted for its role as the nucleus of a cathedral church. Dr. James Caughey was invited to return for revival services. His visit failed to attract many new members. By the end of the century, many Methodists involved in the Holiness Movement he represented left the church to become Pentecostals, Nazarenes, Gospel Workers, Free Methodists, or to join the Salvation Army. Membership of the Adelaide Street Church at the time of its closing reached two hundred and twenty-six. Nearly forty years earlier, the King Street Chapel had had two hundred and sixty-four members.

The church was sold to the Trust and Home Company of Upper Canada for $15,000. Remembering that the King Street Meeting House had been used as a theatre, the Trustees made sure that part of the church would be demolished and the rest rebuilt for an office building. The invitation which had been extended to the Reverend George Cochran was confirmed at the June Conference.

In July, the Trustees of the McGill Square property voted on a name for the new church. Five names were suggested: Wesley Church, Grace Church, Memorial Church, St. Paul's Church and the Metropolitan Church. Memorial was eliminated on the first ballot, Grace on the second, and Metropolitan was chosen on the third.

❁

The cornerstone of the Metropolitan Wesleyan Methodist Church was laid by Egerton Ryerson at an afternoon service on Wednesday 24 August 1870. Morley Punshon had insisted that Dr. Ryerson accept the honour despite his reluctance, for he had taken no conspicuous part in church affairs for more than twenty-five years. Three thousand people crowded the Square for the event. Admission was by ticket only: a twenty-cent ticket to the grounds, a fifty-cent ticket to the 'grounds and collation'. A platform surrounded by flags and banners provided a festive setting. The ceremonies were opened by Dr. Anson Green. The Reverend George Cochran gave out the first hymn:

> Thou who hast in Zion laid,
> The true foundation-stone.

After Scripture readings and prayers by dignitaries of the Wesleyan Methodist Church, W.T. Mason read aloud the contents of the urn: a parchment with details of the service, the Minutes of Conference for 1870, the *Christian Guardian* and city newspapers for 24 August 1870, Sunday School papers, coins in sterling and Canadian coins of twenty-five, twenty, ten, five, and one cents. Mr. Punshon presented the trowel to Dr. Ryerson who placed the urn in the cavity and signalled to Mr. Gearing. The cornerstone, which had been suspended by a derrick to face Church Street, 'descended gracefully' while the choir sang, 'Glorious things of Thee are spoken, Zion city of our God'. Dr. Ryerson was so moved by the proceedings that he could not deliver his address. Mr. Punshon read it for him and then called on the choir and audience to sing 'God Save the Queen' and to raise three rousing cheers for Her Majesty. A marquee had been erected in the valley between the church and Queen Street. There, the Ladies of McGill Square served a 'cold collation' or light meal. When the people were safely gathered in the tent, the elements 'broke loose' and caused an hour's delay before the evening programme could begin with the hymn, 'Before Jehovah's Awful Throne'. After a prayer, Morley Punshon was called upon to speak. The treasurer, Abram Lauder, gave a financial statement. John Macdonald made a witty speech 'punctuated by laughter and applause'. Before the Benediction was pronounced at ten o'clock, seventeen hundred additional dollars had been subscribed.

The following Sunday, the last services were held in the Adelaide Street Church. The Reverend Dr. Anson Green preached in the morning and Egerton Ryerson in the evening. Dr. Green recorded:

> Being requested to preach the last sermon in Adelaide on 28 August, before the hands of spoliation were laid upon those sacred walls, I took for my text, 'They go from strength to strength' (Psalm 84.7). As a proof that we were going 'from strength to strength', I gave them the history of Methodism in Toronto.

For the next ten weeks, the congregation held services in the Music Hall, while the contractor, Mr. Gearing, constructed a wooden Tabernacle at the south end of the Square at a cost of five hundred dollars.

The Methodist community was deeply saddened and shocked when Mrs. Fanny Punshon died after an illness of a few hours. She was the sister of Mr. Punshon's first wife, Maria, who had died in 1859. For ten years Fanny had cared for the children, but it was illegal for a widower to marry his sister-in-law under an English law of 1835. As the law did not apply in Canada, their marriage, conducted by Egerton Ryerson, took place on 15 August 1868, shortly after Fanny's arrival in Toronto with the children. Morley Punshon installed, in her memory, Metropolitan's first stained glass window which was reputed to contain all the colours of the spectrum.

The first McGill Square church service was held in the Tabernacle on 13 November 1870. The congregation faced the future with enthusiasm and no regrets. God had indeed blessed their troubles and sanctified their deepest distress. Week by week they watched the walls of the great church rise. The *Christian Guardian* of 14 September gave a detailed description:

> McGill Square is the centre of unwonted activity. Mr. Gearing is pushing the work with great vigour. Immense masses of Cleveland stone (some weighing over five tons) lie scattered around; a large number of stone-cutters are at work, and the walls are rising rapidly . . .
>
> The building throughout is designed in the French Gothic style of the fourteenth century. Its extreme dimensions are 216 feet in length and 104 feet in width, and when finished will be the largest ecclesiastical edifice in the city. . . The main building will seat on ordinary occasions about 1800 persons, which number can be increased to 2400 when occasion requires. . . The external appearance of the building will be very rich and elaborate, combining at the same time massiveness with elegance and lightness.

The Trustees of the Metropolitan Wesleyan Methodist Church met frequently to make decisions concerning the building and to resolve problems when they arose. Dr. Green observed that Mr. Punshon, in the chair, was 'firm without severity, conciliatory without weakness'. In a letter addressed to the Board in November 1870, Benjamin Chapman (the grandfather of the Misses Marian and Victoria Hanna) offered to provide, gratuitously, a suitable clock for the gallery. In February 1871, the McGill Square Ladies' Association was asked to obtain estimates and facts about upholstery and carpeting. Twelve hundred yards of red carpet and the same amount of rep for cushions were purchased at a cost of one thousand dollars. The McCausland Stained Glass firm was given a contract for leaded glass windows with coloured borders for twelve hundred dollars.

Morley Punshon left in March on an extended lecture tour through the United States to Salt Lake City and San Francisco. From there he travelled by boat to visit the Methodist missions of British Columbia where he ordained the missionary, Thomas Crosby, at the first Wesleyan ordination service held in that province. He returned at the end of May. From June until September he was in England on another lecture tour. On his return, his contributions from lectures, not counting his personal gifts, amounted to $5679.79.

During his absence, the Trustees were dismayed to learn that the contractor was facing bankruptcy and might not be able to complete the building. An added mortgage was assumed and Mr. Gearing was offered a bonus of ten thousand dollars when the church was completed. Costs for lighting, heating and furnishings were approved. A sexton was hired for a yearly sum of four hundred dollars. The expense of a night watchman, hired for a dollar a night, was borne jointly with the contractor.

In March, the organ of the Adelaide Street Church was sold and the proceeds were given to the Young Men's McGill Square Association for their organ fund. In June, the Trustees approved the purchase of a two-manual organ from the O'Dell Company of New York for fifty-five hundred dollars. The case was constructed in Toronto. The Music Committee identified three requirements for an organist: 1. General good character; 2. Good standing as an organist and musician; 3. Possession of administrative ability. Although twenty-one organists applied, none of the applicants warranted an unqualified recommendation. Mr. Thomas Turvey, who had seemed to be the most eligible, was hired for six months at a salary of four hundred dollars per annum. Mr. C.W. Coates agreed to give assistance with the choir.

Metropolitan W. M. Church.

OPENING,

THURSDAY EVENING, 4th April, 1872,

COMMENCING AT SEVEN, P.M.

PROGRAMME.

DEVOTIONAL EXERCISES.

1. ORGAN—*Grand Fantasia*—On " Martha," . . FLOTOW.
   H. E. BROWNE,
   (Organist of the Church of the Holy Trinity, New York.)

2. CHORAL—*Sleepers, wake'!*—Harmonized by MENDELSSHON.

3. ADDRESS . . . . REV. DR. TIFFANY.

4. ORGAN—*Toccata in* F. . . . . J. S. BACH.
   H. E. BROWNE.

5. ANTHEM—*Christ being raised from the dead* . . DR. ELVEY.
   ROM. ch. 6, ver. 9.

6. SHORT ADDRESSES—REV. W. M. PUNSHON, M.A., AND OTHERS.

7. ORGAN—Extempore, introducing the *Storm*, &c., &c., . .
   H. E. BROWNE.

8. CHORUS—*Gloria* { " Glorious is Thy Name, } MOZART.
   { Almighty Lord," }

9. ORGAN—*Overture,* "*William Tell,*" . . . . . ROSSINI.
   H. E. BROWNE.

10. THE HALLELUJAH CHORUS—*Messiah*, ... HANDEL.

THE NATIONAL ANTHEM.

The Metropolitan Church, soon after completion of construction. Note the distinctive pattern in the roof tiles. (Note also the traffic on Bond Street.) At left, a portion of the programme celebrating the church's opening. It consisted mainly of musical performances, with interspersed addresses.

Another striking view of the newly built Metropolitan Wesleyan Methodist Church, showing the Sunday School at the rear.

CHAPTER 5
The Metropolitan Wesleyan Methodist Church

1872 - 1882

Elaborate plans were made for the opening service of the new church on Thursday, 4 April 1872. Mr. Cochran and Dr. Taylor were delegated to arrange reductions in the railway fares of people coming to Toronto for the dedication services. The Reverend Otis T. Tiffany of Newark, New Jersey, one of the most outstanding preachers on the continent, accepted the invitation to preach at the eleven o'clock service on Thursday morning and at the evening service the following Sunday. It was decided that Mr. Punshon, Dr. Green, Dr. Enoch Wood and Mr. Cochran should take part in the service. The idea of a tea-meeting at night was rejected in favour of a programme of speeches and music when the church would be illuminated by gaslight and the magnitude of the organ would be demonstrated by a visiting organist from Detroit, Henry Eyre Browne. The Young Men's Association agreed to sponsor a lecture and an organ recital.

Province-wide excitement mounted as the day of dedication drew near. The Reverend Morley Punshon described the day's events in a letter to his friend, the Reverend Gervase Smith:

> The church was finished and looked perfect. The day was gloriously fine although the streets were muddy. We had succeeded in getting reduced fares from all the railways. Tiffany preached a very fine sermon, rich in old evangelistic truth. At night there were upwards of 2300 people at a public meeting who paid fifty cents each for tickets. My heart is very full this opening day.

Immediately after the service of divine worship at eleven o'clock, the Methodist women of Toronto opened their bazaar in the Tabernacle of 'useful and fancy articles'. A 'cold collation' and refreshments were provided. The *Toronto Mail,* in reporting the evening meeting, noted:

> Mr. Browne delighted the audience by Toccato in F by Bach. It is a rare thing to hear anything of Bach's performed in public in this country and we are greatly indebted to Mr. Browne for the treat he offered us.

The choir sang three anthems and the 'Hallelujah Chorus'. Short addresses were given by Dr. Tiffany and Morley Punshon who acknowledged that he had been suffering from 'Metropolitan on the Brain' and that all he desired to say was summed up in the verse: 'Therefore give us now the proof of your love and my boasting of you.'

Because the meeting took place on a week night, the officials decided that it would be appropriate to launch an appeal and start a subscription list. The amount subscribed exceeded their highest expectations for more than $32,000 was promised. The newspaper published the long list of subscribers, with the amounts, from John Macdonald's two thousand dollars to one dollar from an Alice McNab.

The *Christian Guardian* carried a description of the first Sunday services, written by Dr. Anson Green:

> On Sunday morning the temple was literally crammed to hear Dr. Punshon, our eloquent President, and again in the evening to listen to an admirable sermon from Dr. Tiffany. Large and spacious as the church is, multitudes had to leave, not being able to get even standing room, though about three thousand, it was said, got near enough to hear these learned and eloquent ministers plead the cause of God. . . . On Monday evening, 8 April, Dr. Tiffany interested about two thousand people with his admirable lecture on the Yosemite Valley. . . .

Dr. Green concluded:

> The principal parties engaged in this work have done themselves much credit; but in reviewing the whole, we may have many things to remind us that to God, the first, the best, and the greatest, all praise belongs. Had we known at the beginning when we resolved to build a church for $40,000 that $140,000 would be required to complete the whole, including fencing, I do not think the church would have been built at all; but God, in His wisdom, concealed many difficulties from us until we reached them, and gave us hearts to meet and overcome them; and it now appears that we have accomplished this great work with as much ease as we could have built, after our first impression and purpose, a church costing only $40,000.

The concluding event to celebrate the opening of the great church took place on Tuesday 15 April, when the Young Men's Metropolitan Church Association sponsored an organ recital by Henry Eyre Browne who played selections from Handel, Beethoven, Bach, and Mendelssohn. They were interspersed with sacred vocal solos. The programme began with 'Explanations, Remarks and Words', when due credit was given to the Young Men's Association. Three brothers were leaders in this organization: William T., Thomas G., and Alfred Mason. They had emigrated from Ireland in the 1840s and had worshipped at George Street, Richmond Street, and Elm Street Churches. From the inception of the possibility that a church might be built on McGill Square, they were enthusiastic supporters. Thomas G., who entered the music business in 1854 and established the firm of Mason & Risch, Pianoforte Manufacturers in 1871, became the Treasurer of the Young Men's McGill Square Association and later, the Chairman of the Music Committee of the Metropolitan. Because of his ability and willingness as Secretary of the Young Men's Association, William was made the Secretary-Treasurer of the Board of Trustees. Alfred was appointed the Poor Steward. The three brothers gave years of dedicated service to the Metropolitan Church.

The Sunday services continued to draw about three thousand people, week by week. The Reverend Dr. Morley Punshon acceded to the request of the Quarterly Board to preach twice a month when possible. He had reluctantly received the honorary degree of Doctor of Laws which Victoria College had conferred on him that year. Notices of the times of the services were printed, framed, and distributed to the principal hotels of the city. The church became a show-place. A tour of the premises was included in the first official visit to Toronto of the newly appointed Governor-General, Lord Dufferin. Lady Dufferin recorded in her journal on 15 October 1872:

> D. and I drove to see a fine Wesleyan church. In the same building, forming part of the architectural effect outside, but separate inside, there are Sunday-school and Committee rooms.

Many organizations applied for the use of the Sanctuary or Lecture Room. The Trustees ruled that the property could be used only for sacred or benevolent purposes. They gave permission to the St. George's Society, the Bible Society, the Young Men's Christian Association, and to the Ladies' Aid of Richmond Street Church for a bazaar in the Lecture Room.

The request of the Mechanics Institute for the use of the church for a lecture on Compulsory Education by the Reverend Henry Ward Beecher was refused because of its secular nature.

The Missionary Society decided that a lot along Shuter Street from Bond to Church Streets would be preferable to either the southeast or southwest corners that had been reserved. In January 1873, the Society paid $6,000 for the property on condition that the building should be in the centre of the lot, that none should be erected for domestic purposes and that the site should be sold only to the Metropolitan Church.

For the first anniversary services on 6 April 1873, the Board decided to invite Dr. Punshon, whose term of office was drawing to a close, to preach at the morning service. Dr. Tiffany was asked to come again from Newark, New Jersey, to preach at the evening service and to deliver a lecture on 'Moses' on the following evening under the auspices of the Young Men's Metropolitan Church Association.

The next month both George Cochran and Morley Punshon severed their connection with the Metropolitan Church. Mr. and Mrs. Cochran, who no doubt had been influenced by the missionary zeal of Dr. Punshon, were commissioned with the Reverend Dr. David Macdonald and his wife, as the first Methodist missionaries to Japan. Dr. Punshon conducted the valedictory service, assisted by Dr. Enoch Wood and Dr. Lachlin Taylor and other leading clergy. This was Dr. Punshon's last official act as President of the Wesleyan Methodist Church in Canada. His first official act, five years earlier, had been to conduct farewell services for missionaries leaving for the Northwest. The 'Japan Mission' evinced his vision and administrative abilities. From the seventeenth century until 1858, no person from the Western world was admitted to Japan. By 1871, only fifteen people had been converted to Christianity in that country. In a letter dated 8 May 1873, the day after the service of dedication, Punshon wrote:

> I thank God that I have lived to see this day and that He has honoured me by making me in any way instrumental in bringing it about. . . . In the evening our beautiful church was filled to overflowing when we had the Bible meeting.

Dr. Punshon preached for the last time in the Metropolitan Church on Sunday 11 May. He closed his sermon with these words:

> The long bond which has united us is now of necessity loosened. From other

lips you will listen to the words of eternal life. Our interest in each other, fresh and vivid and hearty now, will become by a law that is common, and of which therefore we may not complain, fainter and fainter, until down the corridors of memory we must gaze to recall with an effort the names and circumstances that are so familiar to-day, but deeply in a heart that does not soon nor readily forget will be graven in distinctest lettering the name of this House of Prayer, and of the congregation that has gathered within its walls. . . . There are prophets who predict your halting,—there are I fear malignants who would rejoice in it. Be it yours to prove the prophets false ones, be it yours to have over the malignants the nobility of a Gospel revenge. As the fathers die, let the children be baptised for the dead, and by a bright succession of manly and intelligent piety prevent the burial ground from becoming richer than the Church.

At the request of many friends, he agreed in 1873 to the publication of a memorial volume with four sermons and six of his lectures: 'Daniel in Babylon', 'Macaulay', 'John Bunyan', 'John Wesley and his Times', 'Florence and the Florentines', and 'The Huguenots'. A publisher's note explained that the front cover had been embellished with a miniature outline of the Metropolitan Church 'which owes its origin to the earnest labour and eloquence of the Rev. Dr. Punshon'. He remarried soon after his return to England and in 1874 served as the President of the British Wesleyan Conference.

During his time in Canada he had worked for a union among the Methodist churches of Canada. In 1871 a union committee had met in Toronto's Music Hall but the Primitive Methodists and the Methodist Episcopals decided to withdraw from any merger. The small Methodist New Connexion Church decided to unite with the Wesleyan Methodist Church in Canada. An invitation to participate in the union was accepted by the Wesleyan Conference of Eastern British America. The first General Conference of the three uniting bodies known as the Methodist Church of Canada took place in the Metropolitan Church on 16 September 1874 when the Reverend Dr. Egerton Ryerson was elected President for a four-year term. Two years later the name of the office was changed to General Superintendent. The General Conference, made up of an equal number of ministerial and lay delegates, severed all connections with the British Methodists.

❀

The Reverend John Potts succeeded George Cochran as the minister of the Metropolitan Church. He was born in County Fermanagh, Northern Ireland, in 1838 and immigrated to Canada at the age of seventeen. He came under the influence of the Reverend George Douglas and was ordained in 1861. Dr. Potts has been described as 'big of frame, big of voice, big of heart, big of brain' and a man of 'cordial ways and strong personality'. He served in St. James Street Church in Montreal before assuming the responsibilities of the Metropolitan Church.

His appointment coincided with that of the new organist, Frederic Herbert Torrington, after a year-long search by Thomas G. Mason and the Music Committee. Torrington was born in Worcestershire, England, in 1837. At the age of twenty he immigrated to Montreal and became the organist of St. James Street Wesleyan Methodist Church where he remained until 1869 when he moved to Boston as organist of King's Chapel. He agreed to come to Metropolitan at a salary of one thousand dollars, 'to be present at special and ordinary services, to train the choir and to interest himself in all the musical service of the church'. The inadequate Mr. Turvey was dismissed with three months' notice.

Dr. Potts' ministry from 1873 to 1876 was a time of growth and activity. His splendid preaching and the beautiful music attracted large congregations and by 1876 three thousand worshippers were still attending the Sunday services. The membership increased from 262 in 1872 to 602 in 1876. The twenty-six weekly class meetings were held on Sunday mornings at ten o'clock, on Wednesday evenings and on Friday afternoons and evenings. Two prayer meetings were held every week on Monday and Thursday evenings. The Sunday School, attended by adults as well as children every Sunday afternoon, grew in numbers from 238 pupils and thirty-eight teachers in 1872 to 581 scholars and sixty-four teachers in 1876. The Sacrament of the Lord's Supper was celebrated every three months; Love Feasts of bread and water took place every month. Seven ordained ministers, in addition to the appointed pastor, were active participants and seven Local Preachers were attached to the congregation.

The Quarterly Official Board was made up of the clergy in the congregation, the local preachers, the leaders of classes, the Sunday School officers, seven representatives of the congregation and three representatives from the Board of Trustees. The minister acted as chairman of both Boards. The Quarterly Board received all Sunday collections which were looked after by a committee of Stewards. They paid the minister's salary, the expenses connected with the parsonage and incidental expenses of church services. This Board was responsible for the distribution of money for the needy. The Poor Steward reported his activities at every meeting. The women of the church organized a Dorcas Society in 1873 to provide clothing for the Methodist poor, and especially for children so that they could attend Sunday School. The Quarterly Board examined and licensed Local Preachers, and appointed Exhorters and Class Leaders. A fixed amount of money was transferred annually to the Trustees. As well as being responsible for congregational matters, the officials had serious concern about social problems, especially alcoholism. In August 1872, a resolution had been forwarded to the Provincial Legislature respectfully requesting the passing of a prohibition liquor law. In 1875 the Board decided to hold a public meeting on 29 December. Mr. Torrington directed the choir in several anthems. The *Toronto Mail* reported the motion that was presented to and adopted by the large audience:

> That in view of the deplorable social and moral evils everywhere manifest as the legitimate fruit of intoxicating liquor as a beverage . . . this meeting is of the opinion that it is the bounden duty of Christians of whatever name or denomination, to put forth all possible effort for the removal of this curse from the land.

The Trustees were appointed for life. This Board was responsible for the music, for the upkeep of the building and grounds, for the rental of pews, for the uses of the Sanctuary and Lecture Room and for the salaries of the organist and sexton. During Dr. Potts' pastorate, many expenditures were authorized. Steam heating was introduced for the Sunday School in 1873 and by 1876 all the furnaces had been replaced. A parsonage at 266 Jarvis Street was purchased in 1874 from the Reverend William Gregg, a former minister of Cooke's Presbyterian Church. The Metropolitan Ladies' Association assisted the Board in the furnishing and carpeting of the Sunday School classrooms. The Trustees purchased an organ for the Sunday School from Mason, Risch and Newcombe at half-price and authorized the architect, Henry Langley, to carry out alterations in the gallery to provide additional seating. The fencing and landscaping of the grounds were given careful consideration. After a meeting with members and pew holders, it was decided that the entire Square should be fenced using Henry Langley's design for an iron fence that echoed the Gothic design of the church. The Missionary Society agreed to pay one-third of the cost.

Landscaping was authorized and 1,268 trees were bought at a cost of $454.04. A Mr. Huggins offered to plant the trees at five cents a tree, and soon after he was engaged to look after the grounds in summer and to shovel the snow in the winter. He later assumed the duties of sexton as well, for $900 a year. The Trustees rejected the request for a fountain in the Square.

Although Mr. Torrington, soon after his arrival, had made known the disquieting fact that the two-manual organ presented by the Young Men's Metropolitan Church Association was too small for the large church, the Trustees did not appoint a committee to investigate and report on the enlargement until June 1875. Thomas G. Mason and Mr. Torrington travelled to Montreal, New York, and Boston to get the best available information and advice. The contract to rebuild and enlarge the organ was given to S.R. Warren & Co. of Montreal at a cost of $7,500. The great organ was opened on Thursday evening 13 January 1876 with a concert of sacred music assisted by the choir. With three manuals and 3,315 pipes and notes, it was the largest and most complete organ in the Dominion of Canada.

❂

The following June, the beloved and highly esteemed Dr. Potts moved to Elm Street Church and the Conference honoured the invitation that the Quarterly Board had extended to the Reverend William Briggs. Soon after his arrival, a glowing tribute appeared in the newspaper series, 'Toronto Pulpit'. He was born in Northern Ireland, was educated in England, and after some years in business he immigrated to Canada with a view to entering the Methodist ministry. The article continued:

> . . . Mr. Briggs has shown himself able, eloquent and painstaking. He has not trusted to the inspiration of the moment or fancied that fluency of talk will compensate for the want of careful preparation and regular systematic study. Accordingly, while others have been best at first, and have gradually degenerated into mere dawdling, goody-goody talkers, Mr. Briggs has gone steadily forward in pulpit power, in broad mental culture, and in general excellence and influence. . . . In short, the present pastor of the Metropolitan is one of the most rising among the younger class of ministers in the Canadian Methodist Church, and, if spared, will in a short time be equalled by few and surpassed by none.

At his first meeting with the Trustees in August 1876, Mr. Briggs brought forward the desirability of the use of envelopes to ensure more systematic giving. After a joint meeting with the Quarterly Board, it was decided that envelopes should be used for all but missionary givings. The Stewards authorized the purchase of a horse and carriage to enable Mr. Briggs to visit his parishioners more frequently. His stipend of $2,000 was increased by $300 to pay for the upkeep of the horse. William Mason resigned because of ill health as Secretary of the Board of Trustees, a post he had held from the first meeting. He was succeeded by his brother, Thomas G. Mason, who served as a most efficient and faithful secretary for the next thirty years.

When Mr. Briggs asked for a leave of absence of six weeks the following Spring, an assistant minister, the Reverend James Sylvester, was appointed to carry on the parish work. In August he reported that he had made three hundred and four pastoral calls, given two Bible readings, officiated at two prayer meetings, filled in four hundred and ninety-six quarterly tickets for admission to the Sacrament of the Lord's Supper, and assisted at six evening services. He continued as the assistant after Mr. Briggs' return.

❂

Mr. Torrington's musical abilities brought him so many pupils that the organ was in use every week-day from eight o'clock in the morning until six o'clock in the evening. One Saturday, a 'Meeting for Holiness' was deeply disturbed. They took their complaints to the Trustees who decided that Mr. Torrington's use of the organ should be restricted to Mondays and Wednesdays. To compensate him for the loss of income, they raised his salary to $1,200 a year. On the occasion of his second marriage in March 1878, they presented him with one hundred dollars in gold.

The maintenance of the church continued to be expensive. In April 1878, after six years of use, the carpeting of the Sanctuary, including the galleries and stairways, was all replaced. Professor Gairdner of Washington, D.C., persuaded the Trustees to install apparatus to make possible the use of gas fixtures for electric lighting at some future date. (A change was not made until 1904). A deficiency was reported at the meeting of the Quarterly Board in November. Steps were immediately taken to reduce church expenditures. Motions were passed to dispense with paid advertisements in newspapers, to sell the horse and carriage, and to terminate the post of assistant minister at the end of the year.

Mr. Briggs left in June 1879 to become Book Steward of the Methodist Book and Publishing House. Under his guidance it became one of the largest publishing houses in Canada. The honorary degree of Doctor of Divinity was conferred on him in 1886. The year after his retirement in 1918, the Methodist publishing venture was named the Ryerson Press. Dr. Briggs died in 1922.

The Stationing Committee of the Conference, in June 1879, confirmed the invitation that had been extended to Dr. Potts to return to the Metropolitan for a second pastorate. He chaired the meeting of the Quarterly Board in September when the recommendation was adopted to hold only one prayer meeting a week on Wednesday evenings, instead of two on Monday and Thursday nights. At the same time the Board resolved to 'bind themselves individually not to allow any mere preference or convenience to prevent them from attending said meeting'. A committee was formed to promote both the spiritual and the social interests of the congregation. A series of revival services, held early in 1880, brought thirty converts into the fellowship of the church.

Dr. Torrington's reputation as an excellent choirmaster brought many new singers to the choir. The Trustees provided money for anthems, shelving for the choir's library, and arranged for the seating area of the choir gallery to be enlarged. Many new choristers had no affiliation with the Methodist Society and, perhaps, were unaware of the strict rules against theatres and play-acting. In February 1880, some choir members joined the Toronto Church Choir Opera Company for a performance of *H.M.S. Pinafore*, the new Gilbert and Sullivan opera that had been first performed in 1878. The Trustees were shocked and angry when it was advertised that some of the soloists belonged to the choir of the Metropolitan Methodist Church! The offending members received the following letter from the Secretary, Thomas G. Mason:

Sir or Madam: The Trustees of the Metropolitan Church, having learned from a Play-bill that you are a member of an organization known as 'The Toronto Church Choir Opera Company' and also that you have announced yourself in said bill as a member of the Metropolitan Church Choir, I am instructed by the Board to inform you that you are hereby dismissed from membership of said choir, and further, that should you hereafter use the name of this church for similar purposes, the Board will take such proceedings to restrain you as they may be advised.

On Saturday 8 March, the *Grip* published a cartoon of the guilty choristers cut adrift from the good ship Metropolitan with an unmistakable Dr. Potts as captain. Underneath was the rhyme:

> They're adrift! they're adrift! and it serves them well right,
> They've to blame but themselves for their sorrowful plight;
> He's a man of his word, is good Dr. P.
> And he vowed he would put down this small mutin-ee.
> With a sweep of authority, certain and swift,
> The Opera-singers are all cut adrift,
> Which will teach all mankind that no *Pinafore* boat,
> At the stern of the Methodist vessel can float!

During the five years from 1879 to 1884, thirteen of the twenty Trustees resigned or died. The Reverend Dr. Anson Green died on 19 February 1879. Born in 1801, he had been connected with the Methodist Church for fifty-five years. As a circuit rider in the early days, he used to travel on horseback four hundred miles every month in all kinds of weather, conducting services at thirty-three monthly appointments. He had served as Book Steward for ten years before he retired in 1863. He wrote his memoirs at the request of the Toronto Conference. The church was 'appropriately' draped in black for his funeral service: pulpit, communion table, front gallery and Dr. Green's pew. Egerton Ryerson, who had been ordained with Dr. Green in 1827, spoke 'in affecting terms' of their long friendship. He also preached the funeral sermon at the Sunday morning memorial service the following day.

Word reached Toronto of the death of Dr. Morley Punshon on 12 April 1881. Canadian Methodists joined with their British brethren in mourning the death of this man of God at the age of fifty-seven. It was a personal sorrow for the people of the Metropolitan for he had continued as a Trustee after his return to England. The church, again draped in black, was filled to overflowing for a memorial service. Egerton Ryerson delivered the eulogy.

In September, a memorial service was held for the Reverend Dr. Lachlin Taylor who had died in Prince Edward Island. The *Methodist Magazine* described him as widely known, deeply loved, vivacious and witty. Dr. Potts preached the sermon for this minister who had been associated with the Metropolitan Church from the beginning.

The Reverend Dr. Egerton Ryerson died on 19 February 1882. The *Globe* reported, in minute detail, his funeral service held at the Metropolitan on 23 February:

> Previous to the arrival of the hearse at the church, His Honour, the Lieutenant-Governor, the Speaker of the House, members of the Legislature and Ministerial Association were in the places assigned for them. The members of the City Council and the Board of Education were present in a body. The pupils of Ryerson and Dufferin Schools marched into the church in a body wearing mourning badges on their arms. Just before the arrival of the casket, there was scarcely an available seat left, and hundreds during the service could not find standing room even in the gallery. There could not have been fewer than 3500 people in the building during the very impressive obsequies. There were representatives of all conditions of society, and it might be said, of all ages. . . . On the funeral *cortège* arriving at the church door, the body was met in the vestibule by the Board of Trustees—the deceased being a member of that Board.

The newspaper gave Dr. Potts' eulogy in full. After speaking of Ryerson's contribution to Methodism and education, he said:

> Dr. Ryerson was regarded by the congregation belonging to this church with peculiar respect and affection. While he belonged to all Canada, we of the Metropolitan claimed him as our own especial possession, for he was a Trustee of the church, and one of its most liberal supporters, for its prosperity he ever prayed, and on its success he ever rejoiced.

Mr. Torrington concluded the impressive service with the 'Dead March in Saul'. The Sunday morning funeral sermon was delivered by the Reverend Samuel Sobrieski Nelles who had succeeded Dr. Ryerson as President of Victoria College.

After twenty years, the trees were growing up around the church, softening the earlier Gothic starkness.

Three of the early ministers of the Metropolitan Church: top, the Reverend Dr. John Potts; centre, the Reverend James Allen; bottom, the Reverend Dr. John Vipond Smith.

CHAPTER 6
The Metropolitan Methodist Church

1882 - 1899

Dr. Potts' term came to an end in June 1882 and the Reverend Dr. Hugh Johnston came from St. James Street Church in Montreal to minister to the Metropolitan. He conducted the funeral and memorial services of the godly William T. Mason who died on 8 November 1882. In an 'impressive and appropriate address', Dr. Johnston spoke of William Mason's remarkable interest in his church: 'much of the success of this great undertaking was due to his clear and vigorous business ability, his sound and cautious judgement, his glowing interest and abounding liberality.' Dr. Johnston revealed that, shortly before Mr. Mason died, he asked those at his bedside to sing the *Te Deum*. When emotion prevented them from singing, he began to sing it himself. Minutes after he had finished it, he peacefully died.

The new Trustees who were appointed included William Gooderham, the eldest son of the distiller. He was converted to Methodism at the age of eighteen and became a teetotaller. He remained an advocate of the temperance cause for the rest of his life. Edward Gurney, who took the place of John Macdonald who had retired, was the President of the Gurney Foundry Company and served on the boards of many organizations such as the Canadian Manufacturing Association and the Ontario Hospital Association. This busy man, who served until his death in 1916, was a faithful and devoted churchman and a generous benefactor. The Honourable John E. Rose, who was a leading lawyer and the son of the Reverend Samuel Rose, a Trustee from 1870, took the place of the late Dr. Anson Green on the Board. Alfred J. Mason replaced Dr. Punshon; James Boustead, the Sunday School Superintendent from 1879 to 1891, replaced Dr. Ryerson.

Dr. J. Branston Willmott, a dentist who was a Class Leader and a Sunday School teacher, and John Mills Treble, a haberdasher who had established his successful business at the corner of King and Bay Street, were both appointed in 1882.

That year, the Trustees decided that the debt of $65,000 should be reduced. They launched a campaign for $30,000 in May, the month after the tenth anniversary. Printed cards were delivered to the pew holders and their wives, and to 'such young ladies and gentlemen as the minister might deem desirable', inviting them to a Tea-Meeting on 11 May at seven o'clock to meet the Trustees and their wives. The ladies were asked to look after the refreshments and the choir was asked to be present. William Gooderham offered to give an additional two thousand dollars if the goal was reached, one thousand dollars if half the amount was raised, and five hundred dollars if twenty-five percent was given. Subscriptions were allowed to cover a five-year period. The Tea-Meeting was a great success. By October, $21,000 had been raised including $10,000 from the Trustees. The choir pledged one thousand dollars.

The Massey family were received as members of the Metropolitan Church at the end of 1882. Hart Massey, the President of the Massey Manufacturing Company, had been living with his family in Cleveland, Ohio, since 1871 while the eldest son, Charles, the Vice-President, conducted the business in Newcastle, Ontario. By 1879, it had expanded to such a degree that a decision was made to move the works to Toronto. Hart Massey returned to Toronto to resume an active role as President. With his wife, his son Chester, aged thirty-three, his daughter Lillian, aged twenty-nine and his two younger sons, Walter, nineteen, and Fred Victor, sixteen, he took up residence in a twenty-five-room mansion on Jarvis Street. They named it Euclid Hall after the avenue in Cleveland where they had lived. The Massey family, who were devout Methodists, had been associated with the Reverend John Heyl Vincent in the summer school he had established on the shore of Lake Chautauqua in the State of New York. Dr. Vincent had been the anniversary preacher at the Metropolitan in 1881, telling about his school for teachers and young people interested in music and fine arts as well as religious studies. The Massey family soon became active at the Metropolitan. In February 1884, the brilliant son, Charles, died from typhoid fever at the age of thirty-five. The sorrowing father appointed Chester to take his brother's place as the Vice-President. Young Walter cut short his course at the Massachusetts Institute of Technology in Boston to assume the duties of Secretary-Treasurer. In March 1886, Chester married the gentle Anna Vincent, the half-sister of Dr. Vincent.

❁

Alfred Mason and James Boustead were appointed as the Metropolitan's representatives on the Union Committee which negotiated union with the Primitive Methodists, the Methodist Episcopals and the Bible Christians. The merger was ratified at the General Conference held in Belleville in September 1883. A Federal Act of Incorporation for the Methodist Church of Canada, Newfoundland, and Bermuda, was proclaimed on 1 July 1884. The Metropolitan's Quarterly Board approved this union in a resolution which expressed 'devout gratitude to God for the practical unanimity of the different Conferences and Church Courts and all District Meetings as well as at the General Conferences'. Two General Superintendents had been appointed in 1883: the Reverend Samuel Dwight Rice, as the Senior Superintendent, and the former Methodist Episcopalian Bishop, Albert Carman, as the Junior Superintendent. Dr. Rice made the Metropolitan Church his place of worship until his death in December 1884. His successor, Dr. John Williams, continued the practice of attending the Cathedral of Methodism. When he died five years later, Dr. Carman became the sole Superintendent and affiliated with Carlton Street, a former Primitive Methodist Church whose fine building, designed by Thomas Storm, had been built in 1874.

It was drawn to the attention of the Board of Trustees that the pinnacles of the tower needed strengthening. Henry Langley's firm estimated that the cost would be about two hundred and fifty dollars but a contract was accepted for half that amount. Complaints about the untidy state of the Choir Library led to the appointment of two librarians at a yearly salary of twenty dollars each.

Although there were always necessary expenditures for the upkeep of the church, many members were also concerned about the work of the Church at large. Every quarter, contributions were forwarded to the Missionary Society. For fifty years, since the demise of the Female Missionary Society of York, the women had not been active in this field. Because of the need for women missionaries in Japan and for Homes for Indian girls in British Columbia, the Reverend Alexander Sutherland, the Secretary of the Missionary Society, was instrumental in organizing a Woman's Auxiliary in Centenary Church in Hamilton in 1880. At the first annual meeting it was reported that a Sewing Circle had been formed in the Metropolitan Church and that they had sewed for the McDougall Orphanage in Alberta. The 'Toronto Auxiliary' was formed in January 1882 and the first Toronto Conference Branch Meeting of the Woman's Missionary Society took place in the Metropolitan Church on 16 October 1882. The next year the Metropolitan Sewing Circle was formally organized as a Mission Band, the name given in the constitution to a group of young women who 'banded together' in aid of the Woman's Missionary Society. The Branch Meeting resolved to organize independent auxiliaries in local churches and at the third annual meeting in 1884, the Metropolitan Church reported an auxiliary with seventy-eight members, including eight life members who had paid the fee of twenty-five dollars. Founding members included: Mrs. J.B. Willmott, Mrs. William Mason, Mrs. B.E. Bull, Mrs. Edward Gurney, Mrs. A.J. Mason, Mrs. W.S. Finch, and Mrs. Abram Lauder. In 1885, the Metropolitan Young Ladies' Mission Circle reported a membership of forty.

Abram W. Lauder, a prominent lawyer and member of the legislature, died on 23 February 1884. A newspaper obituary gave him full credit for the building of the Metropolitan Church! His funeral at the church, where he had been a Trustee from the beginning, was described in detail:

> The church was heavily draped with crepe. All round the gallery, the solemn emblem hung in gracious folds, while pulpit and altar-rail and the deceased's pew were covered over with the same dark emblem of sorrow.

At the conclusion of the service, the Lieutenant-Governor, the members of the Legislature, the Trustees, and the congregation filed up to the front for a last look at the corpse. The next week, the Trustees adopted a motion prohibiting, in future, all draping of the church for funerals, except for the pulpit. They also agreed that no public viewing of the remains should be permitted in the church.

The Quarterly Board, at their meeting in May 1884, heard the report of a committee which had been formed to consider the expediency of hiring an assistant minister. Although it was agreed that the pastor's burden was excessive, the idea of a young assistant was rejected because it was felt that his pastoral work would be 'minimized by his non-appearance in the pulpit as to be practically useless and in some cases positively harmful'. Instead, the Board decided to pay for a summer supply for six weeks and to raise the minister's salary by two hundred dollars.

At the same meeting, Mr. Boustead reported that the Sunday School had outgrown the space provided for it. Six hundred and two pupils were enrolled with sixty-two teachers. Half the scholars had taken the pledge of total abstinence:

> I will abstain from the use of all intoxicating liquors as a beverage and from the use of tobacco in any form, also from the use of profane language and the reading of bad books.

Mr. Boustead also pointed out that it was imperative that the rear part of the building be enlarged.

Henry Langley's firm submitted plans for an extension to provide additional classrooms and a Ladies' Parlour. The Ladies of the Metropolitan, who adopted the name Ladies' Aid in the summer of 1884, offered to raise ten thousand dollars by subscription. The Young People's Society promised fifteen hundred dollars.

The choir of one hundred men and women undertook to raise money and at the request of the Ladies, put on a choir concert at the Pavilion of the Horticultural Society on 30 and 31 May. Billed as 'Ye Musick of Olden Tyme, conducted by Father Helpfull Torrington', the programme consisted of hymns that were sung before 1679, madrigals, and old favourites such as 'The Harp that once through Tara's Halls', 'Ye British Grenadiers', 'Home Sweet Home', 'Auld Lang Syne', and 'Rule Britannia'. The Pavilion was filled to capacity for both performances. Although the music critic gave the concert lavish praise, a letter appeared in the newspaper the following week from a reader who was scandalized that the concert had no 'religious aspect'. The anonymous reader wrote:

> Only two years ago, several members of the choir were expelled for allowing the church's name to be mentioned with theirs at a performance of *Pinafore* at the town hall of Parkdale. . . . The concert is a disgrace and should never have been permitted. If we can't maintain the church's legitimate expenses without resorting to such questionable entertainments as those of Friday and Saturday last, we had better close up!

The choir did not venture into secular music again. For the ninth annual Thanksgiving Day concert on 9 November 1884, they gave a performance of Mendelssohn's *Elijah*. Mr. Torrington, with the Trustees' permission, gave organ recitals in June 1884 during the city's official 'Semi-Centennial Week', celebrating the incorporation of March 1834. The recitals were given daily from four to five o'clock with half the proceeds going to the Choir Fund.

The extensive renovations were not commenced until summertime. Although the Sunday School was holding classes in the Sanctuary, the Trustees gave permission to the Orange Order to hold a service between four and five o'clock on Sunday 6 July, on condition that no band music would be played in the church. The enlarged Sunday School was reopened at a special service of dedication on 20 December when the distinguished Methodist Episcopal Bishop, Randolph Foster, was the special preacher. John Macdonald and William Gooderham also took part in the service.

Dwight L. Moody, the American Evangelist, conducted a three-day revival in the Metropolitan Church that December with three services a day: morning, afternoon, and evening. The *Canadian Methodist Magazine* reported:

> At every one of the nine services, the spacious Metropolitan Church was crowded to its utmost capacity. As early as half-past seven in the morning, people began to gather at the gates . . . At least twenty-five thousand people, or half the population of the city, must have heard him, and overflow meetings were held besides. . . It was a significant spectacle to see Baptists and Presbyterians, Methodists and Episcopalians, taking part in these services side by side.

The Reverend Ezra Stafford, recognized as one of the foremost preachers in the Methodist Church, succeeded the Reverend Hugh Johnston in July 1885. J.V. McAree described him as Lincolnesque, 'a thin spare figure with a wispy beard'. During Dr. Stafford's pastorate, many attempts were made to increase the membership. The Quarterly Board arranged for another revival with the hope that the evangelist, Samuel Porter Jones, a lawyer from Georgia who had become a Methodist minister, would 'attract the masses, from the rinks, the billiard halls, and theatres so that every seat in the church may be filled several times a day on every day of the week, during the effort.' By May 1886, the membership reached seven hundred.

That month the Marquis of Lansdowne, the Governor-General from 1885 to 1886, paid a visit to the Metropolitan. With Lady Lansdowne, he attended the morning service and the afternoon Sunday School. The next year, the special Jubilee service to celebrate the fiftieth anniversary of Queen Victoria's reign was held in the church on 30 June, under the auspices of the Ministerial Association.

At their meeting in November 1887, the Quarterly Board approved a contribution of one hundred dollars for the Church Street Mission which had been started the year before in a room in the Orange Hall by a member of the Metropolitan, Mrs. M.T. Sheffield, for the young 'waifs and strays' of the area south of King Street. It was later moved to Lombard Street and then to Jarvis Street. The young Fred Victor Massey was one of the volunteers who became interested in this work among the destitute children and he used to play his flute for their entertainment.

The Methodist Church, encouraged by Dr. Carman, the General Superintendent, was beginning to realize that as well as seeking the salvation of the souls of the needy, the evils of disease, war, drug addiction, and inadequate wages should be attacked. For years Methodists had been fighting alcoholism. Inspired by the movement of 'social holiness', the Board of the Metropolitan Church, chaired by the new minister, the Reverend LeRoy Hooker, appointed a committee with Mr. John Treble as convenor to look into the possibility of forming a Home Missionary Society to raise money for work with the poverty-stricken in their community and in other parts of the city. The poor of the congregation continued to be assisted by the Poor Steward, John R. James, with the money contributed in special collections at Thanksgiving, Christmas, Good Friday, at the Watchnight services on New Year's Eve, and at all Communion services and Love Feasts. Applications for relief were directed to the Poor Steward from the Class Leaders.

❁

The closing of the Richmond Street Church in 1888 brought new members to the Metropolitan. John J. Withrow was the first President of the Toronto Industrial Exhibition which was held in 1878. He continued as the Chief Executive Officer for twenty-one years. William H. Pearson, the author of *Recollections and Records of Toronto Life,* was the General Manager of the Consumers' Gas Company. He became a Class Leader and taught a Bible Class in the Sunday School from 1888 to 1918. Both these men were appointed as Trustees in 1893.

The Ladies' Aid sent a request to the Trustees in November 1888 for permission to use the Ladies' Parlour one evening a week for the entertainment of strangers who were coming to the church. The Trustees received the request with enthusiasm and suggested that the Parlour might be used on more than one night a week if the Ladies' Aid consulted with the Quarterly Board, the choir, the Home Missionary Society, the Woman's Missionary Society, the Mission Circle and the Sunday School. They suggested a joint committee be formed for the purpose.

The Secretary of the Missionary Society, Dr. Alexander Sutherland, sent a letter, in January 1889, to the Trustees informing them that the Society intended to secure offices in the renovated Richmond Street Church, to be known as the Wesley Buildings. He suggested that negotiations be initiated for the resale of the lot at the north end of the Square to the Metropolitan Church.

No action on this matter had been taken when William Gooderham, a faithful Trustee and a generous contributor, died on 12 September 1889 while conducting a religious service in the Haven on Seaton Street. Dr. Potts delivered the funeral eulogy, praising the good works of this devout Christian. He disclosed that, although Gooderham had been converted to Methodism at the age of eighteen, he had become a backslider in his middle years. In 1873, when Morley Punshon was in Montreal on his way home to England, he met with Dr. Potts who had been recently appointed to the Metropolitan. While giving him some words of advice, Dr. Punshon asked him 'to look after William Gooderham' who had been attending the Metropolitan as an adherent and who had contributed one thousand dollars to the building fund. Dr. Potts had rejoiced in 1875 when Gooderham was reconverted. For the rest of his life he gave lavishly of his time and his money to the Church. The Trustees in a memorial praised his 'noble Christian character, deep piety and widespread benevolence'.

In his will, Gooderham left generous bequests to many organizations. Along with an endowment of $75,000 to Victoria College, he left an additional sum of $125,000 to be paid when the College would move from Cobourg to Toronto. This removal had been under consideration since 1887. When the decision to relocate was made in 1890, the Trustees of the Metropolitan suggested that the north end of their property be considered as a possible site. A committee of Trustees pointed out to Victoria College that the lot was large enough to permit expansion and that by using the Sunday School building for classes and the church for convocations and as a college chapel, the total cost of the new facility would be considerably reduced. A Methodist College built on McGill Square would have been in harmony with the original plan to use it for connexional or denominational purposes. The College authorities, however, selected the site in Queen's Park and the new building opened in 1892.

The Sunday School's printed report of September 1889 recorded that the number of scholars had reached six hundred and seventy-seven with eighteen officers and seventy-seven teachers. The scholars had recited 32,854 Bible verses during the year, 12,447 by the males and 20,407 by the females. A Chinese class was organized in January for the principal purpose of teaching the young men English. The Sunday School library, made up of about sixteen hundred catalogued books, had a weekly circulation of one hundred books. The Sunday School orchestra was conducted by the organist for the school, Mr. Hewitt. The Secretary, W.J. Chapman, described their 'vestibule effort' to invite, personally, young men and women to the Sunday School and the church.

An Epworth League for Christian Endeavour was organized at the Metropolitan in November 1889, six months after Bishop John H. Vincent had organized the first Epworth League in Cleveland, Ohio. The movement spread rapidly to all parts of Canada. All Young People's Societies of the Methodist Church merged into the Epworth League which was named after the Epworth Rectory in England where John and Charles Wesley were born. The motto was: 'Look up, Lift up, for Christ and the Church' and the objects were 'to save souls, to promote an earnest, intelligent, practical Christian life in the young members and friends of the church, to assist them in the study of God's Word and to increase in the service of God and humanity'. The Reverend W.H. Withrow, the editor of the *Canadian Methodist Magazine*, was the first president of the Metropolitan Epworth League. Mrs. J.B. Willmott was in charge of the 'Department of Christian Work', Alderman A.H. Gilbert was the librarian, Mrs. Sheffield looked after Entertainment, and S.R. Hanna (the father of the Misses Marion and Victoria Hanna) was the Social Convenor. He had emigrated from Ireland in 1872 and soon after had joined the Metropolitan Church. Beginning as a scholar, he soon began to teach and for ten years he sang in the choir. He was appointed Leader of Class Number 7 in 1892.

At the request of Dr. Emily Stowe, Canada's first woman doctor, the Quarterly Board invited the Reverend Dr. Anna Shaw to preach at the evening service on 8 June 1890. Dr. Shaw had been licensed to preach by the American Methodist Episcopal Church but the bishops had refused to ordain her. In 1880, the small Methodist Protestant Church, similar in structure to the New Connexion Methodist Church, accepted her for ordination. She served as a minister in the slums of Boston and because of the misery she encountered, she decided to study medicine, graduating in 1885 with a medical degree from Boston University. She came to Toronto as the guest of the Women's Enfranchisement Association. The Board agreed that for her payment the organization would receive the amount in excess of the average Sunday evening collections for the previous three months. Dr. Shaw was such a popular preacher that she was invited to preach again the next year.

Perhaps the influence of Dr. Shaw or Dr. Stowe prompted the Quarterly Board at its meeting in December 1890 to agree, unanimously, that the female Class Leaders should attend the regular Board meetings. The Recording Steward was asked to convey written invitations to the six women Leaders: Miss Segsworth, Mrs. Torrington, Mrs. Vernor, Mrs. (Dr.) Willmott, Miss McGuffin, and Mrs. (Dr.) Williams. At that time, there were eighteen Leaders with four hundred and sixty-six names on their lists. The average attendance was only one hundred and eighty-nine.

Miss Segsworth and Mrs. Willmott were the only women to attend the next meeting of the Quarterly Board when it was resolved that an Aggressive Committee be formed 'to consider and devise means best calculated to attract people to the church by wider publicity or by a systematic canvass of the neighbourhood'. The Sunday School and the Epworth League were both asked to appoint three members to the committee made up of A.J. Mason, A.W. Carrick, Mrs. Willmott, and J.J. Maclaren. The Trustees appointed Chester Massey and the Class Leader, A.W. Carrick, to fill the vacancies on the Board brought about by the resignation of John Morphy, who had been a staunch supporter of Adelaide Street Church, and the death of the Reverend Samuel Rose, the last of the clergy to act as a Trustee. Both had been members of the original Board. W.C. Matthews had taken the place of the late William Gooderham.

Toronto's Methodist Churches marked the centennial of the death of John Wesley at a service in the Metropolitan Church on 2 March 1891 when the Reverend Dr. W.H. Withrow, Dr. Potts, J.J. Maclaren, and the Reverend Dr. W.J. Hunter spoke on 'Facts and Figures of Methodism', 'Wesley: the man and his work', 'Methodism, its universal adaptation', and 'Methodism, its position and influence'.

At the Conference in June 1891, the invitation that had gone forward to the Reverend J.V. Smith was honoured by the Stationing Committee. At this time the Board was in hearty agreement that the services of a second minister were both necessary and desirable. The Reverend J.V. Smith suggested the Reverend William J. Smith who was appointed as the Assistant Minister, at a salary of six hundred dollars per annum.

The Trustees authorized substantial improvements to the building at their July meeting. The choir had frequently complained about the choir gallery which was overcrowded and so situated above the pulpit that they could not see the minister. The architects, Langley and Burke, disclosed that the original plan for the gallery had been altered in 1872 to reduce the cost of the building. They offered to make the necessary renovations for $1,500. The firm of Joseph McCausland & Son was engaged to fresco the walls and the ceiling of the Sanctuary; organ adjustments, made necessary by the alteration of the choir gallery, were approved. The exterior painting of the church and fence was authorized; new carpets were again ordered and arrangements were made for the upholstering of the backs and fronts of the pews. Twelve gaseliers were ordered for the gallery. The total expenditure amounted to $12,000. The church was closed during the alterations and the congregation worshipped in the Music Hall. The Reverend Ezra Stafford was the guest preacher when the church was reopened on 22 November. He died at the end of December from a brain tumour.

A lengthy resolution extolling the virtues of the late Dr. Stafford was adopted at the January meeting of the Trustees before they annulled the life-time appointment to the Board of James Paterson. He had been expelled from the church by the Quarterly Board because he had been charged with drunkenness and the ill-treatment of his family. The Trustees did not declare his position vacant until their legal suit against him had been heard by the courts. When the parsonage was bought in 1874, the deed was signed by William Gooderham, John Morphy and James Paterson. After Gooderham's death in 1889 and Morphy's resignation in 1890, the Trustees tried to persuade Paterson to sign a document so that the title of the property would be vested in the name of the Board of Trustees. Mr. Paterson stubbornly refused to sign it and regularly walked out of the meetings when the subject was raised. He claimed that the deed was none of their business. After consultation with Mr. Justice Rose, the Trustees took him to court. The verdict was decided in their favour in November 1891. Hart Massey was chosen to replace the obstinate and disgraced Trustee.

○

Newton Wesley Rowell, the father of Mrs. Mary Jackman, attended his
first meeting of the Quarterly Board on 19 February 1892. He had come to
Toronto the year before from London, Ontario, to pursue his legal studies.
In 1884, when a lad of sixteen, he helped to organize the London South
Chautauqua Group with his brother and sister and some friends. They
followed the Home Reading Course of the Chautauqua Literary and Scien-
tific Circles, which included the study of Latin, chemistry, political econ-
omy, history, and English literature. The three-year course provided a fair
education for those who could not attend school. In the summer of 1887,
Newton Rowell attended the summer school at Lake Chautauqua and was
one of about two thousand men and women who received certificates at
the graduation ceremony conducted by Dr. Vincent. After a year of study,
Rowell was licensed as a Local Preacher and he organized an Epworth
League in London South Church. When he moved to Toronto in the autumn of 1891, he decided to join the Metropolitan Church, attracted by the
thoughtful sermons of the Reverend J.V. Smith, by the Home Missionary
Society, by the Epworth League and by the Jarvis Street Mission. He
became one of the organizers of the first Epworth League Convention in
1892, when four hundred young people gathered at the Metropolitan
Church. He was sent as a lay delegate to the Toronto Conference and was
made a member of the Committee of Management of the Jarvis Street
Mission Sabbath School along with the lawyer, B.E. Bull, Dr. Willmott,
Miss Alice Withrow, and Miss Bertha Mason. The Superintendent, G.H.
Parkes, became a close friend.

The cost of the parsonage telephone that had been borne by the lawyer, George Kerr, was assumed by the Quarterly Board in February 1892.
In May, Newton Rowell was received as a Local Preacher, licensed with
B.E. Bull and J.J. Maclaren. Later that year, Newton Rowell became a
junior partner in the legal firm, Kerr, Bull and Rowell.

A newly formed Advisory Committee made their first report, identify-
ing as the church's chief weakness the lack of direct touch with the widely
scattered membership and the large 'floating' population. It was recommended that a committee made up of representatives from the Stewards,
Ladies' Aid, Epworth League, Sunday School teachers and Class Leaders
should meet with the minister, Dr. Smith, every Wednesday after prayer
meeting, to report on the strangers, new children and new young people

who had come during the week. The Committee suggested that a section of the gallery should be reserved at the Sunday services for students, that young people should be urged to attend prayer meetings, that some classes should be amalgamated, that advertisements should appear in all the newspapers and that the evangelists, Crossley and Hunter, should be invited to conduct a revival.

The Reverend J.V. Smith lost no time in engaging the team of the Reverend H.T. Crossley and the Reverend John E. Hunter from 26 February to 28 March 1893. Mr. Crossley, who was ordained in 1874 after graduation from Victoria University, has been described as 'an earnest, clear and forcible preacher, logical in argument and persuasive in style'. Mr. Hunter, brought up a Presbyterian, was converted at a Methodist revival at the age of fifteen. Four years later he was called to the ministry. He was ordained in 1882 and almost immediately became an evangelist. He was 'quick, earnest, and outspoken, compulsive, ready-witted and dramatic in style, holding the intense interest of his audience'. They held services for five nights a week and on Sundays. For payment they received the collections of the week-night services and the surplus of the regular Sunday offerings. This arrangement was more than satisfactory for at the end of the revival, they presented the Board with a gift of one hundred dollars.

At the Quarterly Board meeting of March 1893, Hart Massey submitted plans for a building he proposed to erect on the southwest corner of Queen and Jarvis Streets as a new home for the Jarvis Street Mission and as a memorial of his youngest son, Fred Victor, who had been interested in this work until his death in April 1890 shortly before his twenty-third birthday. The Board gratefully recommended the acceptance of Mr. Massey's plans. The Jarvis Street Mission Sunday School was sorely overcrowded with seventy-two children in ten classes and one Bible class for adults.

The ministry of the Reverend J.V. Smith came to a close in June 1894. At his last meeting with the Trustees, they made arrangements to reimburse the Missionary Society with six thousand dollars, the amount that had been paid for the north end of the Square twenty years earlier. The Trustees also decided to comply with the request of Alderman John Hallam to open the church grounds as a public park if the city agreed to provide adequate police protection, to close the gates at dark and to make sure that church services would have no interference. In a resolution, the

Quarterly Board praised Mr. Smith's 'very acceptable labour in the pulpit as a faithful preacher of the Word of God', noting that 'his qualities of head and heart had endeared him to the membership and the congregation'. His successor was the Reverend James Allen who became the father-in-law of Mrs. John B. Allen (Helen) and the late Mrs. Elliott Allen (Ruby). Because of a deficit in the givings, it was decided that the new minister should have no assistant.

The Fred Victor Mission was opened on 25 October 1894, four months after the Massey Music Hall, built in memory of Hart Massey's eldest son, Charles, had held its first concert. The Mission had accommodation for two hundred and twenty-six men who could get a bed and three meals a day for $2.50 a week. Although it was equipped with a gymnasium and baths, the primary purpose was the salvation of souls. All the work of the Mission revolved around the Gospel services held every evening in the lecture hall that accommodated four hundred people. The constitution of the Mission, officially 'The Toronto City Missionary Society of the Methodist Church', stated that the minister of the Metropolitan and one layman should be members of the Board of Management. B.E. Bull was named the President of the Board.

Because the opening up of residential areas in the northern and western suburbs had removed many members from the Metropolitan, steps were taken to attract the people of the district who had no church home. The evening services were made more evangelistic with a song service at 6:45 p.m. The Epworth League obtained permission from the Trustees to use a room in the building on Friday nights for the playing of games such as chequers, chess, and croquinole, to attract young people of the neighbourhood who might not enjoy the more serious League meetings on Monday evenings. A bicycle club was formed about this time.

An effort was made to increase the number of people using envelopes. Leaders were instructed to suggest that class members who did not use envelopes should contribute five cents a week and that those who were able should pay for those who could not afford that amount. Once a quarter, a 'Dollar Sunday' was observed when the minister was requested to preach on Christian giving as a duty and a privilege, stressing the importance of the 'Grace of Liberality'. The Stewards recommended that the amounts contributed by those using envelopes should be published in the Year Book.

Hart A. Massey died in his home on Jarvis Street on 20 February

1896 when Mr. Torrington was conducting his Philharmonic Choir in the performance of Haydn's *Creation* in Massey Music Hall. The news quickly reached the Hall where the curtains of the Massey Box were drawn and the lights put out. At the conclusion of the performance, Mr. Torrington announced the death of Toronto's benefactor and played the 'Dead March in Saul' as the audience stood in tribute to this generous man. His funeral service was conducted by the Reverend James Allen on Saturday 22 February when the church was filled 'to its utmost capacity'. By the will of Hart Massey, the Metropolitan was left $10,000 on condition that the debt would be liquidated within twenty years.

All Massey benefactions had been made in the name of Hart Massey during his lifetime. Within three months of his death, his daughter, Lillian Massey, decorated and refurnished the minister's study. The following January, at the age of forty-three, she became the bride of the highly esteemed John M. Treble, whose wife had died ten years before. He has been described as a 'stout, pompous man, with a benevolent but humorless expression'. After a honeymoon in Europe, they made their home with Mrs. Hart Massey at Euclid Hall.

John Treble and the Massey family had been instrumental in forming the Canadian Deaconess Society of the Methodist Church in 1894. Hart Massey had generously contributed to the erection of a building on lower Jarvis Street for the Toronto Deaconess Home and Training School. The religious order of deaconesses had been revived in Germany and had spread quickly to England and the United States. The American Deaconess Society was largely a nursing order and Hart Massey offered to give $200,000 for a hospital on the grounds of the Metropolitan Church for the Canadian Society. Canadian deaconesses, instead, were trained to assume religious, educational, and social service duties under the direction of the pastors of the churches they served. The Society placed them in churches that applied for them and the stipends were paid directly to the Society.

In January 1896, when Mrs. Torrington was the President of the Ladies' Aid which was made up of fifty members, the women asked the Quarterly Board to request the services of a deaconess. They offered to pay the yearly stipend of one hundred and fifty dollars. Miss Dawdy was appointed in February. Three months later, the Secretary of the Ladies' Aid, Miss Carrick, reported to the Board that Miss Dawdy had made one hundred and forty parish calls, forty-one sick calls, had given out baskets of food and clothing, had found employment for several women and had brought four new members to the church. From 1896 until 1969, a deaconess was on the staff of the Metropolitan Church.

The Epworth League, with the permission of the Quarterly Board, commenced the publication of the monthly *Metropolitan* at its own expense in January 1897. This was the Silver Jubilee Year, marking the twenty-fifth anniversary of the opening of the church. The extant issues give a comprehensive account of the activities of that year. Sixteen Class Leaders conducted meetings on Sunday mornings, Wednesday evenings before prayer meeting, or on Thursdays and Fridays in both the afternoons and evenings. The Epworth League, with a membership of one hundred and thirty-three, met on Monday evenings for lectures or debates on such subjects as: 'Resolved that a Prohibitionary Law should now be enacted in Canada'. The Reading and Social Parlour Committee provided a programme on 'Tennyson's Women' and sponsored social evenings with no attempt to raise money. Their aim was to bring new members to the League. A Junior League reported a membership of seventy-six children. That year they collected 12,189 old stamps and with the proceeds were able to give fifteen dollars to the Junior League of the Fred Victor Mission that met on Sunday mornings with two hundred and twenty-five children on the roll and an average attendance of one hundred and twenty-five. These children, too, raised money for others. Each child was given two cents to invest. Some made forty cents with this capital. With their earned money they made a contribution to a mission hospital in British Columbia. The article on the Fred Victor Mission also reported the activities of the Kitchen Garden and Cooking School, the Girls' Club, the Sewing School, the Savings Penny Bank, the library, classes at night school, the gymnasium and baths. Many Metropolitan members were active volunteers at the Mission.

The May issue of the *Metropolitan* described the anniversary celebrations. The Reverend Dr. Albert Carman, the General Superintendent of the Methodist Church, preached 'a magnificent sermon' to a crowded morning congregation. The Reverend James R. Day, Chancellor of Syracuse University, was the preacher at the afternoon and evening services. At the Wednesday night prayer meeting, past and present members gave 'religious and reminiscent testimonies'. A social reunion to which former pastors and members were invited, was held on Friday evening. W.H. Pearson presided. Addresses were given by Dr. Potts, Dr. Briggs, and several laymen. Letters were received from the Reverend J.V. Smith of Centenary

Church in Hamilton, from the Reverend George Cochran, Dean of the University of Southern California in Los Angeles, and the Reverend Hugh Johnston of Washington, D.C. This issue of the *Metropolitan* printed the text of the 'Historical Sketch' delivered that evening by Dr. J.B. Willmott to the enthusiastic and interested audience. Whole-hearted endorsement was given to the suggestion that the congregation undertake to raise $6,000 to discharge the mortgage on the north end of the property. The sum of $5,241.50 was subscribed within a month.

A bitter headline in the June issue of the *Metropolitan* announced the introduction of Sunday street cars: 'Sunday cars have come! The immoral have triumphed!' On 6 May, Dr. Potts preached an 'impressive' sermon at the reopening of the Lecture Room, 'beautifully redecorated in light green and terra cotta', recarpeted and reseated through the kindness and liberality of Mr. and Mrs. Chester Massey. Mrs. Lillian Massey Treble redecorated and refurnished the schoolrooms, classrooms, parlour and corridors. The death was recorded of Dr. W.T. Aikins, the last surviving member of the first Committee of Management formed in October 1868. He had served as a Trustee since 1870.

The Epworth League paid for the *Metropolitan* through subscriptions (twenty-five cents a year or five cents a copy) and by advertisements placed by church members: S.R. Hanna, Boots and Shoes, 426 Yonge Street; A.W. Carrick, Wedding Cakes and Supplies, 172 Bay Street and 257 Yonge Street; J.M. Treble, Haberdasher, 53 King Street West; Mason & Risch Piano Co., 32 King Street East; Toronto College of Music (in affiliation with the University of Toronto) F.H. Torrington, Director; John J. Withrow, Arbitrator, Building Expert and Valuator, Massey Music Hall; B. Chapman, Watchmaker and Jeweller, 261 Yonge Street; Kerr, Bull & Rowell, Barristers and Solicitors, 62 Wellington Street West; Dr. J.B. Willmott, Dr. W.E. Willmott, Dentists, corner of Bond and Shuter Streets; Methodist Book and Publishing House, 29-33 Richmond Street West.

No copies of the *Metropolitan* survive after 1897 but the annual Metropolitan *Year Book*, first authorized by the Quarterly Board in 1889, continued to be printed until 1930. The booklets provided a list of the officials and officers and a directory of members with their addresses. The amounts of money contributed by members through envelopes and for connexional funds were listed.

At the June meeting of the Quarterly Board, a resolution to honour the departing minister, the Reverend James Allen, was moved by C.D. Massey and seconded by Alfred J. Mason:

> His pulpit ministrations have been earnest, thoughtful and of great profit to
> his hearers. He has always manifested great interest in the financial as well
> as the spiritual interest of the church. We shall remember his kindly minis-
> trations. Mr. Allen bears the graceful title of a Christian gentleman.

It was decided to have the full text of the resolution sent to the *Christian
Guardian*, the *Globe*, the *Mail and Empire* and the *Metropolitan*. Before
he left, Mr. Allen preached at the service for the denomination on 20 June
1897 to commemorate Queen Victoria's Diamond Jubilee. He was appointed to the post of Home Mission Superintendent for Northern Ontario
in 1902 and became Executive Secretary of the Missionary Society in
1906. He and his family became members of the Metropolitan and the
connection has continued to the present day to the third and fourth generations.

The Reverend Richard Pinch Bowles, who became Chancellor of Vic-
toria College in 1913, succeeded the Reverend James Allen. His arrival in
July 1897 coincided with the Third International Convention of the
Epworth Leagues when twenty thousand members from around the world
gathered in Toronto. The main meetings took place in the Metropolitan
Church and the Armories on University Avenue. N.W. Rowell, Chester
Massey, and J.J. Maclaren were leaders in organizing this important event.

The Quarterly Board confirmed the appointment of the Reverend
W.G. Watson as the assistant minister in February 1898. Mr. Bowles
revealed that he had made the arrangement privately because the salary
had been assumed by several members of the church. The board also
authorized the purchase of one hundred copies of the new *Canadian Hym-
nal*, 'prepared especially for Sunday Schools, Epworth Leagues, Prayer
and Praise meetings, Family Circles, etc.' and published by William
Briggs.

The General Conference of the Methodist Church was held in the
Metropolitan for the first time since 1886, in September 1898. As a result
of the deliberations, the term of a pastorate was extended from three to
four years. The Board of the Metropolitan had, through the years, sent
several resolutions to the General Superintendent requesting a longer term.
Because of this new ruling, Mr. Bowles was able to stay until June 1901.

Because of a three-year deficit, the Trustees decided to reduce Mr.
Torrington's salary from $1,200 to $1,000 per annum. A letter was sent to

him explaining that the reduction was due to decreased revenue not from lack of appreciation. The Pew Steward was concerned about the loss of pew rents. At his suggestion, signs reading 'Pew to Let' were placed in unrented pews even though Fred T. Aikins, the son of the late Dr. W.T. Aikins, had resigned the year before as a Local Preacher and a member of the church because he believed that pew rents and money-raising events were 'unscriptural'. He felt that the required money should be directly contributed through free-will offerings. After months of study, a committee convened by N.W. Rowell recommended the purchase of individual communion glasses to be used alternately at the morning and evening bimonthly Sacraments.

At the beginning of his second year, Mr. Bowles sent a circular letter to the officials deploring the church debt of $57,000. He suggested that they take advantage of the Twentieth Century Thanksgiving Fund which was being initiated by the Methodist Church for Educational, Missionary, and Superannuation Funds, or for the reduction of local church debts. He urged them to 'seek to free our beloved Zion from its burdens'. His proposal was so persuasive that the Trustees decided in September 1899 to launch an appeal on the second Sunday in October. The following subscriptions were immediately received: Chester Massey, $10,000; Mrs. H.A. Massey, $10,000; Mrs. Massey Treble, $5,000; John M. Treble, $5,000; Edward Gurney, $5,000; W.H. Pearson, $2,000; Dr. J.B. Willmott, $1,000. It was remembered that the Fund would receive $10,000 from Hart Massey's estate. At that meeting the pastor nominated T. Harold Mason, the son of William T. Mason, to take the place of Hart Massey on the Board, and Alfred R. Clarke to succeed the late Dr. W.T. Aikins.

A canvass of the congregation was organized. The Festival Choir, supported by a paid orchestra, performed *Messiah* with net proceeds of seven hundred dollars. Mrs. Hart Massey assisted in this effort by buying a twenty-five-cent ticket for every workman in her late husband's plant. The Sunday School contributed $256.53 and the Chinese class $135.75. By October 1900, four hundred and seventy-eight people had subscribed $55,600 to the fund.

The choir got new gowns, to go with the church's new organ, and gathered for this picture (top) at Spadina, the great home of Mr. A.W. Austin (bottom left), who was chairman of the Music Committee. Organist and choirmaster Dr. Torrington appears in the second row, far left. Mr. G.H. Parkes (bottom right) went all the way to England to recruit Dr. Fricker as a later Director of Music.

Thomas G. Mason (right) was the Secretary of the Board of Trustees from 1876 to 1906. When he retired, the other members of the Board presented him with this illuminated address (below).

The magnificent interior, before the fire. Note the absence of a centre aisle, in conformity to the Wesleyan Methodist traditions.

Activitities for youth and young people were popular. In 1897, the church had a bicycle club, with regular outings (left). The Epworth League was a forerunner of the Young People's Union.

At left, Judge J.J. Maclaren, Trustee and Sunday School teacher.

CHAPTER 7

The Metropolitan Methodist Church

1900 - 1914

Although the twentieth century did not begin officially until 1 January 1901, the second Sunday in October 1900 was set apart as the Twentieth Century Revival Sunday. The observation began on the previous Friday, a day of prayer and fasting. A public service was held in the evening. The new century was brought in at a Watchnight service on New Year's Eve, 1900. A Love Feast and Sacramental service took place on the first Sunday in January; the second Sunday was 'Sabbath School Sunday'; the third, 'Epworth League Sunday' and the fourth Sunday was one of universal thanksgiving and consecration.

Early in the new century on 22 January 1901, the long life of Queen Victoria came to an end. A memorial service was held at the Metropolitan on Saturday 2 February, at eleven o'clock under the auspices of the Toronto East District. Dr. Albert Carman gave the address, Chancellor Burwash led in prayer, the Reverend James Allen read the Scripture and Mr. R.P. Bowles read the funeral service. Mr. Torrington led the choir in two anthems, accompanied two solos and concluded the service with the 'Dead March in Saul'.

The Metropolitan Church was the scene of another denominational service when the Wesley Portraits were unveiled. Thomas G. Mason, at a meeting of the Directors of the Methodist Social Union, called attention to the fact that no Canadian Methodist Church had a portrait of John Wesley. A committee, under the chairmanship of Mr. Mason, commissioned J.W.L. Forster to paint the Wesley portraits after he had paid a visit to England for reliable information. On 22 April 1901, Mrs. Hart Massey unveiled the portrait of Susannah Wesley, with Chester Massey making appropriate remarks; Dr. Carman unveiled John Wesley's portrait and Dr. Briggs unveiled the portrait of Charles Wesley. The Methodist Social Union, which was organized in 1892 to enhance the spiritual and social welfare of Toronto's Methodist churches, decided that Victoria University should be the portraits' permanent home.

When the Reverend R.P. Bowles' pastorate came to an end, he was highly praised for his initiative, his leadership in the effort to liquidate the debt and for his 'devout presentation of Gospel Truth'. Mr. Bowles was able to report that the Wednesday prayer meetings and the class meetings were well attended, that the after-services on Sunday evenings were encouraging, and that the Epworth League had an ardent desire to promote missionary and evangelistic endeavours. Their open-air summer meetings in the church grounds had been most successful, attracting two hundred and fifty people each week. The Chinese class had a membership of fifty-nine with fifty-five teachers. Thirteen of the class had joined the church. The first Chinese Epworth League of the Methodist Church met at the Metropolitan at two o'clock on Sunday afternoons.

The Reverend William Sparling, who commenced his ministry at the Metropolitan in July 1901, was a man with exceptional skills for organization. At his first meeting with the Quarterly Board, he suggested that a Consultation Committee be appointed to approve and review innovations. At the meeting he brought forward the idea of dividing the body of the sanctuary and the galleries into sections to be 'overlooked' by a member who would be responsible for acquiring the names and addresses of strangers and for introducing them to the pastor. He suggested that young men be invited to be 'Collectors' and that a Convenor of Ushers and Collectors be appointed with the responsibility of preparing schedules three months in advance. The minister made the innovative suggestion that all the Collectors should gather at the back of the church so that the plates could be brought forward simultaneously to the altar. Cards with information about church services and activities were printed for distribution to hotels and boarding houses. Other cards for strangers to fill in were placed in the pews.

A highly unusual impasse took place at the May meeting of the Trustees. No Trustee was willing to sit on the Music Committee. A committee was formed to draft members and in July reported that Edward Gurney, John Treble, T.G. Mason, and Fred Roper had agreed to act with four members of the congregation: Mrs. Lillian Massey Treble, Mr. and Mrs.

A.W. Austin, and Mr. Loudon. At their first meeting, Mrs. Massey Treble offered to assume the responsibility of enlarging the organ and of making changes in the choir gallery which was still unsatisfactory. After consultation with Henry Langley, she preferred to secure the advice of her personal architect.

N.W. Rowell, who accepted the post of Sunday School Superintendent in October 1902, was appointed in March of that year to the Board of Trustees to take the place of the late John J. Withrow. Dr. J.F. Uren was elected as a Society representative to the Quarterly Board. His daughters, the late Frances (Mrs. Arthur Smith) and Isabel Uren, have been lifelong members of the Metropolitan.

The Metropolitan Ladies' Aid sent a message to the Trustees in 1901 complaining about the condition of the parsonage:

> The Society has spent a good deal of money from time to time in the furnishings of the parsonage, and will gladly continue their efforts, but we feel very much discouraged at the prospect of laying out any more on such an unworthy building.

Mr. Treble was asked to look into the matter. He reported at the next meeting that he agreed with the ladies. The parsonage was not only dilapidated but unsanitary. Permission was obtained to sell the building and it was put on the market for $6,000. No buyers came forward to buy such a run-down house.

At the General Conference of the Methodist Church in September 1902, the Ladies' Aid was formally recognized as an organization of the Church, with the President entitled to a place on the Quarterly Board.

The constitution of the Young Men's Society was presented to the Quarterly Board in October 1902. This new organization hoped to attract unchurched young men living in boarding houses in the area. Their Motto was 'Our Brother for Christ'; the Purpose was 'moral, social and physical development'. The President, Dr. F.B. Price (the father of the carillonneur, Percival Price), requested use of the church rooms for two or three evenings a week and permission to make a skating rink in the church grounds. One room was provided for Thursday evenings. The idea of a rink was dismissed. Dr. Uren and S.R. Hanna were appointed as representatives of the Board to work with the Executive. The Society made arrangements with the Fred Victor Mission to use the gymnasium on Tuesdays. During the summer, football was played at the Varsity Athletic Field.

Because the growing number of activities made the Sunday announcements too lengthy, a weekly calendar, prepared by a committee of the Board, was printed and copies were placed in the hands of the congregation for the first time on 2 November 1902.

The Music Committee reported to the Trustees in May 1903 that a paid quartet had been acquired. The soprano and the contralto were each paid two hundred and fifty dollars a year, the tenor and bass, one hundred and fifty dollars. The salary of the librarian was raised to fifty dollars per annum. Arrangements had been made for two concerts by the Westminster Abbey Coronation Choir under the direction of Sir Frederick Bridge.

Mrs. Lillian Massey Treble decided that instead of enlarging the present organ, she would install a new organ in memory of her father, Hart Massey. Dr. Torrington, who had received the honorary degree, Doctor of Music, from the University of Toronto in 1902, drew up the specifications with the assistance of Charles D. Warren. The plans were submitted to Edwin Lemare, the English organist who, from 1902 to 1915, was the resident organist at the Carnegie Institute in Pittsburg. Sir Frederick Bridge was also asked for comments and suggestions. The Karn Organ Company of Woodstock, Ontario was commissioned to build it.

❂

In the autumn of 1903, Mr. and Mrs. Chester Massey, with their two sons, Vincent, aged sixteen, and Raymond, seven, went to Europe where in Zurich they visited Mrs. Massey's brother, Bishop Vincent, who was at that time Bishop of the Methodist Episcopal Church in Europe. Shortly before they were to sail home from London, Anna Massey became violently ill with appendicitis, a dreaded malady at that time. A London surgeon operated, but Mrs. Massey died in England on 11 November 1903. She was beloved by the people of the Metropolitan and the Methodist community and was deeply respected by all for her 'sterling Christian character'.

A member of the Chinese class, Lee King, decided he would like to return to China as a missionary. The Quarterly Board recommended him for appointment by the Missionary Society and authorized a subscription to be taken for his support. A Junior Missionary Society (later known as a Mission Band) was organized in January 1904. Irene Carrick, a member of the Metropolitan until her death in 1977, was the Vice-President.

The members of the choir, in anticipation of the opening of the new organ, thought that it would be appropriate for them to wear choir gowns. A deputation waited upon the Board of Trustees in January 1904, pointing out that 'incongruous colours of dresses were objectionable'. Many of the Trustees did not approve of such formality but the majority gave their consent on condition that gowns were black and that the choir members would pay for them. Subscriptions, however, were received from the congregation. The cost was estimated at seven dollars a gown. Mrs. Massey Treble provided eighty lockers for the gowns, fifty for the women's and thirty for the men's. She informed the Trustees that she would insure the new organ at her own expense and also remove and renovate the old organ which was sent to Central Methodist Church in Sault Ste. Marie. Chester Massey undertook the cost of the renovations to the choir gallery. At that meeting, Thomas G. Mason resigned from the Music Committee.

The dedication of the great new organ in memory of Hart Almerrin Massey took place on Wednesday and Thursday evenings, the 9 and 10 March 1904. The choir, robed in their new gowns, sang Mendelssohn's *Hymn of Praise* on Wednesday evening. On Thursday, Edwin Lemare performed on the organ and the Festival Choir closed the programme with the Hallelujah Chorus.

Albert W. Austin (the grandfather of the late Austin Thompson and the great-grandfather of Evan Thompson) was appointed Chairman of the Music Committee, succeeding T.G. Mason. Mr. Austin, the President of the Consumers' Gas Company and the President of the Dominion Bank, declined the invitation at that time to become a Trustee because of the pressure of business.

At the meeting of the Trustees on 5 January 1905, Dr. J.B. Willmott, who had acted as Treasurer for twenty-one years, was able to announce, in his final report, that the church was completely free from debt. It was decided to celebrate this achievement at the thirty-third Anniversary in April. A membership Social Reunion was planned for 28 April at 7:30 p.m. John Treble, who had been the successful treasurer of the Twentieth Century Thanksgiving Fund, succeeded Dr. Willmott as Treasurer of the Church.

When the Reverend Dr. William Sparling's term ended in June 1905, the membership had reached the highest number in the church's history up to that time. It had increased from 645 to 1,100. Having lived in a cold, dilapidated, unsanitary parsonage for four years, he must have listened with wistful interest to a letter from Chester Massey which was read at his last meeting with the Trustees:

> For some time previous to Mrs. Massey's decease, she entertained a strong desire to do something whereby the Pastor should have a more comfortable home. I am sure, had she lived, it would have been a great pleasure to her to have a part in such an undertaking.
> In fulfillment of her wishes, and in her memory, I write to say that I will be pleased to erect a new parsonage, and furnish it throughout at my own expense, provided that the Trustees of the Church are unanimous in their approval of the choice of the grounds of the Metropolitan Church for its erection.

A second letter from C.D. Massey, as executor of his father's estate, proposed that the estate should buy, for $6,000, the parsonage at 266 Jarvis Street for the Fred Victor Mission to use as a Maternity Home and that the money from the sale should be placed in an endowment fund for keeping the parsonage in repair and for maintaining a proper standard of furnishing.

Before these generous offers could be fully accepted and appreciated, Mr. John Treble, speaking on behalf of the Deaconess Society, suggested that the Society enter into negotiations about the possible purchase of a lot at the north end of the church property for a new Deaconess Home and Training School. The Trustees sent a letter to the Deaconess Society, at the end of the year, offering them a ninety-nine year lease on the site.

The Stationing Committee of the Toronto Conference approved the appointment of the Reverend Dr. Solomon Cleaver, known among Methodists as the 'Prince of the Pulpit'. A parsonage was rented at 94 Gerrard Street, for the sale of the old parsonage had been ratified. The Reverend R.S.E. Large was appointed as assistant minister.

The International Sunday School Convention took place in Toronto from 23 to 27 June 1905. The Honourable Mr. Justice J. J. Maclaren, the Second Vice-Chairman of the Executive Committee, was the Chairman of the 'Local Committee on Places of Meeting'. These Conventions, which had been held every third year from 1875, included Sunday School leaders from Protestant churches in the United States and Canada. Beginning in 1887, World Conventions were held every four years. J. J. Maclaren planned the 1905 convention with meticulous care. *The Official Programme and Souvenir Handbook*, consisting of 161 pages bound in printed boards with a vignette of the Metropolitan on the front cover, was published by the Methodist Book and Publishing House of Toronto. It included a brief history of Toronto, 'some places worth seeing', 'city restaurants', 'street cars' (a five cent fare), 'postal information' (two cents for Canada or the U.S.A.) and details about the excursion to Niagara Falls by steamer (round trip $1.25). An article described the differences that delegates who had attended the Second International Sunday School Convention in Toronto in 1881 would notice. The City had grown from a population of 81,000 to 250,000 inhabitants. The old Pavilion, recently destroyed by fire, in the Horticultural Gardens, renamed the Allan Gardens, had seated less than two thousand people. It was adequate in 1881 but in 1905 'twin' evening sessions were held simultaneously in Massey Hall, seating about four thousand, and the Metropolitan Church which could hold more than two thousand people. Morning and afternoon sessions took place at the Metropolitan. The Sunday School rooms served as the Convention headquarters. A branch Post Office and an Information Bureau were set up on the ground floor. Dr. Torrington gave half-hour recitals before the evening sessions. On Saturday afternoon, concurrent mass meetings for children took place in Massey Hall and in four other large churches. The *Handbook* contained biographies of participants and executive members. About sixty hymns with words and music were included. The book was financed by advertisements.

At the end of the third session on Saturday morning, the Honourable Mr. Justice J. J. Maclaren was elected President for the next three years. Born in Lachute, Quebec in 1842, he had joined the Methodist Church at the age of eighteen and had come to Toronto in 1884 to practise law. He was appointed a Judge of the Supreme Court in 1902 and by 1905 he was Justice of the Court of Appeal. A devout Methodist, he found time to take a leading part in church affairs. From 1885 he had served as a Trustee of the Metropolitan Church. Every Sunday afternoon he conducted the Young Men's Bible Class which met for 'conversational Bible study'. He was a firm believer in the efficacy of the class meeting and regularly attended Dr. Withrow's class. This busy man, with heavy professional responsibilities, had served on the International Sunday School Executive Committee since 1893.

The 1905 Convention was declared successful, 'numerically, financially, and spiritually'. The delegates were so filled with enthusiasm for the cause that when the convention was asked for $50,000 for the enlargement of the work in Japan, the sum of $75,000 was immediately contributed. The *Canadian Methodist Magazine* affirmed: 'Surely the Sunday School is getting at the heart of the World.'

Many Metropolitan laymen took an active part in the courts of the Methodist Church and sat on committees of the General Conference. In 1904, N.W. Rowell was appointed to the first joint committee of the Methodists, Presbyterians, and Congregationalists to advocate church union. He was involved in introducing to Canada the Layman's Missionary Movement with its motto: 'the Evangelization of the World in this Generation'. This interdenominational movement had been organized in the United States by several American leaders, including John R. Mott who won the Nobel Prize for Peace in 1946. The hope of this movement was that it would bring about social betterment for the peoples of the world and international peace as well as personal salvation.

Mrs. J.B. Willmott, who had organized the Woman's Missionary Society at the Metropolitan and was active in many areas of the local church, also served as President of the Toronto Conference Branch and sat on the Dominion Board of Management for twenty-nine years. She was a firm believer in prayer and instituted a women's prayer meeting in 1900, held on Fridays at 10:30 a.m. The women met at the Wesley Buildings at first, but soon came to the Metropolitan. In 1906 the Woman's Missionary Society celebrated twenty-five years of service, during which time it had supported ninety-eight women missionaries in Japan, West China, British Columbia, Alberta, and Quebec.

At the meeting of the Trustees in April 1906, Thomas G. Mason resigned as Secretary after thirty years of faithful service. His fellow Trustees presented him with a bound, illuminated address. He was succeeded by G. Harry Parkes, who was a senior member of the firm of Parkes, McVittie and Shaw, Fire Insurance Brokers. At this meeting, plans for the new parsonage were submitted and enthusiastically approved. N. W. Rowell then proposed that a committee be formed to establish an Endowment Fund and that the principal should remain untouched until it reached twenty-five thousand dollars.

'A Grand Organ Recital' took place on Monday 6 April 1906, when the eminent organist, Edwin Lemare, returned to perform on the Metropolitan organ. The third number, 'Carillon', was by H.A. Wheeldon, the organist of St. Saviour's Church in London, England, 'a composer of many charming pieces'. The last number was 'Concert Overture in C-minor' by H.A. Fricker, organist of the Town Hall, Leeds, and Chorus

Master of Leeds' Musical Festival.

The Music Committee brought to the meeting of the Trustees on 27 December 1906 the draft of a letter addressed to Dr. Torrington, requesting his resignation because of his 'increasing years and failings attendant thereon'. The letter stated that the Committee was prepared to pay him half his salary for the next five years. The other members of the Board felt that this unexpected message should be delivered personally instead of by letter so that Dr. Torrington might be given the opportunity to resign. Dr. Torrington was bitterly offended at the Music Committee's request. His letter of resignation after thirty-four years of faithful service and 'after various expressions of sincere appreciation' was accepted by the Trustees in January 1907. The congregation was stunned when they learned of this action. His choir was indignant and resigned in a body. At the March meeting of the Trustees, Dr. Withrow presented a petition demanding Dr. Torrington's reinstatement, signed by four hundred and sixty-two members. The Board formally received it at its meeting, before confirming the appointment of H.A. Wheeldon, Mus.Bac., F.R.C.O. at a salary of $1,000 per annum. He had been recommended by Edwin Lemare and Sir Frederick Bridge. Dr. Torrington published privately a booklet, *Letters to Dr. F.H. Torrington, Expressing Appreciation of the Musical Services at the Metropolitan Church,* written between 1904 and 1907. He gave a farewell concert on 12 May 1907 for which one thousand programmes were printed. He was appointed as the organist of the new High Park Methodist Church for which Chester Massey had contributed $25,000. Torrington continued as Director of the Philharmonic Choir until 1912.

No report from the choir was included in the *Year Book* for 1906-1907. It did record a new organization, the Young Women's Society, with a membership of sixty. They enjoyed moral and literary programmes, taking part in the Debating League with the Young Men's Society and the Epworth League. A social evening took place once a month: a banquet, a skating party, a picnic, and an 'automobile tour'.

❂

At a formal ceremony on 14 June 1907, Chester Massey presented the memorial parsonage built of gray Credit Valley stone with cut trimmings of Indiana limestone. Built at a cost of $50,000, it was considered to be one of the finest examples of Elizabethan architecture in the Province, with a 'quiet, rich, classic effect seldom seen outside England'. The floors and the woodwork were of the finest oak. The house was elegantly and completely furnished with oriental rugs, Chippendale mahogany, Tudor oak furniture and the most modern appliances of that day. In making the presentation, Mr. Massey 'hoped that the building might long serve as a comfortable home for the pastor of the church'. He gave the keys to Mr. Justice Maclaren who accepted them on behalf of the Trustees. Bishop Vincent, who had come to Toronto for the event, hoped that the parsonage 'would radiate the noblest in social and religious life'. Dr. Cleaver expressed the gratitude and appreciation of the congregation. After a prayer offered by Bishop Vincent, the guests toured the beautiful home, admiring the symbolic stained-glass window in the entrance hall, showing Faith, typified as a graceful maiden, holding an open Bible, with angels on each side in attitudes of devotion and with the legend: 'This house was built and furnished as a memorial to Anna Vincent Massey by her husband, C.D. Massey, 1907.'

Because the minister's salary of $2,500 was not enough to maintain such a large home, Chester Massey added enough money to the Parsonage Endowment Fund, established with money received from the sale of the old parsonage, to provide an additional $2,000 a year to the senior minister's stipend.

The Deaconess Society, meanwhile, was ready to proceed with the building of the new Training School and Deaconess Home in the church grounds. Chester Massey was uneasy for he feared that the building would not be in harmony with the church and the parsonage. Drains for the new parsonage created a problem. The lawyer, Bartle E. Bull, pointed out that the Metropolitan Church did not have the right to negotiate the sale or lease of the property. It was decided to reopen the discussion and to hold a vote concerning it. Five Trustees voted for the building, eleven were opposed to it. They conferred with the Deaconess Society about relinquishing the agreement. Eventually the Training School and Deaconess Home was built at the corner of Avenue Road and St. Clair Avenue.

For the first time, at the Annual meeting in November 1907, a woman was elected to the Quarterly Board as one of the seven representatives of the congregation. Miss Kate Westman was an active church worker: a Sunday School teacher (Mary Frances Uren was one of her pupils), an officer of the Epworth League and the President of the Mission Circle which had a membership of one hundred and ninety-seven young women.

It probably did not occur to her that she had received a singular honour for she did not attend one meeting during her year in office. At the next Annual meeting, seven men were elected as usual. The women Class Leaders and the Presidents of the Ladies' Aid and Woman's Missionary Society had a sorry record of attendance at Board meetings with the exception of the faithful Mrs. Willmott. When no longer a Leader, she was elected as a representative of the congregation, twelve years after Miss Westman's unique appointment.

N.W. Rowell reported for the Committee on Missionary Finances at a joint meeting of the Trustees and Quarterly Board in June 1908. He suggested that weekly envelopes for Missions should be provided, that the congregation should attempt to raise $16,000 for the cause that year, and that monthly missionary prayer meetings should be organized in cooperation with the W.M.S. and the Epworth League. He pointed out that of a membership of 1,100, only 350 contributed regularly through envelopes. The artist, J.W.L. Forster, was commissioned to paint a portrait of Dr. John Potts, their beloved former minister who had died on 16 October 1907. He had served on the International Sunday School Lesson Committee from 1878 and as Chairman from 1896 until his death.

The new organist, H.A. Wheeldon, reported at the end of his first year that the choir had a paid quartet and sixty-eight choristers. In the Spring of 1909, he initiated weekly Twilight Organ Recitals on Saturday afternoons at four o'clock at which a silver collection was received. The Music Committee was so pleased with his performance that they raised his annual salary to $1,200. Mr. Wheeldon, however, was critical of the new Hart Massey memorial organ which he considered to be too American, 'inferior to English construction'. The accommodating Mrs. Massey Treble promised to pay for the improvements that he might recommend even though she and her brother and Vincent Massey had undertaken the cost of the redecoration of the Sunday School.

The Deaconess Society was able to supply the Metropolitan with two deaconesses in September 1908. Miss Bertha Shier replaced Miss Adams who had served since 1903. Miss Mabel Cline was appointed as the Sunday School deaconess 'for the ingathering of scholars'. They were introduced at a meeting of the Quarterly Board when Mr. R. Burrow, who had recently arrived from England with excellent credentials from his former church, was licensed as a Local Preacher of the Metropolitan. He immediately became active in the Epworth League and joined the Sunday Morning Class for men and women conducted by the Reverend Dr. William H. Withrow who had edited the *Canadian Methodist Magazine* since 1874. Dr. Withrow suffered a stroke and died in November 1908. In due course, Mr. Burrow was appointed as his successor. Mr. Justice Maclaren, a faithful member of the Class, agreed to act as the Assistant.

When the Treasurer, John M. Treble, reported a deficit in February 1909, the Quarterly Board, once again, decided to dispense with the services of an assistant minister. A letter was sent to the Chairman of the District advising him that an invitation had gone forward to the Reverend Dr. W. L. Armstrong and that no assistant would be requested for the next Conference year. At the same time, a letter was sent to the Assistant, the Reverend R.S.E. Large, praising his 'unflagging interest in every department of church life', especially his work with young people and his success with the 'Home Sweet Home' meetings held on Sunday evenings after church. Mr. Burrow succeeded him as President of the Epworth League.

John Treble died at his home on Jarvis Street on 17 May 1909, seven months after the death of his mother-in-law, Mrs. Hart Massey. He had served as Trustee for twenty-seven years and as Treasurer for four. He had been the Board's representative at the Fred Victor Mission from its beginning. Vincent Massey was appointed as his successor to the Board of Trustees, Dr. Charles E. Treble assumed his father's place as a Director of the Fred Victor Mission, Mr. A.R. Clarke took over the duties of Treasurer of the Church. In a resolution, the Trustees paid a grateful tribute to Mr. Treble's efforts in liquidating the church debt. His widow, Lillian, offered to provide funds for a memorial window, the design of which was to be submitted to the Robert McCausland firm.

The request of the Fred Victor Mission to hold tent meetings on the church grounds was approved at the May meeting of the Quarterly Board. Chester Massey and his sister, Lillian Massey Treble, offered to provide the stipend for the summer supply if the Reverend Dr. George C. Workman of Montreal were appointed as the guest preacher. He was a liberal theologian who denied that the Old Testament prophecies referred to Christ. He had been dismissed from Victoria College in 1891 and again from the Wesleyan Theological College in Montreal through the express efforts of the General Superintendent, Dr. Carman. In 1907 and 1908 the Workman supporters, including Chester Massey, had attempted unsuccessfully to have the dismissal reversed by the Court of Appeal. Dr.

Workman's ministry at the Metropolitan was so successful that he was invited to return for eight weeks the following summer at a cost of twenty-five dollars a Sunday, despite the harsh criticism of Dr. Carman.

❂

The Reverend Dr. W. L. Armstrong commenced his ministry without an assistant. He soon claimed that he needed an organization of one hundred men and women to welcome the strangers who were coming to the church. By November it was evident that with the large membership, the services of an assistant minister were essential to meet the pastoral demands. A committee was formed to secure a lay assistant and in December, R. Burrow, the Local Preacher, was appointed at a salary of $800 per annum.

Shortly after Dr. Armstrong's arrival he noticed, one day, a group of girls eating their lunches on the church lawn. He wondered where they went in cold weather. This question persisted in his mind. After consultation with the Deaconess, Miss Shier, and with the Trustees' permission to use the church kitchen and parlour, he made an announcement at the evening service one Sunday in February, inviting young women who worked in the nearby stores or factories to come to the church during their noon-hour to meet Miss Shier and to enjoy the quiet of the church parlour. The following day four girls arrived, the next day seven came, the next day ten, and soon one hundred and fifty girls were coming daily for rest and relaxation. Three paid workers and two volunteers prepared the tables and served tea and coffee. The Metropolitan Business Girls' Club, with the motto, 'Each for the Other', was organized under the guidance of Miss Shier and with the support of the Ladies' Aid. All the officers of the Club belonged to the church. Members were charged ten cents a month for club privileges. New members were added when they were recommended as girls of good character. Short meetings were held once a week when physicians, dentists, ministers, and others gave short addresses. Sometimes a musical concert was provided. At other times, a prayer meeting was held. Many of the girls joined the Metropolitan, attended class meetings and Bible classes or sang in the choir. An extant clipping about the club concludes: 'No wonder so many hundreds of young people attend the services at the Metropolitan on Sunday evenings.'

The Trustees, at their meeting in April 1910, received a letter from Chester Massey and his sister setting forth their offer to pay for the redecorating, reseating, and relighting of the church on condition that the membership should assume responsibility for the improvement of the heating, ventilating, and drainage systems and, as well, increase the Endowment Fund to $25,000. C.D. Massey was prompted to make this generous offer because the Metropolitan Church had had the honour of being selected to host the fourth decennial meeting of the World Methodist Conference in October 1911. Although the exterior of the church was imposing, the interior was shabby, the upholstery on the pews and the carpets were in tatters, and the heating system inadequate. The offer, with its stipulations, was gratefully accepted on the motion of Judge Maclaren and W.H. Pearson. The church was closed from June until October while a narthex, with oak panelling, was constructed within the existing vestibules. The old pews installed in 1872 with cast iron ends and upholstered seats and backs were replaced by solid oak pews, some of which are still in use in the gallery. The pews were arranged to provide a centre aisle; a flooring of cork tiles replaced the carpets. Stone floors were laid in the narthex and in the tower. Protective glass covered the windows in the nave; the lighting was improved. The interior was tastefully redecorated. The congregation, for its part, repaired the foundations, installed steam-heating and new plumbing, fixed the drains and poured a concrete floor in the basement. The total cost of these improvements was $45,000. Of this amount, Chester Massey and his sister contributed $33,000.

The church was reopened on 23 October 1910 with Dr. T.B. Kilpatrick of Knox College as the preacher at the morning service. Dr. S.P. Rose, whose father had been a minister in the old Adelaide Street Church and a Trustee until his death in 1890, preached in the evening.

A meeting to discuss the future of the Metropolitan was called in December. Dr. Armstrong prepared a report suggesting new ways of reaching the young people who lived in the boarding houses of the district. He envisaged a building or 'institute' erected on the property with accommodation for eighty to one hundred young men. These should be selected with care so that they could be used as Sunday School teachers, in Classes, the Epworth League or Young Men's Society, and as an 'army of power' at the Sunday evening services. The Institute, he maintained, should have rooms where clubs for boys and girls might meet and a Convocation Hall for lectures and concerts. He suggested that the 'English Pleasant Sunday Afternoons' could be emulated. He felt the emphasis should be on singing, music, and art. He concluded:

Shall we rise to this opportunity? In a few years it will be impossible for her to rise save by spoiling this magnificent property by commercializing it. Let us spiritualize it, that it may be used for Christ and his Church. . .We do not need to sigh for the past—we do not need to fear the future. The consciousness of the problems which face the church today is indicative of progress. To look forward with courage and upward with faith is the key-note of solution.

The meeting, impressed with Dr. Armstrong's report, set up a committee to investigate the feasibility of building an 'Institute'.

Six months later the committee presented its report, giving wholehearted approval of the concept of a 'parish or church house' but doubting that such a venture could be financed by the membership. It was suggested that other Toronto churches might be asked to support the project, assuming the role of supporters rather than rivals. The committee deplored the fact that the Metropolitan had a reputation of being wealthy and somewhat exclusive, when in reality it was difficult to make ends meet.

The Trustees gave approval for tennis courts to be laid at the north end of the property. They endorsed the motion of Vincent Massey and T.H. Mason that the church be open every day but Tuesday from ten until four o'clock for prayer and meditation. At the suggestion of Mr. Burrow, the Quarterly Board agreed to have the Apostles' Creed printed in the calendars, to be repeated by the congregation at every service. A portrait of the late Dr. Withrow was commissioned. The Board decided to change the laconic name of the Poor Fund to the more charitable term of Benevolent Fund.

The reopening of the improved Hart Massey memorial organ took place on Monday evening 16 January 1911. Mr. Wheeldon was assisted by Mrs. Will Merry, the soprano soloist, and Frank E. Bemrose, the tenor soloist. The programme noted:

> With the object of keeping in touch with recent developments in the art of organ building in England, large additions and alterations have been made, the result being, that though to outward appearances it remains the same, this is now the largest and most up-to-date organ in the Dominion. The improvements and additions have been planned and supervised by the Organist of the Church, Mr. H.A. Wheeldon, who was formerly organist of St. Saviour's, Belgrave, London, England, and deputy organist of Ripon Cathedral. The writer of the above (Wheeldon) wishes to express his personal indebtedness to Mr. C.D. Warren, the pioneer organ builder of Canada, for his untiring efforts to make this organ the crowning effort of his career.

The programme announced that on Saturday the free afternoon Twilight Recitals would be resumed and that in addition, the organ would be played every day, except Saturday, from twelve to one o'clock. The ailing Mrs. Massey Treble made an arrangement to hear the organ in her home over a special telephone receiver. The Music Committee raised Wheeldon's salary, but sent him a letter containing a list of suggestions for the betterment of the musical portions of the services. Because he needed time to prepare for his public recitals, the Committee in April appointed A.L.E. Davis as the choirmaster at a salary of one thousand dollars.

The Fourth World Ecumenical Methodist Conference took place at the refurbished Metropolitan for a fortnight from 4 to 17 October 1911, hosted by the General Superintendent, Dr. Carman. First organized in 1881, this world body of Methodists met every ten years. Four hundred official delegates gathered in Toronto and about one thousand unofficial observers attended the sessions. Chester D. Massey spoke at the first session on the training of ministers. Methodist literature was discussed at the second, the Church and education at the third. At the closing session, the Church and the Evangelization of the World was a matter of discussion and special prayer. Resolutions were put forward against the opium trade, divorce, and mob violence. The Conference resolved to constitute the Methodist Historical Union to include existing and future Historical Societies. The Honourable Mr. Justice Maclaren was named to the committee to draft the constitution.

At the General Conference of the Methodist Church of Canada held in Victoria, B.C. in 1910, a vote on the desirability of church union had been requested. The subject had been under discussion since a committee was formed in 1904. By 1906 the name, the United Church of Canada, had been selected. The General Conference decided that the vote of all officials, members and adherents should be taken in 1912. The report of the Metropolitan vote was tabulated in the minutes of 12 May 1912. Twenty-two officials supported union, six were opposed. Three hundred and forty-one members over the age of eighteen voted 'Yes', and twenty-seven voted 'No'. Twenty-four members under the age of eighteen were in favour, one was against it. This was the only vote taken by the Methodists. The Presbyterians voted in 1910 and again in 1916 and 1924 with the number of opponents to union growing with every vote.

When Mr. Burrow reported the shocking information that fifty-five dollars had been stolen from the church office, a safe was acquired and it was regretfully decided that the basement windows should be barred with heavy wire. The Quarterly Board adopted a resolution expressing congratulations to the Business Girls' Club after three successful years. Special mention was made of the services of the Misses Parkes, Mrs. Francis, Mrs. Menzies, and the Deaconess, Miss Agnes Thompson, who succeeded Miss Shier in September 1912. When the services of the Sunday School Deaconess had been discontinued, Mr. Burrow was named the Director of Religious Education at a salary of $1,400 per annum. That year four hundred and fifty books were added to the Sunday School Library through the generosity of Edward Gurney. A letter from T.G. Mason requested permission to install a window in memory of his brother, William, as a gift from the Mason family. The City of Toronto installed lighting in the church grounds at no charge.

In February 1913, Mr. Wheeldon submitted his resignation to take effect on 31 July. He was succeeded by T. J. Palmer, A.R.C.O., who had acted as the Canadian agent for the organist, Edwin Lemare.

The pastorate of the Reverend W.L. Armstrong came to an end in June 1913. At his last meeting with the Board, a resolution three pages long, extolling his outstanding ministry, was adopted by a standing vote. T.G. Mason and the genial Mr. H. Horsman, an usher and collector, rose in turn to give 'eulogistic remarks'. Dr. Armstrong made a 'fitting reply'.

When his successor, the Reverend Dr. John Wesley Aikens, took the chair at his first meeting with the Board, he asked for their sympathy and prayers. The new St. Paul's Anglican Church was opening in November 1913 and the evangelical preaching of the Reverend Canon H. J. Cody was expected to draw worshippers away from the Metropolitan. The Timothy Eaton Memorial Church on St. Clair Avenue was expected to open the next year. Dr. Aikens soon made some innovations which included a Sunday morning talk to the children before the second hymn chosen especially for them. He introduced Sunday Afternoon Meetings and song services held after Sunday School, assisted by the Alexander Choir. An organization, 'Home Care for the Sick', was favourably discussed. The Board agreed that it would meet a need not supplied by the City. Church calendars were delivered on Saturdays to the principal hotels. In December, Mr. Burrow reported that the Endowment Fund had been fully subscribed and was invested with the National Trust. The interest went into the general fund of the church. A small Benevolent Loan Fund was formed to supply members with interest-free loans should they become sick or unemployed.

The Trustees provided a bowling green for the Young Men's Club. In April, an arrangement was made with the City to take charge of the church grounds during the summer months. Many complaints had been received about their 'deplorable condition' and the fact that in the evenings the grounds had become a rendezvous for dissolute characters. The Ladies' Aid petitioned the Trustees for permission to use the grounds during the summer for children's recreation.

The members of the Quarterly Board in February were stunned when Mr. Burrow tendered his resignation. One after another rose to praise his work: B.E. Bull, A.W. Carrick, Hon. Mr. Justice Maclaren, T.G. Mason, S.R. Hanna, W.G. Francis, and A.R. Clarke, the Treasurer. A committee was formed to urge his reconsideration. Mr. Burrow agreed to continue until May 1914 at a salary of $1,800 a year and then to take a six-month leave of absence to visit his son in Nevada. During his absence, Mr. McCutcheon acted as the lay assistant.

In the summer, Mr. McCutcheon conducted a Vacation Bible School for the children of the area under the auspices of the Ladies' Aid. This was a new and untried undertaking. Because of its success, other churches soon adopted this novel plan of summer activity for children.

Mrs. J.B. Willmott, president of the Woman's Missionary Society in Toronto Conference for twenty-nine years.

Reverend Trevor Davies came to the Metropolitan from Wales in 1917.

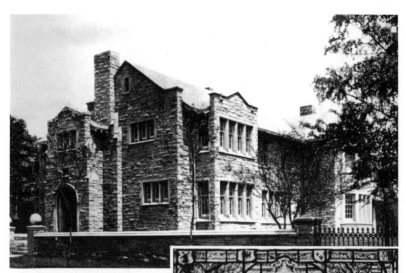

The parsonage (above), presented in memory of Anna Vincent Massey by her husband, Chester D. Massey (below left), in 1907, and the memorial window (right) commemorating the generous gift. Mrs. Lillian Massey Treble (below right) was also a generous benefactor.

The interior, renovated to
include a centre aisle. Right, a
side gallery of the church, before
the fire. Below, a tent set up on
the grounds for evangelistic
meetings, 1909.

CHAPTER 8
The Metropolitan Methodist Church

1914 - 1925

The Great War was declared on 4 August 1914. The Metropolitan Methodist Church, like the rest of the Dominion, plunged into war service. The Home Care for the Sick scheme was put in abeyance for the duration of the War and was not revived. Practically all the members of the Young Men's Club enlisted. Their clubhouse on George Street was rented. The President, Mr. George McCann, a barrister-at-law, kept in touch with the men and prepared a framed Honour Roll. In November, the fourth brigade of the Second Contingent, camping at Exhibition Park, was invited to attend a Sunday service. The church supplied their carfare. A new flag was mounted on the church tower. The Ladies' Aid became involved in Red Cross work and raised money for the Prisoners' Bread Fund. Mr. Hanna's Class Number 7 raised $1,020 for the Belgian Flour Fund. The Epworth League carried on with a greatly reduced membership. The Business Girls' Club flourished as women became a part of the work force in munitions. The Trustees gave permission for classes in musketry in the schoolroom and target practice in the basement.

Many laymen were engaged in the war effort. Vincent Massey and P.L. Mason, the Secretary of the Sunday School, accepted commissions in the army. The government made use of Holt Gurney's business abilities in the placing of contracts for munitions. J.H. Gundy and his brother, W.P. Gundy, sons of a Methodist minister, were requisitioned for important assignments. N.W. Rowell, as Leader of the Ontario Liberal Party, travelled from coast to coast recruiting young men for active service. He sincerely believed that the purpose of this war to end all wars was to create a more Christian society. In 1917 he entered the Union Government of the

Prime Minister, Sir Robert Borden, as Chairman of the War Committee. Vincent Massey became the Secretary. Because of the added responsibilities of the various Trustees, the Board met on only four occasions during the War.

Alfred J. Mason died on 23 October 1914. The Trustees and the Quarterly Board joined in a resolution in tribute: 'His faith was unswerving, his nature bright and optimistic, his trust in God implicit, his daily life quiet and unobtrusive, ever thinking of others more highly than himself.'

A German submarine on 7 May 1915 torpedoed the *Lusitania*, a passenger ship of the Cunard line, off the coast of Ireland. Of the 1,924 passengers, only 726 were rescued. Mr. A.R. Clarke, the Treasurer of the Metropolitan, was among the survivors, but he died in a London hospital on 20 June from the injuries he had sustained. His funeral took place on 7 July at the Metropolitan where he had worshipped for thirty-five years. In a resolution adopted at their meeting on 18 July, the Trustees and officials described him as a man of 'sterling Christian character and kindly disposition which endeared him to all who came within the influence of his cheerful personality'. His widow requested the Quarterly Board to keep the names of her late husband and daughter, Isabel, on the church roll, promising to contribute weekly offerings in their names.

At the same meeting, the Board paid tribute to the late Dr. J.B. Willmott who had died on 14 June. He had been associated with the Metropolitan for forty-two years as a class leader and Bible class teacher. For thirty-five years he had served as church Treasurer. He had been a delegate at every Toronto Conference since the union of 1884 and he represented the church at four General Conferences. His tribute read: 'In his death, Toronto has lost one of its best citizens, the dental profession a leader, the Methodist Church a lifelong, zealous and consistent member, the Metropolitan an official of sterling character and great usefulness and a liberal contributor to its funds.'

The congregation was again saddened when they learned of the death of Mrs. Lillian Massey Treble in Santa Barbara, California, on 3 November 1915. She had been a generous benefactor in providing the organ and contributing substantially to the upkeep of the building. Every week she had supplied flowers for the Lord's Table. The Metropolitan was munificently remembered in her Will, which directed that the income from her bequest of $61,000 should provide money for the maintenance of the organ, for the salary of an organist holding specified English qualifications (probably suggested by Mr. Wheeldon) and for free organ recitals. A further sum was bequeathed to provide for the service of a deaconess. Mrs. Massey Treble also left one hundred thousand dollars to endow a hospital if the building were commenced at the north end of the property within ten years of her death. This legacy was forfeited.

Edward Gurney died in September 1916. The tribute of the Quarterly Board described him as a

> man of magnetic personality, of a disposition kind and considerate, of religious feelings strong and tenacious. In temperament he stood unique, cheerful, optimistic, and light-hearted, with a kindness of spirit which won him the affectionate regard of his brethren. . . . His gift of one thousand books to the Sunday School Library proved his readiness to spend and be spent for the cause of the coming preachers and prophets of a better day.

His son, E. Holt Gurney, was appointed to the Board of Trustees that year, along with Henry H. Mason, the son of the late Alfred J. Mason and Managing Director of Mason & Risch, Pianoforte Manufacturers, and Griffith B. Clarke who succeeded his late father in the management of A.R. Clarke Co. Ltd., Leather and Glove Manufacturers. S.R. Hanna took the place of Dr. Willmott on the Board. Because the Sunday School had decreased in numbers without the encouragement of a special deaconess, the Quarterly Board appointed a member, Miss Margaret Armstrong, at a salary of four hundred and sixteen dollars a year, to carry on the duties of keeping in touch with Sunday School scholars.

New members were added to the Music Committee: Major Vincent Massey, George E. McCann and G.H. Parkes, the President of the Mendelssohn Choir. Mr. Parkes was given the responsibility of going to Great Britain to interview eligible organists with Methodist sympathies to take the place of T.J. Palmer whose qualifications did not comply with Lillian Massey Treble's endowment. On his return, Mr. Parkes recommended the appointment of Herbert Austin Fricker, M.A., Mus.Bac., F.R.C.O. He had held the post of City Organist of Leeds, England from 1898 to 1917 when the Trustees of the Metropolitan Church confirmed his appointment commencing in September. Fricker had studied under the eminent Sir Frederick Bridge who recommended him for the post.

Mr. Parkes submitted to the Quarterly Board the name of the Reverend Dr. Trevor Davies of Brixton, London. After extensive enquiries about him, Mr. Parkes was convinced that he was the best qualified of all the ministers whom he had heard preach during his stay in England. An invitation was extended to Dr. Davies and steps were taken that would secure his appointment by the Stationing Committee. After receiving his letter of acceptance, arrangements were made for him to become attached to the Toronto Conference.

That winter, Dr. Torrington returned to the Metropolitan for his first visit since his dismissal ten years before. Mr. Burrow, with the permission of Mr. Palmer, invited him to play the organ. When the Board was told of his great pleasure at this opportunity, it was unanimously agreed that he should be afforded every facility whenever he wished to use the organ. The old wounds were healed. When he died the following November, his funeral took place at the Metropolitan. Dr. Fricker played the 'Dead March in Saul' in his memory.

At Dr. Aikens' last meeting with the Quarterly Board he, too, was accorded a resolution praising his ministry, adopted by a standing vote. It read:

> He has laboured faithfully and zealously with but one end in view, namely the promotion of the Kingdom of Christ . . . . While remaining true to the old standards of biblical interpretation, he has not neglected to take advantage of the light which modern scholarship has thrown on the Sacred Page.

At the meeting, E. Holt Gurney recommended that the Reverend Peter Bryce, the minister of Earlscourt Methodist Church, should be invited to make a report on all downtown churches in Toronto with suggestions that might be adopted for a more aggressive policy on social work. It was moved by B.E. Bull and carried unanimously that one thousand dollars should be made available for expenses and for part-time help to free Mr. Bryce for twenty-five percent of his time. A committee was appointed to wait upon him. He agreed to assume this responsibility. Commencing on 29 September 1917 he submitted one-page bulletins week by week to keep the committee informed of his progress. He reported on his survey of the resources of the Metropolitan, King Street Church, the Fred Victor Mission, Berkeley Street, Queen Street, Crawford Street, Euclid Street, Parliament Street, Elm Street, and Carlton Street Methodist Churches. He surveyed the communities and the work of other denominations in the area. He visited downtown churches in Pittsburgh, Montreal, Chicago, Syracuse, New York City, Brooklyn, Boston and Detroit. He surveyed the Sunday Schools in downtown Toronto. By February 1918 he began to issue weekly recommendations which included the hiring of a Social Worker to whom the minister and deaconess could refer difficult cases. She would be a connecting link with other social agencies. He recommended a trained Boys' Worker to cooperate with the Big Brothers. At that time, sixty percent of the boys appearing in the Juvenile Court claimed to be Methodists. He advocated a trained Girls' Worker and suggested the formation of a Downtown Workers' Association. He recommended that the social work of the area should be directed from the Metropolitan. He revealed the need for an office to deal with homes affected by the War. Fathers of 11,000 homes had been killed in action. He suggested that there should be a well-equipped office to welcome immigrants and to befriend boys and girls coming from the country to the big city. As well as giving advice, he emphasized that every effort should be made to bring these people into the fellowship of the Church. Finally, Dr. Bryce recommended a building on the north side of the property, in harmony with the church, with a lunch-room for girls, a well-equipped Sunday School, a good auditorium, a Board Room, and social and recreational facilities. He suggested that revenue could be acquired by renting rooms to such organizations as the Lord's Day Alliance. He emphasized that there should be no commercial business on the grounds. He felt further study was necessary before he could recommend the erection of a hotel as some American churches had done. The first Conference with Downtown Workers and the clergy of the area took place on 17 February 1918. Other recommendations were not to take effect for years to come.

○

From his first Sunday at the Metropolitan on 7 October 1917, the ministry of the Reverend Trevor Davies was abundantly successful. He was born in Llanfyllin, North Wales, the son of a minister. After ordination by the Wesleyan Conference in 1895, he served with distinction on circuits in Manchester, London, and Edinburgh. His powerful sermons and the excellent music provided by Dr. Fricker brought large congregations which once again filled the Metropolitan Church at both the morning and evening services. Chester Massey arranged for an annuity fund to compensate Dr. Davies for the years he would not be contributing to the British Methodist pension fund. A church automobile was acquired to assist him in his pastoral duties.

With the coming of the new minister, the genial Fred Roper, 'an ever welcome member of committee meetings', resigned as Recording Steward of the Quarterly Board, after thirty-four years in the post. He was associated with the Metropolitan from 1875 until his death in 1922. He was succeeded by B.E. Bull whose duties as Treasurer were transferred to W.G. Francis. The new official *Methodist Hymn and Tune Book* was published by William Briggs in 1917. It had been authorized at the General Conference of 1910 before the vote on Union. The Reverend Dr. J.V. Smith, who died in 1916, was a member of the Committee chaired by Dr. S.P. Rose. A section at the end contained Doxologies, Ancient Hymns and Canticles, the Lord's Prayer and the Apostles' Creed. Chester Massey and A.W. Austin each paid one third of the cost of seventy-five copies for the choir and one thousand copies for visitors. By an arrangement with the publisher, these copies were supplied with all the Psalms. Members were supposed to bring their own hymn books and Bibles to church.

By 1918 only four classes were holding regular weekly meetings at the Metropolitan. W.H. Pearson, at the age of 86, was still conducting his class on Friday evenings. These continued until his death in January 1920. Miss Bessie Starr was the Leader of the Young Women's Class that met before prayer meeting on Wednesday evenings. For ten years Mr. Burrow had conducted the late Dr. Withrow's Sunday morning Class which the Honourable Mr. Justice Maclaren faithfully attended. Class No. 7, with its motto 'Not to be ministered unto but to minister', was made up of young men and women who also met on Sunday mornings at ten o'clock. The first Leader, Dr. Frank Price, was succeeded in 1892 by S.R. Hanna who continued as Class Leader for twenty-six years until his death in January 1918. A deep sense of loyalty existed among the members. Class anniversaries were celebrated every January when Mr. Hanna received letters from former members living in all parts of Canada. Miss Marian Hanna recalls that children came with their parents: 'The meeting consisted of hymns, prayers, readings from the Bible, a few words pertaining to this message by the Leader, Bible verses recited by the children and testimonies or interesting remarks by the members present.' As well as the Sunday meetings, the Class enjoyed picnics to the Island, banquets prepared by the members and concerts of solos, piano selections, and recitations. They mourned the death of their popular Leader and commissioned J.W.L. Forster to paint a portrait which now hangs in the narthex stairway. It was unveiled at the Class meeting on Sunday 2 June 1918 when the Reverend

James Allen read the one hundredth Psalm. This proved to be Mr. Allen's last Sunday at the Metropolitan for he died on 29 June. Mr. J.V. Denike succeeded Mr. Hanna, with A.W. Carrick as his assistant.

Dr. Trevor Davies preached at the Anniversary services which were held as usual in April but the Metropolitan joined with all the Methodist churches in the city in celebration of the Centenary of Methodism in Toronto in November 1918. The Methodist Union planned the city-wide events. On Monday 18 November, 'a grand entertainment' and pageant took place in Massey Hall under the auspices of the Epworth Leagues. On Wednesday, the Methodists of the city filled the Metropolitan for a prayer meeting of thanksgiving for the end of hostilities and for guidance in the future. On Friday 22 November, four concerts presented by the Methodist choirs of the city were held in four churches including, of course, the Metropolitan.

A committee was formed to welcome returning soldiers and former members at the special Sunday services. The Sunday School, which had celebrated the November anniversary for the whole century with special services and entertainments, launched a campaign to add one hundred scholars to the roll during the centennial year. By November the goal was reached with a membership of five hundred and forty-four children and adults.

Mr. Burrow prepared a *Souvenir Historical Sketch* of the Metropolitan Church, published in 'the month and the year of peace'. The well-illustrated booklet contained short biographies and photographs of four ministers, twenty-four laymen and Mrs. Lillian Massey Treble. It pictured the parsonage memorial window, the 'Ascension' window installed by Chester Massey in memory of his mother, Eliza Phelps Massey, in 1911, and the 'Sermon on the Mount' window erected in memory of Edward Gurney by his wife in 1918. These great windows were over the gallery at the northeast and northwest sides. Mr. Burrows described the windows on the west side: 'The first Miracle' in memory of W.T. Mason, 'Christ healing the sick' in memory of James Billington Boustead, the Sunday School Superintendent from 1879 to 1891, and 'Christ feeding the multitude' in memory of Alfred Russell Clarke. The last two were erected by Mrs. Clarke to honour her father and her husband. On the east side were 'Christ blessing the little children' erected in memory of John Mill Treble by his children, and 'Christ among the doctors' erected by Chester Massey in memory of his sister, Lillian. The McCausland firm was responsible for the scheme of placing windows depicting the 'Miracles' on one side of the church and 'Scenes in the life of our Lord' on the other.

As well as giving details of all the organizations of the church, Mr. Burrow supplied a paragraph about the church office which he had inaugurated in 1909. In addition to keeping financial accounts and membership registers, it was responsible for newspaper advertisements, the preparation of the calendar, of circulars about church events and the gathering of reports for the *Year Books*. It also acted as an employment bureau and kept lists of reliable rooming and boarding houses. Miss E.E. Withrow, the daughter of J.J. Withrow, was appointed as Mr. Burrow's assistant in 1918 at a salary of thirty-five dollars a month. She continued as Church Secretary until March 1933.

Little had been done during the war years to maintain the church property. In March 1919, the Trustees decided that a cement walk should be laid from Queen Street to the church with suitable lights on each side to be lighted at dark, year round. At the next meeting, Chester Massey submitted plans for landscaping the grounds, for providing the walk with stone pillars at the Queen Street entrance to support new and attractive iron gates. The Board approved the plans and gratefully accepted this new evidence of Mr. Massey's generosity.

Midweek activities were at a low ebb in 1919 with the exception of the Business Girls' Club which was attracting two hundred and twenty girls every day at lunch, the Ladies' Aid and the two Missionary Societies that had a combined membership of two hundred and fifty women. The Epworth League had an average attendance of only thirty; the attendance at Sunday School was declining. The Chinese Class was in need of teachers. The Quarterly Board established a Comradeship Committee for the development of work among boys and young people. By 1920, a Boys' Club, under the direction of T.H. Mason, had a membership of twenty-four and received $140 for a baseball team. It became known as the Baseball Club.

The urgent need for special work with young people was forcibly put forth by the Reverend F. Langford at a meeting of the Quarterly Board in January 1920. The Sunday Schools of the day were supplying ninety percent of the new members of the Methodist Church, but of that number, seventy percent were lost to the church after the age of twelve. The Board decided that a young man should be procured as an assistant minister. At the next meeting Mr. Burrow tendered his resignation. He had given twelve years of faithful service as a Local Preacher, a Class Leader, a Sunday School teacher, and as the Lay Assistant. At the presentation of a purse of more than five hundred dollars, his executive ability, his deep religious convictions and his kind affability were praised. His Sunday morning Class was disbanded.

In June, the Conference appointed the Reverend Wilfred Scott as the Assistant Minister. In taking over the duties of Mr. Burrow, he became the President of the Epworth League. He reported that the attendance had dwindled to seventeen people. The reactivated Young Men's Club suggested that an Athletic Association be formed. Years later, Dr. Scott recorded some recollections of his year at the Metropolitan. He praised the polished sermons of Dr. Davies, 'one of God's gentlemen', and recalled his admonition: 'If a sermon requires more than twenty minutes, it has not been prepared adequately.' During the year Mrs. A.R. Clarke and her daughter, Vivian, furnished the Sunday School rooms and club rooms with expensive carpets, draperies, and furniture, 'all in exquisite taste'.

Mr. Scott, who decided to return to College, was succeeded by the Reverend J.E. Griffith. In September, the Jubilee Committee, made up of Vincent Massey, B.E. Bull, J.H. Gundy, and G.H. Parkes to plan the fiftieth anniversary in April 1922, reported that arrangements were being made with the Reverend Campbell Morgan to hold a week of evangelistic services as part of the celebration. Chester Massey approached the Committee with the suggestion that he install a carillon in the church tower in memory of his wife, Margaret Phelps, the cousin he had married in 1909. She had died in Pasadena, California, on 29 January 1921 after a long illness. The bells of a nearby church had given her such comfort that it was her wish that the people of Toronto could know similar helpfulness and enjoyment. Mr. Massey suggested that the bells might be dedicated on the fiftieth anniversary Sunday.

The bells were cast in Croyden, England by the firm of Gillett & Johnston, the firm that had made the clock for the City Hall. The bells were designed to the specifications decided upon by Dr. Fricker while on a visit to England, the largest bell, eight feet in diameter, weighing 8,456 pounds or 3,836 kilograms. Prior to their shipment to Canada, H.R.H. Princess Beatrice and the Duchess of Albany, the daughter and daughter-in-law of Queen Victoria, attended by Sir George Perley, the Canadian High Commissioner, and Lady Perley, visited the plant to inspect the bells and to enjoy a recital by Mr. April Johnston, the head of the firm. Princess

Beatrice was greatly interested in bells and in this harmoniously tuned carillon which was the first to be mounted in North America.

Dr. Davies was the anniversary preacher on Sunday 2 April 1922. Dr. Chown, the General Superintendent, assisted in the service of dedication. The inscription on the main bell reads: 'This chime of twenty-three bells was presented to the Metropolitan Methodist Church, Toronto, in loving memory of Margaret Phelps Massey by her husband, Chester D. Massey, 1922.' Each of the original bells bears the inscription: 'May the spirit of the Lord reach the heart of every one where the sound of these bells is heard.' Dr. Davies prayed that the bells 'might be a reminder to all who hear them of the comfort and inspiration of the Church of God'. Crowds of people lined the streets to hear the first dedicatory recital by Mr. Harry Withers of Birmingham, England.

At the evening service, Dr. Davies' sermon was followed by two cello solos, a duet with organ and cello, and soprano and tenor solos accompanied by the cello. The postlude was composed by Healey Willan. A reunion was held on the next Tuesday and on the following Sunday, the Reverend Dr. G. Campbell Morgan began a mission which he continued during the week with services every day at three o'clock and again at eight.

Percival Price (1901-1985) commenced his duties as the first professional bell-ringer on 9 April, a position he held until 1926 when he accepted the post of carillonneur at the Rockefeller Carillon in New York. At first, an automatic electric player produced a hymn tune every day at nine o'clock, noon, three o'clock, and at six. Recitals were played before the morning and evening Sunday services. Mr. Price's salary was thirty-three dollars and thirty-three cents a month.

❂

Members of the Elm Street Methodist Church, between Yonge and Bay Streets, made unofficial overtures regarding a union with the Metropolitan. In May 1922, a committee of the Quarterly Board met with officials of Elm Street and their pastor, the Reverend David Wren, to complete the arrangements. The resolution of amalgamation, moved by E.T. Berkinshaw, was seconded by W.G. Watson (the grandfather of Mrs. Eleanor Walker, Mrs. Ruth Peckover and Mrs. Margery Roden). The union was approved at the Toronto Conference in June. Mr. Wren was appointed as an Assistant Minister for a year. The Elm Street Sunday School of 160 scholars united with the Metropolitan Sunday School on 18 June. The congregation of 350 members were welcomed at an impressive communion service on 25 June. The proceeds of the Elm Street church property, after liquidating church debts, were used to establish the Elm Street Church Memorial Fund, the income of which was to be applied to the funds of the Metropolitan in perpetuity.

At the June Conference, the Stationing Committee approved the Board's request for a year's extension of Dr. Davies' pastorate. Steps were at once initiated to find his successor for Dr. Davies had already accepted an invitation from the Timothy Eaton Memorial Church to take effect in June 1923. An invitation was extended to the Reverend A.E. Whitham of Leeds, England, who had been highly recommended by the Honourable N.W. Rowell. Mr. Whitham declined the invitation when Dr. Chown, the General Superintendent, ruled it obligatory for him to join the Canadian Methodist Church. The Board then prevailed upon George H. Parkes to make a second trip to England in search of another preacher. At considerable personal sacrifice, Mr. Parkes complied and strongly recommended the Reverend Dr. J.T. Wardle Stafford, commenting on his 'genial and attractive personality'. Because he, too, was unwilling to join the Canadian Church, the Board invited him to come for two years as a 'Visiting Preacher' at a salary of $5,000 and the use of the parsonage. The Stationing Committee appointed the Reverend Dr. George H. Williams, who had been at Sherbourne Street Church, to be in charge of the pastoral affairs for the next two years, or until Union, at a salary of $3,500. The Ladies' Aid furnished a rented parsonage for him and his family at 526 Sherbourne Street. The Reverend J.E. Griffith continued as the associate pastor of religious education.

The congregation was sorry to bid farewell to Dr. and Mrs. Davies who had been with them for almost six years. Chester Massey, presiding at the reception in their honour, recognized that 'the revolving wheel of our itineracy has made another revolution and we are obliged to part'. A resolution of appreciation commended Dr. Davies' power in the pulpit, described as 'unique, quiet, very seldom impassioned, free from sensationalism, scholarly, appealing to the heart and mind rather than the emotions'. Both Dr. Davies and Mr. Wren received purses 'of a substantial sum'.

On Sunday 9 September 1923, Dr. Williams dedicated the memorial window, 'to the Fallen'. Two plaques were placed beneath the window listing the forty-one young men from the Metropolitan and Elm Street Churches who had lost their lives in World War I. (A third plaque with the names of ten who were killed in World War II was added in 1946). Commissioned in 1921, the window showed 'David and the Mighty Men' with the legend: 'Is this not the blood of the men that went into jeopardy of their lives? therefore he would not drink it.' (II Samuel 23:17)

The Reverend Wardle Stafford began his ministry in September. The Quarterly Board was called to a special meeting in October to discuss the novel opportunity offered to the Metropolitan of broadcasting the morning service once a month by means of a radio set connected with the Star Broadcasting Station. Mr. A.W. Austin, the Chairman of the Music Committee, strongly endorsed the idea and offered to assume the cost of the broadcasts for one year. Although the Board could see the value to shut-in members, some feared it would appear to be 'journalistic propaganda'. Others felt it would place a restraint on the preacher. Although Dr. Stafford was willing to carry out the Board's wishes, he was not personally in favour of radio services and the matter was laid on the table. No service was broadcast from Metropolitan until 1928.

The ministry of Dr. Wardle Stafford proved to be so successful that the Board asked him to extend his time at the Metropolitan. He agreed to continue as the Visiting Preacher until June 1926. The morning services were liturgical, the evening services evangelistic. The congregation was pleased to look forward to two more years of his inspiring and effective preaching, which continued to fill the church Sunday by Sunday at both services. The resignation of the Reverend J.E. Griffith was regretfully received.

On 20 April 1924, a special meeting was called to frame a petition to be sent to the Parliament of Canada in favour of the organic union of the Methodists, Presbyterians, and Congregationalists, 'after lengthy negotiations extending over twenty years'. The discussions pertaining to Union, which were begun in 1904, had been discontinued during the War. Meetings were resumed in 1921 when a joint committee of the three churches met to bring to fruition the Union which all the leaders of the Methodists and Congregational churches and the majority of Presbyterian leaders felt was the Christian solution to the postwar problems of the expanding Western population brought about by massive immigration. The Honourable N.W. Rowell, Chester Massey, and Judge J.J. Maclaren served on the committee. Rowell, who had resigned in 1920 from his post in the cabinet of the Union government in Ottawa, accepted the demanding task of Chairman of the Sub-committee on Law and Legislation.

The last General Conference of the Methodist Church, held in the Metropolitan Church, approved in principle the doctrine and polity of the Basis of Union. The Joint Committee asked the Metropolitan to issue an invitation to hold the first General Council of the United Church in the 'Cathedral of Methodism' beginning on 10 June 1925, the day the union would be consummated.

In some ways it was not difficult for many Methodists to enter union. Times had changed the Methodism of the twentieth century. Attendance at class meetings was no longer mandatory. Although some people, like Judge J.J. Maclaren and Mr. Pearson, were loyal to the class meeting as long as they lived, most members had given up attendance or had never experienced this opportunity. The General Conference of 1910 had reinterpreted John Wesley's *Discipline* to permit social dancing. Emphasis on salvation had given place to a more social gospel for the betterment of life on earth. Prayer meetings, when they existed, were sparsely attended and usually by the aged.

The last meeting of the Board of Trustees of the Metropolitan Methodist Church took place on 9 January 1925. At this meeting complaints were once again received about the choir gallery. Chester Massey, who had already paid for alterations, offered to give one thousand dollars for the suggested improvements. This was the last time that this generous benefactor contributed to the fabric of the church. New Trustees were appointed: W.G. Watson, in place of the late Edward Gurney; John Carrick, in place of Fred Roper; E.T. Berkinshaw replaced W.H. Pearson; Dr. H.M. Tovell replaced G.B. Clarke; Colonel P.L. Mason took the place of his uncle, the late T.G. Mason, who had died in September 1924. He had been the last surviving member of the original Board appointed in 1870. It seemed appropriate that the Trustees' *Minute Book* that he commenced in 1887 should end with a tribute to this 'tireless and devoted member and official, a Christian gentleman and a brother beloved'. His full minutes, written in his exquisite hand, noted important matters, occasions, and various activities of the ministers and members. The last entry accurately predicted that the book 'would greatly assist any archivist'. The Sermon Registers, giving the date, preacher and text for every sermon preached at the Metropolitan Church from 1872, was continued until 1935.

On the motion of Chester Massey, seconded by G.H. Parkes, the

Quarterly Board in February 1925 agreed to extend an invitation to Dr. W.H. Sedgewick, a Presbyterian minister, to take effect in July 1926. The Board hoped that this example of Christian brotherhood would demonstrate to other churches the meaning of amalgamation. Dr. Sedgewick accepted the invitation with hearty enthusiasm. Dr. Williams left, as planned, in June 1925 to take up his duties in Ryerson United Church, Hamilton.

William George Watson (right) seconded the motion that Elm St. Methodist Church (below) join with the Metropolitan in 1922.

CHAPTER 9
The Metropolitan United Church

1925 - 1928

The service inaugurating the United Church of Canada was not held in the Metropolitan because of the numbers who planned to attend. It took place instead in the Mutual Street Arena which seated eight thousand people. For half an hour before the service on Wednesday 10 June 1925, the bells of the Metropolitan rang out over the city as the people gathered to form a procession from the church to the arena. The General Council convened the next day at the Metropolitan and agreed to meet in 1926 to organize a new form of government.

Although few changes were made at the Metropolitan until 1930, the Board decided to introduce gowns for the ministers in February 1926. These had been forbidden at the 1906 General Conference of the Methodist Church. Dr. Stafford admitted that he had hidden in a cupboard the gown he had brought from England. The Ladies' Aid raised money to provide a gown for the assistant minister, the Reverend A.E. Black, who had succeeded Dr. Williams in 1925. Delegates were appointed to the newly organized Presbytery which replaced the old District Meeting. One layman was appointed for every minister connected with the congregation. In 1926, N.W. Rowell was appointed Chairman of the Missionary and Extension Fund. Dr. Peter Bryce became the Secretary in 1927, and A. Elliott Allen, a son of the Reverend James Allen, was made the Treasurer. This fund took the place of the Methodist connexional funds for missions, education, the superannuation fund, evangelism and social services. The Presbyterian method of allocation was adopted. The fiscal end of the church year was changed from the end of April to 31 December.

Soon after the Anniversary, which was celebrated in May 1926, the congregation bade farewell to the 'eloquent, fluent and forceful preacher', the Reverend Dr. Stafford, and his 'much beloved' wife. The resolution prepared by the Board 'regretted that the congenial relationship extending over three years was to be severed'. His 'remarkable adaptability combined with a genial and kindly disposition' had won him a place 'in the hearts and homes of the congregation'.

The life of Chester D. Massey ended 2 June 1926. He was praised as a generous and cheerful giver who avoided publicity. The great absorbing interest of his life centred in the advancement of the Kingdom of God. His simple funeral service took place in the Metropolitan Church where he had worshipped for forty-four years. Permission was given to his sons, Vincent and Raymond, to erect a memorial tablet in the church. In October 1927, Vincent Massey resigned from the Board of Trustees on which he had served since 1909. He joined the Anglican Church and rose in public life to the high honour of Governor-General.

A month after Chester Massey's death, the Honourable John James Maclaren, 'a man of sterling Christian character', died at the age of eighty-four years. He had represented the Metropolitan at every Toronto Conference and at every General Conference since the union of 1884. He was a prominent member of the World's Sunday School Association.

At Dr. Sedgewick's induction on 11 July 1926, the Reverend Dr. J.R.P. Sclater referred to the Metropolitan as 'one of the most important preaching stations in the British Empire'. Dr. Sedgewick had served at Central Presbyterian Church in Hamilton for nineteen years, first as assistant and from 1910 as the minister. When the church voted to remain out of Union, Dr. Sedgewick went for a year as an assistant at St. James in Montreal before taking up his duties at the Metropolitan.

At a meeting of the Official Board on Friday 20 January 1928, J.B. Allen, W.E. Segsworth and N.M. Squire were welcomed as new officials. Enthusiastic reports were received from the Lunch and Rest Room Committee, the Woman's Association (formerly the Ladies' Aid), the Woman's Missionary Society and Evening Auxiliary, the C.G.I.T. (Canadian Girls in Training) led by Doris Moss and Eleanor Sedgewick, the Athletic Association, the Crusaders' Club, the Young Women's Guild, the Metropolitan Young Men's Club and the Metropolitan Young Girls' Club made up of girls in Mrs. A.R. Clarke's Sunday School class.

That month, Dr. Sedgewick planned a series of evening services with the sermons on the Prophet Elijah and with the choir singing, week by week, portions of Mendelssohn's *Oratorio*. At the evening service on Sunday 29 January, Dr. Sedgewick chose as his text, 'The God that answereth by fire, let Him be God', taken from I Kings 18:24, where Elijah challenges the prophets of Baal to pray for fire to ignite their sacrifice of a bullock laid on wood. No fire came. Then Elijah built a stone altar, surrounded by a trough. He laid pieces of bullock on wood, poured four barrels of water over it three times and prayed to the Lord God to send fire. The fire 'consumed the burnt sacrifice and the wood and the stones and the dust and licked up the water that was in the trench.' All the people fell on their faces, proclaiming, 'The Lord, He is God.' Dr. Sedgewick told the large congregation:

> It is not permitted to us in these days to appeal to any material proof that God is with us. We do not expect the visible fire from heaven. Sometimes we wish it were otherwise. Sometimes we wish that the spiritual world might be made more manifest—that it might be quite visible indeed.

Early the next morning, shortly after four o'clock, an employee of St. Michael's Hospital noticed smoke issuing from the church door facing Bond Street. He alerted the Sister-in-Charge who called the Fire Department at 4:20 a.m. The night was clear and desperately cold with no wind. Deputy Fire Chief Sinclair arrived at 4:26. He tried to enter the west door but he was driven back by smoke. Wisps of flame were seen through the flooring. Eerie sounds from the organ were heard as the fire advanced. Sinclair immediately sounded a second alarm and trained six lines of hose through six memorial stained-glass windows. The window in memory of Mrs. Punshon was smashed. A third alarm was turned in at 5:31 when the fire was at its height. The floor of the church burned through and collapsed into the basement. Slates rained down from the blazing roof. Twenty-six lines of hose were put into action, pumping two million gallons of water at tremendous pressure from the pumps. Fourteen lines were trained on the sanctuary from the west side, nine from the east. Three high-pressure streams were hurled across the south end causing a curtain of water to tumble constantly against the church. Two hundred firemen from ten different stations were on the scene taking turns holding the lines that carried so much pressure that the Fire Chief, himself, was knocked down by the force when he tried to give assistance. Thirty-five policemen guarded the Square, keeping it free from traffic. The coats of the firemen became covered with ice; icicles formed on their hats. All effort was concentrated on the tower. Chief William Russell said afterwards: 'I did not care what happened as long as the men kept the fire from the tower. We wanted to save those bells, and we did!' The fire was extinguished at 8:30 that morning. The tower, narthex and rear balcony were saved. The Sunday School was intact. The parsonage was unharmed. The well-built brick walls of the sanctuary stood firm. The organ was completely destroyed. The pipes were twisted into grotesque shapes. The choir gallery, unsatisfactory from the beginning, was reduced to ashes. The church looked like an 'ice-bound skeleton'.

❂

At four o'clock that afternoon, members of the Official Board gathered in the Board Room of the Toronto General Trusts Corporation (W.G. Watson was the General Manager). Messages of sympathy and offers of hospitality were read from Cooke's Presbyterian Church, the Unitarian Church on Jarvis Street and from three United Churches: Sherbourne Street, Carlton Street and St. James Square. Resolutions were adopted in praise of the Chief of the Fire Department and his men for their efficient and heroic service, to the Reverend Mother and staff at St. Michael's Hospital for their assistance and hospitality to the firemen and police, to Mr. and Mrs. T.F. Wickes of 76 Bond Street who brought kettles of coffee, and to the proprietors of the Castle Café for their kind hospitality. The owners of this Chinese café had refused to accept payment for the coffee, tea, and food they provided for the firemen. An honorarium of one hundred dollars was contributed to the Firemen's Benefit Fund. N.W. Rowell's motion, seconded by W.G. Francis, that the Metropolitan Church should carry on as an entity as far as possible without interruption, and that the calamity should be considered a challenge rather than a defeat, was passed unanimously.

On Friday, a second meeting was held when arrangements were made for the Sunday School and midweek activities to take place in the Unitarian Church. A committee was named to explore reconstruction of the damaged church, or building on the same site or elsewhere. The committee, under the chairmanship of N.W. Rowell, included Dr. Sedgewick, W.G. Watson, T.H. Mason, W.G. Francis, E.J. Howson, and the Recording Steward, G.R. Munnoch. The cause of the fire was declared unknown, although the Fire Chief thought it might have started in the organ. His assistant thought a burner on the gas stove had been left on. Arson was not considered.

The morning and evening services on Sunday 5 February 1928 were held in Massey Hall. That morning, Jack Skillicorn, the bell-ringer since 1926, mounted the steps of the tower to ring the bells for half an hour as the people gathered, proclaiming the spirit of a church that would someday rise again. The front cover of the Order of Service carried a message from the words of John Ruskin:

> When we build, let it be such a work as our descendents will thank us for, and let us think, as we lay stone on stone, that a time is to come when these stones will be held sacred because our hands have touched them and that men will say as they look upon them, 'See, this our fathers have done for us.'

The Scripture lesson was from Isaiah, Chapter 40, beginning, 'Comfort ye, comfort ye my people, saith your God.' The congregation read responsively Psalm 40, 'God is our refuge and strength, a very present help in trouble.' The sermon was entitled 'Divine Providence'. Mr. Rowell made a brief address 'characterized by good taste and delicate expression'.

On Sunday 12 February, the congregation worshipped in Elm Street Church in the morning and in the Tivoli Theatre at night. On the next five Sundays, services were held in the Victoria Theatre. From 25 March until the reopening of the church in December 1929, the former Central Methodist Church was rented. The members of that church, at the corner of Bloor Street East and Park Road, had united with Westminster Presbyterian Church to form Westminster-Central United Church, later renamed St. Andrew's.

Church activities were carried on. The Business Girls' Club arranged for temporary premises at 60 Bond Street. The Athletic Association was given permission to use as much of the church and parsonage property as possible. Women's organizations met in members' homes. The Reverend Mr. Black accepted a call to East Aurora. The Reverend Mr. Strangways was appointed as the Associate Minister.

The committee appointed to study the future of the Metropolitan heard many suggestions. Some felt a new site should be chosen; Sherbourne Street Church welcomed a union with the Metropolitan. A new church for Carlton, Sherbourne and the Metropolitan was considered. Some thought a Bloor Street site would be advisable, others suggested a new building beside Victoria College. The City of Toronto made it known that it would be willing to acquire the property for a new Police Administration Building. The Parks Department wanted the site for a public park. But many in the congregation felt that the church should be rebuilt. They recalled the story of the ointment in the alabaster box that 'might have been sold for much'. The committee consulted Dr. Peter Bryce, who again surveyed the district and visited Central Methodist Church in Detroit where Lynn Harold Hough had been minister for seven years. Dr. Bryce appreciated the many advantages of a union with Carlton Street, with a new church built on that site, but he came to the conclusion that 'sacred tradition would appear to demand reconstruction' and that the needs of the downtown area should be the only consideration. He felt that the Metropolitan was a 'National Church Extraordinary' and that it should continue to be a witness and a great preaching centre in downtown Toronto. He strongly advised the construction of a modern building at the rear to serve as a centre for church activities and community service. The Executive of the General Council heartily endorsed reconstruction and permitted the congregation to solicit funds from United Churches across Canada.

At a joint meeting of the Trustees and Official Board in June 1928, a motion to rebuild the church on its present site was adopted. Holt Gurney voiced his opposition and in due course removed his membership to another church. Mrs. A.R. Clarke withdrew before the church was reopened. In August, at a joint meeting attended by Dr. Bryce, the plans of the architect, J. Gibb Morton, were approved in principle. He was asked to investigate costs for a building as an extension of the parsonage, to be used for social work while keeping the residential character of the Massey Memorial Parsonage.

At a congregational meeting on 8 October 1928, the architect's design for the new Gothic sanctuary to be built within existing walls, was projected on a screen. The vaulted ceiling was to be fifteen feet higher than the original church. A chancel would extend into the Sunday School with organ chambers on either side. Gothic stone arches would replace the cast iron columns that had supported the side galleries which would not be replaced. The transepts were deepened by eight feet. The Victorian spires and turrets at the rear of the church would be removed. Clerestory windows would be installed at each side of the upper nave. On the motion of J.H. Gundy, the congregation approved the plans for the reconstructed church on the present site and decided to build and equip a community house in which social service programmes and church activities would take place.

The architect secured the services of the Globe Furniture Co. of Waterloo, Ontario to build and install the memorial screen, throne, choir stalls, organ screens, pulpit, lectern, communion rail, font cover and pews. The Robert McCausland firm was commissioned to replace all the stained-glass windows using the original themes and inscriptions and, as well, to design a memorial chancel window. The window in memory of Mrs. Punshon could not be replaced for there was no record of its design. Robert McCausland, the head of the firm founded in 1857 by his grandfather, Joseph McCausland, borrowed ten artisans from England for two years to assist in this massive commission. The firm paid the travelling expenses by sea and rail of the craftsmen and their families.

The laying of the Foundation Stone took place on Saturday afternoon, 15 December 1928. Many members and friends gathered under a large white tent at the northeast corner of the building. Special guests on the platform included the Honourable G. Howard Ferguson, the Premier of Ontario, Controller Robbins, representing the mayor of Toronto, Sir Robert Falconer, the President of the University of Toronto, the Reverend Dr. A. Gandier, the Principal of Emmanuel College, and Rabbi I. Isserman of Holy Blossom Temple. The senior surviving minister of the Metropolitan, Dr. R.P. Bowles, Chancellor of Victoria University, relaid the original corner-stone of 1870. Lieutenant-Colonel P.L. Mason placed the historical documents in the new stone: the *Holy Bible*, R. Burrow's *Souvenir Historical Sketch*, the final issue of the *Christian Guardian*, 10 June 1925, and the first issue of the *New Outlook* on the same day, the Metropolitan *Year Book* for 1928, calendars of the last Methodist Sunday service on 7 June 1925 and the first service after church Union, 14 June 1925. The stone was laid by Sir Joseph Flavelle who had contributed $50,000 towards the cost of rebuilding. The Right Reverend Dr. George C. Pidgeon, the Moderator, offered the prayer of dedication, Dr. James Endicott and Canon Cody brought greetings, the National Anthem (God Save the King) followed prayers for the recovery of King George V by the Reverend L.B. Gibson of Cooke's Presbyterian Church. The Reverend John MacNeill, President of the World Alliance of Baptists, pronounced the benediction.

At the Annual Meeting on 25 January 1929, the Chairman, W.G. Watson, praised the splendid reports of the organizations that had carried on successfully during the year. The Sunday School, however, meeting in the Unitarian Church, had been reduced in number to eighty scholars. Despite all the problems of the year, the Missionary and Extension Fund, which changed its name during the year to the Missionary and Maintenance Fund, had reached the allocation of $35,000. The total amount raised during the year was more than fifty-five thousand dollars.

Top, Dr. W.H. Sedgewick. Top right, N.W. Rowell; below, his daughter Mary just married to Harry Jackman.

The great fire of 1928 reduced the formerly mighty cathedral of Methodism to rubble. Little stood but the walls and the tower. Firemen, as seen in newspaper photographs, struggled with freezing temperatures. Next morning, icicles wreathed the wreckage.

ARISING ANEW FROM ITS ASHES!

But soon work began to restore the Metropolitan.

*Undaunted hope: above, two former ministers,
Chancellor Bowles and Dr. Sedgewick, take
part in the relaying of the cornerstone. Right,
P.L. Mason places historic records into a metal
box, to be sealed under the cornerstone.*

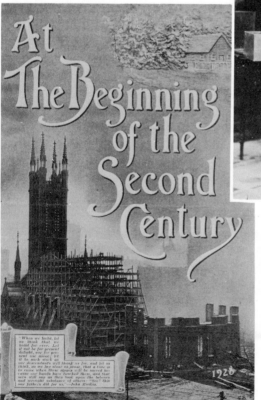

*Despite the fire, the
congregation of the
Metropolitan celebrate
the beginning of their
second century with a
booklet whose cover
shows the original chapel
and the present church
surrounded by contrac-
tors' scaffolding.*

CHAPTER 10

The Rebuilt
Metropolitan United Church

1929 - 1938

Plans for the reopening of the church were set in motion in the summer of 1929. The Order of Service, prepared by Dr. Sedgewick, was printed at the Ryerson Press. When it was ascertained that the new Casavant organ could not be installed for the opening service, Dr. Fricker was given authority to assemble an orchestra for the dedication services on 15 December. Arrangements were made for the service to be broadcast. The Chairman of the Music Committee, A.W. Austin, at his own expense, provided the choir with new cassocks, white surplices, and mortar-boards in place of the old black gowns acquired in 1904. The Official Board decided to permit a Processional by the choir and clergy even though this formality had not been approved by the Methodist *Discipline*. Tickets were distributed to members, known adherents, and special guests who were instructed to enter by the north door before 10:30 on Sunday morning. The front doors were opened to the public at twenty minutes before the hour.

By the day of the reopening, five lofty stained-glass windows were in place: the 'Ascension' window and the 'Sermon on the Mount' window in the transepts, the windows in memory of J.M. Treble and Mrs. Massey Treble, and the magnificent Chancel window, the gift of the congregation, 'to the Glory of God and the Holy Cause of Christian Unity, in Him made One'. In the centre of the window, Jesus is shown as the Sovereign Christ, enthroned on the orb of the world, with crown and sceptre, as 'King of Kings and Lord of Lords'. In the upper portion are the words: 'And I, if I be lifted up from earth, will draw all men unto me.' His Nativity is portrayed on the upper left, His Crucifixion on the right. An integral part of the window, below the figure of the Sovereign Christ, is the empty stone niche symbolizing the presence of the Holy Spirit, guarding and empowering the work and worship of the Church. In the lower portion, the three lights on the left portraying Christian charity show St. Peter with Cornelius: 'God hath showed me that I should not call any man common or unclean.' The east lower lights illustrate the vision of St. John when 'all nations and kindreds and tongues stood before the Throne and before the Lamb'.

The intricately carved screen designed by the architect, J. Gibb Morton, stretches across the chancel beneath the window. Soaring up to the niche in the window are the pinnacles of the crowning canopy of the throne or sedilia, ornamented with symbolic carvings: clouds signifying the unseen God; the 'bursting sun', a sign that Christ is the 'Sun of righteousness' as affirmed in Malachi 4:2; a torch signifying Christ, the 'Light of the World'; the open book representing God's Word; and the vine showing Christ's relationship with his disciples, 'I am the vine, you are the branches.'

The Communion Table, before the Throne, is the focal point of the chancel. The front face is a carving of the 'Last Supper' after the painting by Leonardo da Vinci, carved from soft oak imported from California. The designs were made from many pieces dovetailed together with the grain running in alternate directions to prevent warping. The disciples are arranged in groups of three with Christ set apart in the centre and the centre of interest for all. From left to right on the left side are Bartholomew, James the Less and Andrew, Judas, holding the money bag, Peter, with a dagger in his hand, and John, the favourite disciple. On the other side of Jesus are Thomas, with his finger upraised in question, James the Greater (the brother of John), Philip, Matthew (the publican), Thaddeus, and Simon. The table was the gift of the Mason family, dedicated 'to the glory of God and in loving memory of Bertha Elizabeth Mason, 1864-1929'.

The canopied choir stalls with carved roses to signify Christ's birth and trefoils (three-part circles representing the Trinity) are surmounted by tall Gothic organ screens on both sides of the chancel. The pulpit, placed upon a massive stone base, has finely carved pillars. The lectern and the font cover in the shape of a crown, are ornamentally carved in harmony with the motifs. The portable communion rails, which occupy the spaces in front of the pew screens when not in use, are also enriched by decorative carvings. Eighteen angel heads on each side at the base of the ceiling of timbered oak look down on the worshippers as agents of God's love and knowledge. All the carvings were fashioned under the supervision of Andrew Brown of the Globe Furniture Company, with a staff of hand-carvers trained in Russia, Switzerland, England, Scotland, Belgium, Holland, and Roumania. Small pieces of glass from the shattered stained-glass windows are reputed to have been used in making the impressive chandeliers.

With awe and with thanksgiving, the congregation gathered on 15 December 1929 to dedicate their beautiful church to God's service. Despite the bitter windy weather and icy sleet, the church was filled to capacity at eleven o'clock. Dignitaries were welcomed and escorted to the front pews by Charles Matthews, who became known as the Metropolitan's 'Chief Protocol Officer'. Extra chairs were placed at the front and people stood two deep along the walls. When the doors had to be closed, hundreds of people, four abreast in a long line stretching from the front steps to Queen Street, were turned away.

For the first time, the congregation of the Metropolitan Church witnessed a Processional, rising to join with the choir and clergy in the triumphant hymn of praise, 'Christ is made the sure foundation, Christ the Head and Corner-stone.' Sir Robert Falconer and Chancellor Bowles read the Scripture lessons, the Very Reverend George C. Pidgeon conducted the act of dedication. The prayer of dedication was offered by the Reverend Dr. S.D. Chown. The choir, accompanied by the orchestra, sang Attwood's setting of 'Come Holy Ghost, our Souls Inspire'. The preacher of the day was the Reverend Lynn Harold Hough of Montreal. In the morning, he traced Christian history, basing his sermon on a verse from the Revelation: 'Behold the tabernacle of God is with men, and He will dwell with them and be their God.' After the National Anthem and the Benediction, the congregation remained standing while the Lieutenant-Governor, W.D. Ross and his party, Mayor Sam McBride and Mrs. McBride, Sir William Mulock and other dignitaries withdrew. At the evening service, Dr. Solomon Cleaver led in prayer and Dr. Bryce read from Holy Scripture. In the afternoon, Denton Massey's York Bible Class of about two thousand young men met in the Metropolitan at the invitation of the Board.

Special services continued for four weeks. Although filled with admiration for the restored church and thankful that it would again proclaim God's presence in downtown Toronto, the congregation faced the staggering cost of $400,000 for the church and Church House, just when the crash of the stock market had heralded the Depression that strangled the country's economy for a decade. With bitter disappointment the people realized that the fine acoustics of the original church had been lost and that those of the rebuilt church were woefully inadequate.

The introduction of the Processional Hymn met with such favour that the Board decided to continue it at both morning and evening services. The introduction of a Recessional needed further study in the Board's opinion. A motion of appreciation praised Dr. Sedgewick for the 'perfection of word and spirit' that was achieved in the liturgy of the Opening Service. The character of the evening service was changed after the first Sunday. A more formal evensong was introduced in place of the evangelistic services. The evening congregation dwindled until only a few dozen attended.

❂

The Reverend J.E. Graham was inducted as the Assistant Minister and Director of the Memorial Church House on Wednesday 5 February 1930. The Church House was officially opened on Monday 14 April. All members were invited to attend this service of dedication. Dr. Bryce spoke on behalf of the Metropolitan; Dr. Archer Wallace represented the United Church of Canada. Young people, only, were invited to a social evening on Tuesday to inspect the new dining room, gymnasium, classrooms and offices, and the Board Room, lounge and Chapel in the converted parsonage which had been included in the Church House complex with the consent and approval of Vincent Massey. A new parsonage was acquired at 94 Binscarth Road. Later that month, Class No. 7, that had continued to meet socially in the homes of its members, put on a concert to raise funds to furnish the Chapel. Admission was thirty-five cents. A plaque on the wall reads: '"Be still and know that I am God." A Sanctuary for quiet meditation, furnished by former members of Class No. 7, in loving memory of their leader, S.R. Hanna.'

On Easter Day, 20 April 1930, the magnificent new organ, for the first time, thrilled the worshippers with its power. Built by the Casavant Frères of St. Hyacinthe, Quebec, it was the largest in Canada and one of the finest in the world, with its five manuals, 7,852 pipes, and with five hundred miles of wire in its construction. On that Easter day, the choir, for the first time, sang an Introit at the morning service.

All the stained-glass windows were in place for the Easter services, including the window in memory of Margaret Phelps Massey which had originally been erected in 1921 by her husband, Chester Massey. Those on the west aisle, as before, depict the miracles and parables of Christ; scenes from our Lord's ministry are on the east side. All the windows contain liturgical symbolism and representations of the Holy Land.

On the Saturday after Easter 26 April 1930, while Dr. Fricker played the organ, the Honourable N.W. Rowell, who had borne a large share of the responsibility of the rebuilding of the church, escorted his daughter, Mary, down the impressive aisle to give her in marriage to Henry Rutherford Jackman, a young financier of the city. This was the first formal wedding to be solemnized in the completed church. The first marriage ceremony had taken place in the chancel when Miss Grace Adella Gooderham became the bride of T.H. Mason, the son of the late W.T. Mason.

At a membership meeting on 7 May 1930, almost five years after Union, it was decided that the administration of the church should be in accordance with the *Manual* of the United Church of Canada. The Quarterly Official Board was dissolved and twenty laymen were elected for five years to serve as elders on the newly formed Session, along with the six ministers who were associated with the Metropolitan. Twenty-one Stewards, including Mrs. Willmott, Miss Bessie Starr, A. Elliott Allen, and G.R. Munnoch, were elected for one year. The Session, the Stewards, and representatives from church organizations comprised the Official Board. The *Manual* limited the Board of Trustees to fifteen members. The Metropolitan had sixteen. Resignations were accepted from George Kerr and B.E. Bull (who died on 30 May 1930), both Trustees for forty-six years; from E. Holt Gurney; E.T. Berkinshaw (who died in September 1930); T.H. Mason and G.H. Parkes (a Trustee for thirty-five years). Five new Trustees were appointed: Sir Joseph Flavelle, E.R. Wood, G.H. Wood, W.B. Woods, and Denton Massey. The Board of Trustees relinquished its reponsibilities for music and the use of the church. It was empowered to look after financial investments and endowments and had special responsibilities regarding property.

The United Church had no place for class meetings. William Atley's class that had met on Sunday mornings at ten o'clock became a Fellowship meeting. Miss Starr's class of loyal women, organized in 1907, continued to meet 'for fellowship' before the Wednesday night prayer meeting. Pew rents were abolished although free reserved sittings were permitted for a time. The Young Men's Club changed its name to the Men's

Association in accordance with Rule 62 of the United Church *Manual*.

The radio broadcasts of the church services begun on 15 December continued at a cost of fifty dollars a Sunday until the end of June 1930. That month the congregation bade farewell to Miss Helen McGregor who had served for nine years as the Deaconess. She was succeeded by Miss Louise Pirch. The Board was able to borrow, from the Book Room of the United Church, copies of the *Methodist Hymn Book* for use by the choir and the congregation. It had been replaced by the *Hymnary* which was published that year.

On 15 June, the Reverend J.E. Graham commenced a series of open-air services held in the church grounds immediately after the evening services. These proved to be so successful that the last service at the end of July attracted more than two hundred people who probably could not have been persuaded to enter the church for a regular service.

The Moderator, the Right Reverend E.H. Oliver, preached at the evening service on 14 December to mark the first anniversary of the rebuilt church. Dr. Strangways, the Pastoral Visitor, continued to serve until the end of the year. His valuable services were recognized at the Annual Meeting on 18 February 1931. As a gift from the church, he was allowed to keep the parsonage furniture that he had been using. He was appointed as an Elder, along with H.H. Mason, George Blow, and A. Elliott Allen. Two new Stewards, H.R. Jackman and Lloyd Wood, were elected.

The inadequacy of the acoustics had a serious effect on the attendance at church services. The York Bible Class decided to leave the Metropolitan for the spacious Yorkminster Baptist Church at the end of June 1930. The Reverend J.E. Graham's resignation was accepted and the Reverend Ray McCleary was called as his successor. The Depression and smaller congregations affected church givings. Mr. McCleary's stipend, set at $1,600 per annum with free living quarters in the Church House, was $900 a year less than that of his predecessor. The carillonneur, J. Leland Richardson, was dismissed. Two members of the choir, Edmund Milroy and Sidney Giles agreed to act without payment.

A special meeting was held in December 1931 concerning a Remit from the General Council to substitute the word 'members' for 'men' in the phrase to read, 'members in good standing'. Before the Council met in the summer of 1932, the Honourable N.W. Rowell declined the nomination for Moderator put forward by former Presbyterians, strongly supported by a group of Methodists. They had wanted him to be the first layman to be elected to that high office.

Mr. McCleary organized a Daily Vacation Bible School for a week in July. At the closing, the girls danced around a maypole, the boys acted scenes from *Robin Hood.* In the autumn he edited the first, and possibly the only issue of the *Chimes.* Similar in format to the *Metropolitan* published thirty-five years earlier, the *Chimes* recorded the activities of the Church House and the various organizations such as the Woman's Missionary Society, the Evening Auxiliary, the C.G.I.T. and the Sunday School. The Woman's Association sewed for the needy and raised a thousand dollars towards the church debt at a garden party at the home of the Social Convenor, Mrs. N.W. Rowell. A Junior W.A. was organized by Mrs. Sedgewick in 1931 with Mrs. T.H. Mason as President, Miss Victoria Hanna as Secretary-Treasurer, and Mrs. Harry Jackman as Convenor of Social Service. The Business Girls' Club flourished with a membership of three hundred. The Young Women's Guild met on Thursdays, the Mothers' Club met twice a month with nursery care provided for the children. The Young People's Department of the Sunday School was organized into clubs for midweek activity. Friday night was boys' night when they came with their teachers to the Church House. A community club for boys met every Saturday morning, and in the afternoon, the Chinese Boys and Girls Club conducted their meetings. A Young People's Society was being organized to meet on Wednesdays for supper, group games, and a meeting. Friendship Teas took place on Sunday afternoons. In addition to these activities, the elders held Family Fellowships on Wednesday evenings when the families in each district met for dinner and sociability. (When Miss Starr's group disbanded in 1934, prayer meetings came to an end.) In November, the Governor-General, the Earl of Bessborough, with the Countess worshipped at the morning service.

The dark days of the Depression meant hardship for many people. The Benevolent Fund assisted one hundred and eighty families in 1932. Twenty-five children were sent to fresh-air camps. The Unemployed Men's Club met in the Church House on Saturday nights when more than one thousand found a warm welcome. No welfare was available in those days. About four hundred letters were mailed that year for men who did not have the price of a two-cent stamp. About one hundred and sixty men gathered for a party in the Church House after the evening service on Christmas Sunday. Each man received a pair of socks provided by the Woman's Association.

The Metro Boys' Club, made up of a group of wild boys who earned the title the 'Allan Gardens Gang', had an average attendance of thirty. They came to the church on two evenings a week and on Saturday afternoons. In the summer they entered the Inter-Church Baseball League. According to Mr. McCleary, these boys 'did not indulge in things sacred' but they were given the opportunity of being reclaimed and saved from a life of crime. Contributions towards the cost of maintaining the Church House were gladly received. With an annual subscription of seventy-five dollars, it was possible to become an Honorary Member of Church House.

About this time, the Book Room asked the Metropolitan to return the *Methodist Hymn Books* borrowed in June 1930 and to buy copies of the *Hymnary*. The Board replied that no money was available for new hymn books and that the church would continue to use the borrowed books. Two years later, in 1935, an anonymous donor supplied the church with a sufficient number of copies of the *Hymnary* for use by the choir and congregation.

The Reverend Dr. Joseph S. Cook died on 27 May 1933. He had been an active member since 1920 when he retired from the ministry because of his health. He was described as 'a very dear and prized friend of the church'. His Christmas hymn 'Gentle Mary laid her Child, Lowly in a Manger' was included in the *Hymnary* and also in the *Hymn Book* of 1971. When his daughter, Alta-Lind Cook, died in 1980, she left a generous bequest to the Metropolitan in memory of her father.

In October 1933, Dr. Sedgewick sent a letter of resignation to the Official Board to take effect the following June. 'For some time,' he wrote, 'I have been increasingly convinced that radical changes must be met at the Metropolitan if the church is to maintain its ministry.' He had been in charge of the church for a longer time than any previous minister. He had held the congregation together during the dark days of decision after the fire. He had ministered during Depression years when the church was saddled with a debt of more than two hundred thousand dollars. The Board acknowledged his outstanding service during critical and difficult periods. N.W. Rowell said that he had sat under no minister more inspiring or helpful.

At the Annual Meeting in February 1934, the Missionary and Maintenance Committee reported a splendid response to the Cent-a-Meal Boxes that had been distributed in June 1933. The Stewards reported a deficit of more than four thousand dollars. The Sunday School had doubled, reaching an enrolment of two hundred and thirty. Dr. John McIntosh (the father of Mrs. Jean Lee), was appointed the Superintendent, succeeding H.H. Mason who had been in office since 1922.

❖

The City of Toronto's Centennial celebrations took place in 1934. On the Anniversary Sunday 29 April, the Metropolitan celebrated the 116 years since the opening of the King Street Methodist Episcopal Chapel in the town of York. The Reverend Dr. George A. Dickson was invited to be the special preacher that day.

Born in Lanarkshire, Scotland in 1886, Dr. Dickson had been recruited by the Presbyterian Church in Canada for service in the Canadian West. He was ordained by the Manitoba Conference in 1914. For ten years he had been the minister at Knox, a downtown church in Calgary which had been deeply in debt after Church Union. He attracted large congregations; the church debt was reduced from $165,000 to $76,000. He was blessed with a good voice. Despite the poor acoustics at the Metropolitan, the congregation could hear him adequately on that Anniversary Sunday. He received and accepted a unanimous call and he assumed his new duties on 1 August 1934 at a salary of five thousand dollars.

That summer, Ray McCleary invited the Toronto Silver Band to play on the church lawn after the evening service. These Christian bandsmen had been connected with the Salvation Army before forming their own band in 1931 under the direction of Alfred Pearce. The next year they became associated with the Avenue Road Tabernacle. The band played occasionally at the Metropolitan evening services that summer of 1934 and on 9 September began an official association with the church, playing regularly at every evening service. The next year it became known as the Metropolitan Silver Band.

Many of the bandsmen were from England. They suggested the formation of a P.S.A. (Pleasant Sunday Afternoons), a feature of Wesleyan Methodist Churches in England. The Metropolitan P.S.A. was an immediate success. The audiences were largely made up of the single unemployed men of the area. After a programme of hymns and songs, the wives and daughters of the bandsmen served tea and sandwiches. By June 1937, the average attendance reached about two hundred and fifty every week.

Dr. Dickson welcomed the participation of the Band. He told the Board at his first meeting with them that he was 'attempting to make the morning services devotional and expository, the evening services wholesomely popular'. The evening congregation returned to the Metropolitan in large numbers.

At Dr. Dickson's request, he and his wife, who was seriously ill, moved to an apartment in the Church House from the parsonage at 94 Binscarth Road. For some time this house could be neither rented nor sold. Because the church grounds were in a most undesirable condition, the Board asked the City of Toronto to contribute to their care and upkeep and a grant of $450 was received. The Deaconess, Louise Pirch, who left on 31 March after five years of faithful service, was succeeded by Miss Louise Mollenhauer. The Reverend Ray McCleary, because of his experience in a downtown ministry, received a call to WoodGreen United Church which was on the verge of closing. He served there with exceptional success for several years.

The Reverend Noble Hatton became his successor. Although Noble was born in Atherton, Lancashire, he was only a year old when his parents immigrated to Penetanguishene, Ontario. During his student days at Victoria, he served one summer as the Director of the Boys' Camp at Bolton; for another as a student minister at Delburne, Alberta. Mr. Hatton has recounted how he came to receive his call to the Metropolitan. After graduating from Emmanuel College in 1935, he was at his parents' home in Penetang awaiting ordination when he received a long-distance telephone call from Dr. Peter Bryce asking him to come to his office in the Wesley Buildings to discuss the possibility of an appointment as Assistant Minister and Director of the Memorial Church House at Metropolitan. When Mr. Hatton said that he had already volunteered for service in Northern Ontario, Dr. Bryce suggested that he should give some consideration to this new proposal. During the interview, Dr. Bryce made a telephone call and then told Noble that an appointment had been made for him to see Mr. W.G. Watson, the General Manager of the Toronto General Trusts. The young theolog became acutely aware of his need for a new suit for both knees of his trousers had been patched. To avoid embarrassment, he decided that he would not take his topcoat off during the interview. The receptionist, eyeing him doubtfully, asked if he had an appointment. He was soon ushered into Mr. Watson's opulent office. After a brief interview, Mr. Watson informed the young candidate that a luncheon had been arranged at the National Club in an hour's time so that he might meet the other members of the Committee: N.W. Rowell, Harry Jackman, and Dr. Bryce. In dismay, Noble realized that the patches on his trousers would have to be exposed. In distress he telephoned his fiancée, Evelyn, who advised him to have his trousers pressed while she bought him a new tie. At the appointed hour, the young Mr. Hatton, with his new tie and pressed pants, met with the Committee in that exclusive club. They asked him if he were married. Noble told them that he was in debt to Victoria College and could not afford to get married. 'The Committee has felt for some time that we should have a married assistant,' Mr. Watson explained. 'Could you get married if we advanced a month's salary?' So Noble and Evelyn were married in July. The Committee reported to the Board that Mr. Hatton 'gave splendid indications of his fitness for the position of Assistant Minister'.

The newlyweds, in August, took up residence in an apartment on Wellesley Street, furnishing it with furniture that was stored in the church basement, and commenced their association with the Metropolitan. Mr. Hatton was not only responsible for the activities and social work of the Church House, but in addition, he looked after the pastoral duties of the congregation with the Deaconess and the Retired Assistant, the Reverend Arthur Terryberry.

Dr. Dickson's chief responsibility was as a preacher. He also assumed a leading role in the undertaking of a campaign to reduce the huge debt of over $200,000. Steps were taken to reduce church expenditures. The annual allocation of $1,600 to the choir was discontinued. Dr. Dickson made a voluntary reduction of ten percent of his salary. A committee was formed, under the chairmanship of N.W. Rowell, to try to liquidate the debt. The General Council gave permission for the campaign to extend outside the church membership.

At the Annual Meeting in February 1936, Alfred C. Pearce, the conductor of the Band, Sidney Giles who had resigned as a voluntary carillonneur, and John McIntosh were elected to the Session. The elected Stewards included Furnivall Francis and W. Lloyd Wood. Miss Bessie Starr and Mrs. Willmott (listed as inactive) were still included on the Committee of Stewards. The godly Mrs. Margaret Taylor (Bowes) Willmott died on 28 June 1938 at the age of ninety-five, the oldest member of the congregation. She had been an active member since 1871. A memorial tablet, erected by her son, Dr. W.E. Willmott, was placed under the window commemorating the life of her husband, Dr. J.B. Willmott.

While attending the General Council in Ottawa in September 1936, the Honourable N.W. Rowell accepted the appointment of Chief Justice of the Supreme Court of Ontario, succeeding Sir William Mulock. The delegates were delighted to congratulate this devout churchman on his well deserved honour. That day he nominated Dr. Peter Bryce as Moderator of the United Church. Dr. Bryce was elected on the first ballot because the Reverend W.L. Armstrong and other nominees moved that the election be unanimous. Dr. Bryce resigned as Secretary of the Missionary and Maintenance Fund to give his full time to this high office. During his term, he and Mrs. Bryce attended the Coronation of King George VI in Westminster Abbey on 12 May 1937.

A special morning service to mark the Centennial of Victoria University was held in the Metropolitan on 11 October 1936. The Governor-General, Lord Tweedsmuir (John Buchan), read the lesson. The Reverend Dr. Jesse H. Arnup preached the sermon.

The Sunday evening services continued to fill the church to capacity. Mr. Hatton recalls one Sunday when the doors were barred so that no more could enter. A woman hammered on the door with her umbrella until he opened it to explain that the limit set by the Fire Marshall had been reached. She replied in anger: 'Well, this is the last time I'll come to this church.'

About two hundred and fifty people attended the Annual Meeting on 10 February 1937. The reports of the organizations were encouraging, the budget was balanced. The Junior Band had been organized in 1936, conducted by the founder, John Wood. Edwin Milroy had taken up his duties as carillonneur. Mr. Donald Tow (the son-in-law of W.G. Watson) was appointed for the first time to the Committee of Stewards. Mr. Chief Justice Rowell paid tribute to the services of Dr. Dickson and his staff. Dr. Dickson thanked the members for their support and surprised them by saying that he felt his period of usefulness was over. He spoke of the stress under which he had laboured since 1934 and announced that he wanted to be relieved of his duties in a year's time.

That summer Mrs. Mary Jackman became concerned about the young children of the district who were excluded from the Daily Vacation Bible School for boys and girls from five to twelve years of age. She organized a Nursery School for the little children who were from two to four years old. It proved to be so successful that a year-round Nursery School was inaugurated in September, directed by Miss Ruth Thompson, who was a graduate of the St. George's School of Child Study. The Bond Street Nursery has continued to the present day, financed by an independent Board which includes at least one representative appointed by the Metropolitan Church.

The successful campaign of the Building Committee was closed at the Annual Meeting in February 1938. The debt of $215,000 had been reduced to $85,436. About $90,000 had been contributed by friends across Canada. Mr. Elliott Allen, the Chairman of the Board of Stewards, again reported a balanced budget. His brother, John B. Allen, reported that the membership had reached 592. It was announced that commemorative tablets to honour the memory of the late A.W. Carrick, W.G. Francis, and P.L. Mason would be placed in the church. W.H. Carruthers (the father of Miss Ruth Carruthers and Mrs. Beatrice Maxwell) was elected to the Committee of Stewards. A former member of Elm Street Church, he had recently decided to move his membership to the Metropolitan at the invitation of Dr. Bryce. The Pastoral Relations Committee appointed to search for a new minister included W.G. Watson, T.H. Mason, E.J. Howson, J.H. Gundy, H.H. Mason, J.B. Allen and H.R. Jackman.

Dr. Dickson's pastorate came to an abrupt end in March. The deaconess, Miss Mollenhauer, submitted her resignation to take effect in June. The Pastoral Relations Committee added other members including N.W. Rowell, W.H. Carruthers, Mrs. T.H. Mason, Miss Isabel Uren and the Right Reverend Dr. Peter Bryce who was well acquainted with United Church clergy from coast to coast. He submitted several names for consideration. At the first meeting that he was unable to attend, the committee seized the opportunity of discussing the possibility of asking Dr. Bryce himself to be the minister. On the motion of J.B. Allen and E.J. Howson, which was unanimously endorsed by the committee and subsequently by the congregation, Dr. Bryce received a call to the Metropolitan Church.

Dr. Bryce was hesitant about accepting the call. He was in his sixtieth year. He felt that he did not possess the necessary preaching skills for the Metropolitan pulpit. Long-time friends, such as Dr. Archer Wallace, tried to dissuade him from assuming this heavy burden. Dr. Bryce, however, had been a member of the Metropolitan for almost ten years. He knew the people and the problems. He had been vitally interested in this downtown church since he had made the survey in 1917. He asked Noble Hatton to remain as his Assistant for the next year and he accepted the call to take effect in September when he would be relieved of the duties of Moderator.

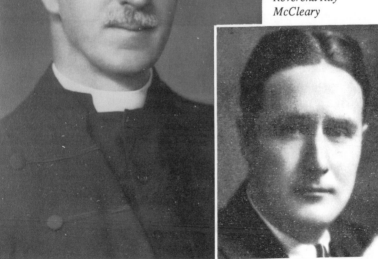

The Metropolitan Silver Band, shown here with conductor Alfred Pearce at centre, became affiliated with the church in 1934.

At left, Dr. Peter Bryce; below, Reverend Ray McCleary

The rebuilt chancel: above, decorated for 'Roses in December' Sunday ; right, detail of the 'Last Supper' carving on the communion table.

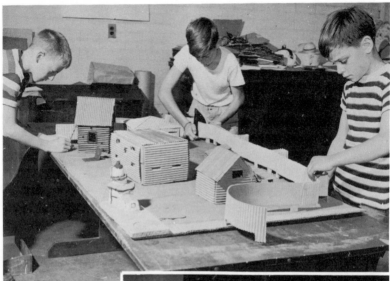

*During the 1940s,
Christian Education
programmes began
increasingly to make
use of innovative edu-
cational techniques.
Miss Ruby Brown
started a 'Play Hour'
for children living in
the neighbourhood
(right); the Boys'
Work Board created a
Boys' Centre in the
basement (above).*

CHAPTER 11
The Metropolitan United Church

1938 - 1950

Peter Bryce was born in a humble home in Blantyre, Scotland (the birth-place of David Livingstone) on 31 December 1878. When a boy, he read with tremendous interest a biography of the social reformer and evangelist, John Wesley. 'Father,' he asked, 'Who are these Methodists?' Andrew Bryce, a strict Presbyterian, replied, 'The Methodists, my son, are very good people and kind to the poor.' Peter was later converted to Methodism and after a 'singular experience', offered himself as a candidate for the Methodist ministry. He travelled in England and Scotland as an evangelist before being posted in 1903 to Newfoundland. For three years he ministered to the fishing communities on the west coast, rowing, at his peril, from one charge to another. During his stay in Newfoundland, the handsome young missionary became engaged to Julia Bemister Woods, a kindergarten teacher at the Methodist College, and the daughter of the Honourable H.J.B. Woods, later to become the Postmaster-General of Newfoundland.

Dr. Bryce decided to enter Victoria University for theological training in 1906. As a newcomer to Toronto, he volunteered to assist the minister of the King Street East Methodist Church, the Reverend Gilbert Agar, who told him of the need in the Earlscourt district, an industrial suburb known as 'Shacktown'. Peter Bryce went to Earlscourt as the student minister in charge of Boon Avenue Church in 1907. He was ordained in 1908, married in 1909, and he continued to serve as Superintendent of the Earlscourt circuit until 1920.

From the first, he was deeply concerned about the poor and the destitute for whom no government help was available. In December 1906, he took a list of thirty families with one hundred children, who faced a bleak Christmas, to Joseph Atkinson, the publisher of the *Toronto Daily Star*. Mr. Atkinson, who had known poverty in his youth, decided to make a public appeal for contributions to the 'Star Santa Claus Fund'. That year $151.15 was collected, enough to look after the people on Dr. Bryce's list. (Sixty-five years later, the Fund received $2,600,000.) A firm friendship developed between the two men. Mr. Atkinson placed the columns of the *Star* at Peter Bryce's disposal, either for regular contributions by him or for occasional articles about the work in which he was engaged.

During his years at Earlscourt, he built seven churches, organized eight Sunday Schools and established the Earlscourt Children's Home. He supervised the seven clergy attached to the circuit. The Reverend Archer Wallace, a friend from Newfoundland, was the Assistant Superintendent. As well as excelling as an administrator, Dr. Bryce was always deeply interested in individuals. He carried coal from his own cellar to parishioners in need; he wielded a hammer to assist unskilled newcomers, mostly immigrants from the British Isles, who were trying to build their own shacks on their Earlscourt lots. He found ways and means of making it possible for promising teenagers to remain at school; he badgered the Council to make the sidewalks of the area wide enough for baby carriages.

Dr. Bryce had the ability of making the plight of the poverty-stricken the concern of affluent people and government officials. He played an active role in the campaign which resulted in the Ontario Temperance Act of 1916. After years of effort, the Federation of Community Service was founded in 1918. He became the first President of this body which has developed into the current United Way. In 1920 he left Earlscourt to head the National Campaign for the Methodist Church and was instrumental in raising about $5,000,000 for this fund. With the permission of the Toronto Conference, he served as a Director of the Child Welfare Social Service Council of Ontario and as the first Chairman of the newly formed Provincial Mothers' Allowance Board, a post he held until 1927. He was influential in organizing the Neighbourhood Workers Association (now known as Family Services) and the Bolton Fresh-Air Camp for underprivileged mothers and children. He was a member of the Toronto Housing Commission. His vision of Old Age Pensions was realized by the Province of Ontario in 1929.

In 1923, he took on the added responsibility of ministering to the struggling Woodbine Heights Methodist Church, serving there with energetic zeal until 1927 when he was appointed Secretary of the Missionary and Maintenance Fund. When the Metropolitan was reopened in 1929, he and his family placed their memberships in this church. Mrs. Bryce became the President of the Woman's Missionary Society, and John Bryce began his long official connection with the Metropolitan in 1931 when he was made an Officer of the Sunday School. Dr. Bryce was well known, respected and beloved by the congregation when on 18 September 1938 he entered the pulpit as the Senior Minister of the Metropolitan United Church.

He was tall, erect, silver-haired and immaculate, with a saintly countenance and kind, blue eyes. His manner had an old-world graciousness that never varied. He spoke to the most unfortunate derelict in the same way that he addressed people of wealth and prominence. To Dr. Bryce, they were all children of God. He could always detect and deal with insincerity. He possessed a gentle, merry sense of humour. A young student once asked him for advice about preaching. Dr. Bryce replied: 'Always preach about Christ and about twenty minutes.' His own sermons, simple yet profound, brought to large congregations messages of hope, admonition, and the tenets of the Christian faith. His preaching was effective, for he seemed to speak directly to each individual in the pew. His prayers took the worshippers to the very Throne of God for he prayed as one who 'spoke oft with the Lord'. At the conclusion of the services, Dr. Bryce always stood at the foot of the chancel steps to speak to the people who crowded the centre aisle, glad of the opportunity to shake his hand and thereby to receive a special blessing.

❂

In October 1938, at Dr. Bryce's invitation, Miss Ruby Brown came to the Metropolitan as a deaconess. She was born in 1895 in Northern Michigan where her Canadian father was working for a few years. Ruby was always interested in children. At the age of fifteen she became the Superintendent of the Primary Department of her Presbyterian Sunday School. Shortly afterwards, at a Young People's Rally, she felt called to offer herself as a missionary to India. After finishing her High School course, she entered the Presbyterian Deaconess Training School (Dr. Bryce was one of her lecturers). After graduation, she was rejected as a missionary to India because of her health. Instead, she went to College Street Presbyterian

Church as the Deaconess. After Church Union, she was invited to Queen's Avenue Church in New Westminster, B.C. She had been at Zion United Church, Brantford, for ten years when Dr. Bryce persuaded her to come to the Metropolitan, where she served with exceptional distinction for seventeen years.

Dr. Bryce, Mr. Hatton, and Miss Brown lost no time in getting to work as a team, building on the organizations and activities already in place while opening up new avenues of opportunity with fresh vigour and wide perspectives. Dr. Bryce made the rule that everyone who came to the church seeking help should receive a home visit. A Deaconess Committee with Miss Ruth Carruthers as Chairman was formed in that month of October to assist Miss Brown with visiting, with the distribution of clothing and with providing leadership for the Mothers' Club that had an average attendance of seventy women. It was decided that four groups should be formed; one met for cooking (with Mrs. Ruby Bolt), another to learn how to sew and knit, a third group went to swimming classes, the fourth group met for games and recreation.

Miss Brown was appalled at the conditions under which some people were living in the neighbourhood. She found families with five and six children huddled into one room in the rooming houses of the area. Realizing that the children had no place to play after school, she organized a 'Play Hour'. About seventy-five children attended regularly. Volunteers staffed the gymnasium, the Quiet Room for crafts and quiet games, and the Housekeeping Room equipped with thirteen dolls' houses made from wooden soap boxes and furnished by the Woman's Association. Each had a set of doll dishes and a high chair or doll carriage. The children were taught how to set tables and how to entertain at tea-parties. A retired librarian read to the children in a room upstairs or helped them to read for themselves. Miss Brown liked to be there always, to greet the children. They were given a piece of cherry cake, donated by a bakery, when they went home.

The 120th anniversary, celebrated on 21 November 1938, was attended by His Honour, the Lieutenant-Governor and Mrs. Matthews. Dr. Lynn Harold Hough and Dr. E. Crossley Hunter were the special preachers. That Sunday, a new loudspeaker was installed to improve the acoustics. The Junior Congregation was large enough to meet in three sections. Miss Isabel Uren looked after the Nursery; Mrs. Olive Broley soon succeeded Miss Frances Horning as the leader of the middle group; Miss Brown looked after the children from ten to twelve years of age. The afternoon Sunday School now numbered 356 scholars and teachers. Dr. McIntosh's I.H.S. (the first three letters of the Greek name for Jesus) Class for young people met every Sunday afternoon.

In December, Dr. Bryce distributed folded sheets bearing 'Greetings to our Friends':

> The Metropolitan Church rejoices in its many friends as another year draws to a close. Their prayers and their confidence have been a constant source of strength.
>
> The Metropolitan last month celebrated 120 years of life. At no time in its history have the opportunities for service been greater and more insistent than now. In this downtown area the poor are always with us, many of them noble people, and in a multitude of ways our workers are doing everything in their power to help them. . . . The Church House is full of activity from day to day.
>
> Large numbers of young people are finding their Church Home at the Metropolitan, and the great crowds at the Sunday evening services are obtaining, we believe, comfort and strength and inspiration for their daily lives. We pray that we may be worthy of the task committed to us.

This modest brochure had a picture of the chancel as it had been on the first Sunday of December, filled with one thousand roses, provided anonymously by C.L. Burton, for later distribution to the elderly, afflicted, or lonely who lived in cheerless rooms. 'Roses in December Sunday' became an annual event. Dr. Bryce often quoted from J.M. Barrie's *Courage*:

> God gave us memory so that we might have roses in December.

Dr. Bryce's love of roses prompted Miss Emma Hardy, a former nurse, to place a rose in the pulpit every Sunday as long as Dr. Bryce lived.

Christmas Day fell on a Sunday that year. At the Metropolitan, a group of sixty young volunteers prepared and served breakfast for two hundred and seventy-seven 'forgotten men'. The food was donated by merchants and wholesale dealers. The P.S.A. met as usual at three o'clock. Special Christmas services were held at eleven and seven o'clock with Christmas music by the carillon, organ, and Silver Band. White gifts for the needy were received at the morning service. At the evening service Dr. Fricker led the church choir of sixty voices in Part I of Handel's *Messiah*.

Dr. Bryce soon made administrative changes. He organized a Boys' Work Board in the spring of 1939 made up of T.H. Mason, John McIntosh, J.B. Allen, and Arthur Uren. They had the responsibility of creating a Boys' Centre in the basement of the church, under the Sanctuary. Six rooms were partitioned, electric lights were installed and cupboards were built to hold the woodworking tools donated by Simpson's store. Volunteers took charge of teaching other crafts as well, such as clay modelling and soap carving. The Centre was open two nights a week.

A Christian Education Council of fifteen members was also inaugurated under the chairmanship of Dr. John McIntosh, the Superintendent of the Sunday School. He conducted monthly supper meetings for his Sunday School teachers, giving lectures one term on 'Teachers of Religion, or, The Principles of Teaching'.

Mr. and Mrs. Hatton left in June 1939 to go to Cobalt United Church. His successor, the Reverend G. Howard King, reported to the Annual Meeting that thirty-four weekly activities took place in the Church House, not counting outside groups. The Metropolitan Young People's Club was divided that year into two groups, one for devotional study, the other as a Married Couples Club. The Pleasant Sunday Afternoons, the Fireside Teas, and the Fireside Hours continued to flourish.

Mrs. Elliott (Ruby) Allen, the President of the Woman's Association, reported an active year, achieving in large measure the constitutional purpose of this organization, 'to assist in the social and welfare work of the congregation, to raise funds for church purposes and to promote a spirit of good-will and Christian fellowship throughout the congregation'. The Sewing Committee finished two hundred and fifty new articles of clothing, made felt slippers for the Nursery School and provided quilts and knitted garments for distribution by Miss Brown. The W.A. cooperated with the W.M.S. in sending a bale of clothing to the West. This work was carried on in the upstairs Work Room which was redecorated that year and named the Morley Punshon Room. The women paid half the cost, put a name-plate on the door and hung Dr. Punshon's portrait on the wall.

❂

Canada entered World War II on 10 September 1939. A War Service Unit was soon organized at the Metropolitan. The Study, 'Our Church and its Time', conducted under the leadership of Mrs. Jackman and Miss Brown, was discontinued because of the pressure of war work.

On 12 October, the wives of the bandsmen and the mothers of the boys of the Junior Band organized the Allegro Auxiliary. For years they had served refreshments after the P.S.A. gatherings. From October to December that year they made one hundred and fifty Christmas stockings, filled fifteen boxes of fruit for shut-ins and made eighteen gowns for the Christmas pageant. These industrious women provided comforts for the twenty-eight bandsmen who enlisted for active service. The Allegro Group continued to assist in the social service work of the church for fifteen years.

The Metropolitan Silver Band became associated with the Toronto Scottish Regiment in August 1940. They wore the kilted uniform of the regiment and adopted the name, 'The Metropolitan Toronto Scottish Band' until July 1944. In addition to their military duties, they carried on with their church commitments as best they could. The Junior Band disbanded in 1940 and was not reorganized until 1945.

Dr. Bryce made a point of entertaining service men who attended church in uniform and encouraged members to invite the boys to their homes. Through the generosity of C.L. Burton, a table was reserved for Dr. Bryce in Simpson's Arcadian Court on Mondays when he could entertain guests free of charge: visitors to the city, church officials, friends or ordinary members of the congregation who valued this opportunity to become personally acquainted with their minister.

The Metropolitan Church was filled to capacity on 24 November 1941 for the funeral of Newton Wesley Rowell. Colleagues, friends, and representatives of governments gathered to pay tribute to this devout man of God who had served the church with life-long devotion, his profession and his country with distinction. His death followed an illness of three and one-half years. In May 1938, he had suffered a massive stroke which deprived this fluent orator of the power of speech. At his request, there were no pallbearers nor eulogy at his simple funeral service conducted by Dr. Bryce, Chancellor R.P. Bowles, Dr. Trevor Davies and Dr. Sedgewick.

The Japanese attacked Pearl Harbor in December 1941. The Reverend Percy Price, who had served as a missionary to Japan since his ordination in 1912, was in Canada on furlough when the hostilities made it impossible for him to return to the mission field. He was called as the Assistant Minister to succeed the Reverend Howard King in 1942, bringing to the post exceptional experience in inner-city work. Before entering the ministry Mr. Price had practised law in Toronto. In Japan he developed, in 1912, the East Tokyo Mission, a social service enterprise of the Methodist Church. He played a key role in the formation of the Tokyo Methodist

Federation for Social Service and served as the National Secretary for Social Welfare for the Japanese Methodist Church. When at the Metropolitan, Mr. Price was instrumental in organizing Toronto's first Alcoholics Anonymous group.

One day in 1942, Dr. Bryce received a telephone call from the Office of the United Presbyterian Church of the United States. A prospective missionary to India, Miss Gertrude Nyce, was coming to Toronto to study Urdu with a student from India who was attending the University of Toronto. Miss Nyce needed part-time work and as Miss Brown was sadly overworked, Dr. Bryce arranged for her to join the team of Bryce, Price, Nyce, and Brown on a part-time basis as 'Girls' and Young Women's Worker'. According to Ruby Brown, 'everyone fell in love with her.' Because of the war she was able to stay in Toronto for two and a half years. She organized C.G.I.T. groups which met on Wednesdays for sewing lessons and other handicrafts, on Thursdays for healthful exercises, and on Fridays for the regular C.G.I.T. programmes to enable girls to fulfil the purpose 'to cherish health, seek Truth, know God and serve others'. Margaret Martin (still a member of Metropolitan) was invited to assist. When Miss Nyce left, she acted as the Superintendent for fourteen years. The girls were sent to Camp during the summer.

The boys were able to experience camp life too. Mr. Douglas Wright, who owned a farm near Georgetown, invited the Boys' Work Committee to arrange for three camps at his farm and he sent a cheque for $1,500 to cover expenses. In 1943 every boy had at least two weeks at the camp which lasted from 8 July to 17 August. Jim Ludford, a student at Emmanuel College, was Camp Leader from 1941 to 1944.

In 1943, the Council of Women was organized under the Chairmanship of Mrs. Ruby Allen, to coordinate the activities of the many women's organizations. That year, at the request of the Board of Education, the Metropolitan undertook to serve lunch at the Church House to about fifty children attending the Duke of York School whose mothers were enagaged in war work. Miss Ruth Carruthers, a graduate in Household Science, assumed the responsibility of planning menus and buying food. A cook and a helper were engaged. Women of the church assisted as volunteers. The children were told that they could have as much as they wanted to eat. Many had never before experienced regular, nutritious and satisfying meals! Their health, behaviour and studies improved. They were the envy of the other children in the schoolyard. The Board of Education provided the money for this service that continued for three years.

Dr. Fricker, who had retired early in 1943, died on 11 November that year. He had served as organist of the Metropolitan for twenty-six years and as the conductor of the Mendelssohn Choir for twenty-five years. His funeral took place at the Metropolitan on Saturday 13 November. The next year a memorial tablet was dedicated at the Sunday morning service of 19 November 'erected as a mark of affection and esteem by choristers who served under his leadership'. Dr. Fricker was succeeded by John Reymes-King, F.R.C.O., who had formerly been organist of Pembroke College, Cambridge.

The Metropolitan celebrated the 125th Anniversary for the whole month of November 1943 when a campaign was launched to liquidate the church debt of about $82,000. The campaign committee was chaired by W.G. Watson and H.R. Jackman. The Vice-Chairmen were Lloyd Wood and Donald Tow. The Executive Secretary was Austin Thompson. The women of the church were represented by Mrs. J.B. (Helen) Allen, Miss Ruth Carruthers, Miss Victoria Hanna and Miss Ruby Brown. Permission was once again granted to seek contributions from United Churches across Canada. The parsonage at 94 Binscarth Road, which had been rented since Dr. Dickson's day, was sold. A sale of parsonage furniture and fixtures netted four hundred dollars. The daily press gave excellent coverage about the Metropolitan, the activities and the campaign to retire the debt. Church members were encouraged to give generously to the Glory of God and also as a sixty-fifth birthday present for Dr. Bryce.

The campaign was amazingly successful. The members gave about $31,000, in addition to their annual balanced budget. 'Friends of the Metropolitan' contributed more than $50,000. A Trust Fund was established with the surplus. At a special service of thanksgiving in 1944, Mr. Jackman presented the Moderator, the Right Reverend J.R.P. Sclater, with a cancelled note. Mr. Watson presented the congregation with a complete list of contributors without the amounts of their gifts. The church was free from the heavy burden of debt she had carried since 1929.

When World War II ended in 1945, the Reverend Percy Price left the Metropolitan to return to Japan and Miss Nyce was able to go to India as a missionary. The Reverend Victor Fiddes succeeded Mr. Price and the Reverend S.T. Martin was appointed as a Pastoral Visitor.

❂

Although Dr. Bryce had recommended in 1917 that a trained social worker should be added to the Metropolitan staff, this appointment did not take place until 1 June 1945 when Miss Esther Highfield joined the staff. Born in Saskatchewan, she graduated from the University of Toronto's School of Social Work in 1941. For three years, she was connected with the Neighbourhood Workers Association. In 1944 she decided to attend the Deaconess Training School, graduating in the Spring of 1945. At the suggestion of Miss Brown, she applied to the Metropolitan and was appointed as Deaconess and Director of Social Service, a position she held until 31 December 1947 when she was succeded by Miss Vivian Jarvis.

After the war, Miss Florence Bird was appointed by the Woman's Missionary Society as a W.M.S. Worker with Japanese Canadians. Her office was at the Metropolitan. Mrs. Fumiko Ioi, when a girl, had been in Miss Bird's C.G.I.T. in Vancouver and had continued to correspond with her after the Japanese people living on the Coast had been forced to leave their homes, their belongings, their property and their businesses by a misguided Government. When the war was over, many Japanese young people wanted to come to Ontario but they could not come to Toronto without a job. Mrs. Ioi has recalled that Miss Bird found employment for her, met the train on a Saturday and brought her to the Metropolitan Church the next morning. Because she had been a missionary in Japan, Miss Bird was fluent in Japanese. Although she tried to integrate the Japanese young people into church life in Toronto, she organized the Metropolitan Nisei Young People's Union and the Metropolitan Nisei Mission Circle which met in the Morley Punshon Room until 1953. Both Mrs. Ioi and her husband, Masayuki Ioi, who died in 1986, have been active members of the Metropolitan.

The Junior Band was reorganized in October 1945 with John Wood acting as the conductor until his son, Alan, returned from overseas in December. Thirty-one boys reported on the first night. Dr. Bryce persuaded the Tamblyn Drugstore firm to sponsor the Band. They continued their support until 1958, providing uniforms in the Tamblyn colours of dark green with yellow trim. At the age of seventeen, the boys transferred to the Metropolitan Silver Band. When Alfred Pearce became ill, Alan Wood took over the Senior Band and Gordon King became the conductor of the Junior Band.

On 1 March 1946, S. Drummond Wolff was appointed Organist and Choirmaster, succeeding John Reymes-King. When only twenty-one years of age, Drummond Wolff became the Master of Music at St. Martin's-in-the-Fields, in London, England. He had been a chorister at Hereford Cathedral and later, Solo Boy at H.M. Chapel Royal of the Savoy. During World War II he conducted the Canadian Military Headquarters Choir in London. At the Metropolitan he initiated noon-hour organ recitals on Wednesdays. That first year the choir prepared both *Messiah* and the *St. Matthew Passion*. Miss Eleanor Tait was the assistant organist.

One Sunday, a broadcast of the Metropolitan Church service was heard by a New York mining magnate, Thayer Lindsley, who was in Toronto on business. He had personal worries at the time and he telephoned Dr. Bryce to ask if he might see him. This was the beginning of an enduring friendship. Lindsley was deeply impressed with the work that the Metropolitan was attempting to do. He offered to give $6,000 a year for programmes and $6,000 a year towards the upkeep of the property. Dr. Bryce set up the Thayer Lindsley Committee made up of Dr. and Mrs. Bryce, Mr. and Mrs. H.R. Jackman, Mr. and Mrs. Lloyd Wood, Mr. and Mrs. T.H. Mason, Mr. and Mrs. J.B. Allen, Dr. John McIntosh, Mrs. N.W. Rowell, Miss Irene Carrick, Mr. Austin Thompson, and Miss Brown. Suggestions were set forth, subject to Mr. Lindsley's approval: the appointment of Directors of Girls Work and Boys Work, improved acoustics, improved lighting, better care of the grounds, oil heating, a new souvenir booklet, chairs and curtains for the dining room. There seemed to be no limit to the projects that should be carried out. The most pressing need, it was decided, was to transform the Intermediate and Senior Sunday School room, now known as the Chancel Room, into a Youth Worship Centre, with a triptych to serve as an altar, mounted on wood with doors that could be closed when the Centre was not used for worship. A Picture Committee with W.G. Watson as Chairman selected the artist, Gordon Couling, A.O.C.A., to paint a picture in three panels with the three-fold theme: 'Come unto me, Abide in me, Go ye into all the world,' incorporating as many suggestions from the young people as possible. The triptych, mounted on carved oak wood found in the basement, was equipped with concealed lighting. Dr. McIntosh reported on the interest of the students in the project, noting that the attendance of the Intermediate Department had doubled in two years. Mr. Lindsley suggested that $1,500 should be set aside for new chairs and lighting for the Centre. A new piano was provided. The old one was transferred to the Morley Punshon Room which was known as the Young Adult Centre for a short time.

The Lindsley Fund made possible the appointment of a Girls' Work Secretary. At the suggestion of the Deaconess Committee, Mrs. Mabel Jickells was appointed as Church House Hostess to coordinate all the luncheons, teas, and dinners that were served day by day. Gracious and beloved, she has been described as a 'woman of legendary energy and achievement'. She continued in this demanding role until she married and retired in 1962.

❁

The Reverend Victor Fiddes was succeeded by the Reverend Frank G. Brisbin who had served in two multi-point pastoral charges in Alberta. He arrived in August 1948 with his friendly, unassuming wife, Louise, and their little daughter. With the encouragement of Louise, Frank had entered a doctoral programme at the Toronto School of Theology. He had been advised to seek a post as an assistant minister in a city church so that he would not have sermons to prepare. At the interview, Dr. Bryce had seemed in good health. In August he was in hospital and although he was back at work in September, his health was broken. Mr. Brisbin, with the able assistance of the pastoral assistant, the Reverend E.W. Stapleford, assumed more responsibility than might have been expected under normal circumstances. Dr. Bryce, in an article, 'Ten Years at Metropolitan', published in the *Toronto Daily Star* as the 130th anniversary was approaching, wrote that he had just completed 'ten of the happiest years of a rich and full life'.

To celebrate the 132nd anniversary, Dr. Bryce asked Mr. Brisbin and Mr. H.D. Tresidder to prepare a souvenir booklet which was available for the first time on the Anniversary Sunday, 5 November 1950, the last service Dr. Bryce was able to attend. He concluded his 'Personal Word' or Foreword:

> A staff of fourteen workers is now employed at the Metropolitan to meet the ever growing demands for larger service. It is our hope and prayer that the Metropolitan, at the heart of a great and growing city, may be increasingly a vital Christian witness and a centre of humanitarian service.

On that Anniversary Sunday, the Honourable Leslie Frost, Premier of Ontario, read the Lesson. Dr. David MacLennan, then of Yale Divinity School, was the special preacher. On Wednesday night, Drummond Wolff conducted the choir in Mendelssohn's *Elijah*.

The Canadian Broadcasting Corporation broadcast a programme, 'Sermons in Stone', on 26 November about the work of the Metropolitan under Dr. Bryce whose voice was heard in a recorded message for the last time. He died on 30 November 1950 after a protracted battle with cancer.

The funeral took place on 2 December. At his request, members of the Metropolitan Silver Band stood a twenty-six hour vigil by the open casket in the church from noon on Friday until two o'clock on Saturday. Throngs came in grateful tribute for the life and influence of this good man. Despite harsh winds and a driving rain, the church was filled to capacity for the funeral service by a cross-section of the whole community. The honorary pallbearers included Thayer Lindsley, Timothy Eaton, C.L. Burton, W.G. Watson, T.H. Mason, and several ministers including the Reverend Gilbert Agar, his first Toronto friend who had advised him to apply for the Earlscourt charge. Active pallbearers included J.B. Allen, H.R. Jackman, Donald Tow, Percy Slighte, Lloyd Wood, Dr. John McIntosh and representatives from the City and Province. The service, conducted by Mr. Brisbin, began with Isaac Watts' hymn,

> Give me the wings of faith to rise
> Within the veil, and see
> The saints above, how great their joys,
> How bright their glories be.

The choir sang the anthem, 'Let not your heart be troubled', composed by Dr. Drummond Wolff. Two close friends, the Very Reverend Jesse Arnup and Dr. Archer Wallace, gave the eulogies.

Long obituaries appeared in the newspapers extolling the life and career of Dr. Bryce. *The Globe and Mail* reflected editorially:

> The external successes have their place in any tribute. But to many thousands the sense of loss will be keenly personal. It was as a friend that Peter Bryce excelled. Nobody will ever know how many faced life again with renewed confidence in themselves because he believed in them. He had reverence for the courage with which people met their problems and sought to strengthen their souls with the aid of a religion for which he lived.

The ministry of music: right, Dr. S. Drummond Wolff, at the five-manual Casavant Frères organ, in 1950; below, the choir, led by Dr. Melville Cook (in the front row centre) in 1968.

Metropolitan's famed 23-bell 17-ton carillon, installed in 1922 and expanded over the years; right, two carillonneurs, James Slater with his son Gordon.
Below, two of the Metropolitan's organists: Dr. H.A. Fricker (right), and Dr. Melville Cook (left).

*Metropolitan clergy over recent years: counterclock-
wise from top, Noble Hatton and Frank Brisbin at a
Christmas party; a younger Frank Brisbin; George
Birtch; Jim
Norquay,
baptising
Philip Ivey;
Doug and
Ethel Lapp
after his
induction.*

CHAPTER 12

The Metropolitan United Church

1951 - 1966

During the months that followed Dr. Bryce's death, the young Mr. Brisbin, ably supported by the staff, carried on the work of the church. With unpretentious dignity, wisdom, and unfailing tact, he planned the Sunday services with no visible alteration in form. A Pastoral Relations Committee, chaired first by Mr. Jackman and then by John B. Allen, began a year-long search for a new Senior Minister. From the first, Frank Brisbin had made it known that he was not a candidate for he intended to complete his studies before returning to Alberta. Although many ministers in Canada and abroad were approached, no one was willing to accept the heavy responsibilities of a downtown church. At the year's end, John Allen came to Mr. Brisbin and said, 'You have now been in charge for a year. Things are going well, the people like you and you have survived. What excuse do you have against staying?'

Although the prospect seemed terrifying, Frank Brisbin decided, with the encouragement and support of Louise, to accept the challenge and to abandon his studies. At the Annual Meeting in January 1952, the report of the Pastoral Relations Committee was followed by strong debate for some members felt it unfair to place this heavy burden on such young people. However, a unanimous decision was reached and from that night they received the total support of the congregation. The Reverend Edgar G. Cowan, who was appointed as the Assistant Minister, moved into the Church House apartment. After a year in a rented furnished home, a manse on St. Clair Avenue East was acquired. The Brisbin family lived there until 82 Ridge Drive was purchased in 1957.

The many activities of the church carried on with undiminished vitality. During 1951, a new organization for people over sixty was inaugurated by the Social Worker, Miss Vivian Jarvis, and named 'Roses in December' in memory of Dr. Bryce. Members of the Guild, convened by Mrs. Hilda Potten, served tea at the weekly meetings. An A.O.T.S. (As One That Serves) Men's Club had been organized late in 1950 to serve in Christ's name in practical ways. With Mel Angove as President, the men undertook useful projects: tables were repaired, cupboards were built, Christmas hampers were packed and delivered, the church garden was planted. The Young Adults' Council coordinated the A.O.T.S., Sunday Evening Firesides, Monday evening bowling, Friendship Teas, Sunnybrook Hospital visiting, the 'Metro' newsletter, Easter Sunrise services, Easter pageants, and the Couples Club.

Miss Rita Rafelton, who had been appointed as Youth Worker to assist Miss Brown, organized the Metro Teens Club with Jean McIntosh (now Mrs. Jean Lee) as the President. It developed into the Teen-Agers Club which met on Saturday evenings from 8:00 until 11:30 o'clock. The City of Toronto continued to give a grant of $4,000 for the Play Hour, the Boys' Club and the Summer Programme in the park for all were open to the children of the community. Miss Isabel Cleland (now Mrs. Isabel Rowe), the Director of the Nursery School, reported that half the mothers had joined the Young Mothers' Club and that many of the children attended the Sunday School. The Junior Congregation was organized as a Sunday School in 1952, following the same programme as the Afternoon School. Each had its own Superintendent and staff of teachers. Dr. McIntosh provided a Leadership Training Class for volunteer church workers in addition to the regular staff meetings for Sunday School teachers. Under the guidance of Miss Brown, the first Labour Day Weekend was held at Whitby Ladies College when forty church members spent two days of study, worship, fellowship and planning for the coming school year. The Camp was such a rewarding experience that it was an annual event as long as Miss Brown was the Deaconess.

The Afternoon Woman's Missionary Society and the Afternoon Woman's Association decided to hold joint luncheon meetings on the first Wednesday of each month in 1952, anticipating by ten years the formation of the United Church Women. The Guild continued to raise money for the church and other worthy causes. Mrs. Jickells, the Church Hostess, reported that 4,580 meals had been served in 1952 for church affairs and to outside groups such as the Christian Business Men, the Canadian Israel

Association, Public Health Nurses and to the Christian Business Girls which met monthly. The meals were provided, not for profit, but as a service to people working in the downtown area.

In July 1952, John Sidgwick, F.R.C.O., succeeded Dr. Drummond Wolff who had taken up duties as organist of Christ Church Cathedral in Montreal. According to the *Annual Report*, Mr. Sidgwick 'quickly endeared himself (as did his wife) not only to the choir but to the congregation and its various groups'. The choir, numbering thirty-three members, was divided to occupy both sides of the chancel. He organized a Junior Choir. (Muriel Cairns was a member who graduated into the Senior Choir and became the Choir Librarian, a post she still retains). A programme of cleaning and overhauling the organ was commenced for no major renovations had taken place since it was installed in 1930.

Mr. and Mrs. Lloyd Wood approached Mr. Brisbin in 1951 about the possibility of placing a brass Cross and matching vases on the Communion Table in memory of their parents. Realizing that some members might not consider it an appropriate gift, Mr. Brisbin brought the matter to the Session. The elders deliberated at length and proposed that the Official Board be asked to make the decision. The Board decided to take the proposal to the next congregational meeting, where it was accepted gratefully. Mr. Brisbin dedicated the gift on 2 November 1952 and preached a sermon on the history of the Cross as a symbol in the Church.

The Metropolitan had 1,099 members in 1952 with about 800 adherents under pastoral care. Mr. Brisbin felt that one of his chief responsibilities was to encourage the people to believe that they could maintain the church and the programmes without the dynamic influence of Dr. Bryce and without the financial support of his wealthy friends. He encouraged lay leadership and suggested the theme for a financial campaign, 'One Great Hour of Sharing', recommending that church contributions should, at least, be equivalent to the amount earned for one hour's work a week. Many people realized that their meagre givings were sorely out of proportion to their incomes. Though the funds of the church were considerably strengthened, they remained insufficient to carry on the social service programmes that were in place. In April 1953, the Official Board launched the Peter Bryce Memorial Foundation, under the patronage of the Reverend Ray McCleary, C.L. Burton, C.L. Gundy, and Thayer Lindsley. The Campaign Committee, chaired by W.G. Watson and H.R. Jackman, included Lloyd Wood, Donald Tow, E.J. Howson, J.B. Allen, Dr. John

McIntosh, Austin Thompson, Dr. Douglas Bryce, John Bryce and Helen
Allen, Ruth Carruthers and Victoria Hanna. At the end of the year, the
Fund had received more than $65,000. Ten years later it reached $140,000
and was able to provide more than $5,000 a year for social service pro-
grammes. The large Peter Bryce memorial window, showing the conversion of Paul on the road to Damascus, was erected in the gallery.

❂

Changes came in the mid-fifties to the Metropolitan, the City, and to Society as it had been known. J. Bascom St. John described the changing times
in the booklet, *The "Fifty Years" at Metropolitan*, which he and Mrs.
Jackman compiled in 1975:

> And yet, if one had looked, there was a small cloud "no bigger than a man's
> hand", rising over the horizon, in the person of a civic candidate for public
> office in Toronto, whose main plank was the promotion of Sunday sport. He
> did not get in on his first try, but he made it a year later. A loophole in the
> Lord's Day legislation had been found, and with the co-operation of the
> Provincial Government, Sunday sport became a reality which has grown
> continuously over the whole quarter century.
>
> Following on its heels were Sunday movies and all kinds of other forms
> of secular amusement, capping the climax in the arrival of television, giving
> the public still further reason to stay at home on any or all nights of the
> week. And as if these problems were not enough, the rise of the weekend
> rush to the country, in defiance of traffic and convenience, made the viabil-
> ity of the downtown churches enormously more difficult to maintain.
>
> Still another factor was the establishment of the Metropolitan Toronto
> form of government, which made possible the tremendous growth of the
> suburbs, and incidentally encouraged the dispersal of the main family sup-
> port on which the 'inner city' church relies for maintenance. The old hous-
> ing in the core area was at the same time demolished for redevelopment.
> The one important compensation for these conditions was the building of
> the subway, which provided relatively cheap and rapid transportation to the
> downtown area for those who wished to come.

The Reverend P.J. McCready and Mrs. McCready came from Montreal
in September 1954 to take the place of Mr. and Mrs. Edgar Cowan who
had gone to Hanover, Ontario, in June. That year the 8:15 meeting became
known as the 'Acquaintance Hour' with programmes organized by Mr.
George McLeish. To assist Miss Jarvis, a Welfare Advisory Committee

met once a month under the chairmanship of Morris Yates. On Good Friday, John Sidgwick conducted the Choir in their presentation of the *St. Matthew Passion*, with the Junior Choir led by the Assistant Organist, Suzanne Welsh.

More changes came in 1955 when Miss Ruby Brown, held in affectionate esteem by everyone connected with Metropolitan, resigned after seventeen years of creative, fruitful service to become Deaconess at St. James-Bond United Church, a less demanding post. Miss Margery Stelck proved to be a worthy successor, carrying on the projects initiated by Miss Brown and promoting new activities. That summer, the children's programme became known as the Summer Fun Club. The Deaconess Committee ceased to function at the end of the year.

Dr. John McIntosh, who had been Chairman of the Christian Education Council since its inception in 1939, resigned from this post and as a Leader of the IHS Bible Class which disbanded at the end of the year. He was succeeded by Lloyd Perry who also maintained his position of Chairman of the Metropolitan Boys' Work Board. That year the original Mothers' Club became the Fidelis group of the Woman's Association. The Younger Mothers' Club then became the Mothers' Club. The number of Sunday Communion services held in the Chapel at ten o'clock was increased from five to ten during the year.

The community surrounding the church was changing drastically day by day. The old rooming houses were torn down to make way for commercial enterprises. The Session authorized a committee, chaired by Mr. McCready, to survey the area bounded by Yonge and Jarvis Streets, Gerrard and Queen Streets during the first week of October 1955. The next year, the Official Board established the Evaluation Committee with Austin Thompson as the Chairman, to make a detailed study of the congregational structure of the church. They developed a questionnaire, solicited briefs from all elements of the congregation, and conducted detailed conversations with most of the groups. The Report published in 1957 had numerous recommendations but few fundamental changes. The intention was 'to encourage efficiency, conserve human energy and to maintain the essential religious functions of the church'. The Church House Board and the Property Committee amalgamated at this time.

The *Annual Report* of 1956 reflected the changing times for the number under pastoral care was reduced by about six hundred people. About one hundred inactive families had been removed from the list. Two hundred young people had moved out of the area. Miss Vivian Jarvis resigned at the end of the year after nine years of dedicated service. Miss Hazelle McManus succeeded her as 'Welfare Worker'. The President of the Afternoon W.A. and W.M.S., Mrs. H.R. Jackman, announced that the group had adopted the name, The Women's Federation. The President of the Evening W.A., Mrs. Margaret Yates, reported the publication of the second edition of their popular cookbook. The Allegro group disbanded early in 1957.

The trip that Mr. and Mrs. Brisbin took around the world in 1958 brought vicarious pleasure to everyone. He was sent as a delegate of the United Church to the World Conference on Christian Education, formerly known as the World Sunday School Convention. Mr. Jackman, when he realized that the meetings were being held in Japan, suggested that they go around the world. The generous Thayer Lindsley made it possible. The congregation rejoiced that this honour and opportunity had come to their popular young minister and his wife who had both served the church with selfless dedication. Mr. Brisbin (his degree of Doctor of Divinity was not conferred until 1969) accepted a call to St. Giles United Church in Hamilton in June 1959, after eleven arduous years at the Metropolitan. In his last 'Word from your Minister' in the *Annual Report* of 1958 which recorded an income exceeding $100,000, he wrote:

> Spread the news of the vitality of your church wherever you go. Tell your friends that we are not merely content to hold our own but are determined to grow in number, in service, and most of all in obedience to the great Commission of Christ to take the Gospel to every creature.

❂

Mr. McCready remained as minister for the following year, supported by Miss Stelck and Miss Hazelle McManus who tendered her resignation to take effect in September 1960. The Evening Woman's Association voted to become part of the Women's Federation on 1 January 1960, to be known as the Evening Federation. That year they invited Mr. McCready, an expert in the field, to speak on Canadian Art. The Young People's Fireside, later known as the Young Adults' Group, continued to meet in the Morley Punshon Room after the evening services. The President, in her report added, 'Mr. McCready has been our counsellor and we are grateful to him for his leadership and fatherly care.' The eighty members of the 'Roses in December' seniors group received membership cards, useful for identification and as tangible evidence of belonging to the Metropolitan Family. The half-hour chapel services conducted by Miss Esther Moffatt prompted one man to remark: 'This Club is different from the others, it emphasizes the spiritual part of the meeting.'

The Metropolitan Silver Band, after celebrating its twenty-fifth anniversary in 1959, made an arrangement to play at only one evening service and one P.S.A. meeting a month. In July 1960, John Sidgwick, the highly respected organist and choir leader, resigned after eight successful years. The Junior Choir disbanded but was reorganized in September as the Junior and Intermediate Choir.

Meanwhile, the Pastoral Relations Committee, chaired by Dr. John McIntosh, was seeking 'the best Christian personality the United Church can provide. His pulpit should speak with authority and eloquence for Christ and His Kingdom and interpret the Christian verities in terms of twentieth century living.' The Reverend Dr. George W. Birtch, possessing these attributes, was called to the Metropolitan from Melrose United Church in Hamilton. Dr. McIntosh, in a letter to the Visiting Elders, wrote that Dr. Birtch 'was regarded for his scholarship, his warmth of human understanding and his ability to preach'. He had spent six years as a missionary in China, returning to Canada in 1945. The Induction service took place on 8 September 1960.

At the morning service on 6 November, Dr. Birtch dedicated twelve new bells presented by Mr. Charles W. Drury as a gift from his late wife and himself. J. Leland Richardson, the former carillonneur, played the dedicatory recital. The bells had been cast by the 300-year-old Dutch firm of Petit and Fritsen. Formidable difficulties were overcome by Gerald Fritsen who came from Holland to install the bells with the help of a Canadian assistant. James Slater has recorded:

> The new equipment could not be admitted through the slit window immediately below the bell chamber because of the narrowness of the openings. The only alternative was to carry all the material up the narrow spiral staircase (ninety steps) and then up a ladder to the mezzanine that holds the keyboard. From there, the beams and bells were raised through a small trapdoor into the bell chamber and on up to their proposed position above the original bells.
>
> The actual installation took eight days. During much of the time, the weather was bitterly cold, with high winds blowing snow in through the tower.

The bells weighed from fifty to one hundred and fifty-five pounds. The old wooden keyboard was taken to the vestibule where it is still on view.

The Christmas White Gift service was televised on CBLT. Shortly afterwards, the radio station CFRB made arrangements to broadcast six services on six Sunday evenings during Lent. The response was so encouraging that a Radio Committee made arrangements for the morning services to be carried over station CJRH (Richmond Hill), commencing in September. A 'Friends of the Metropolitan' was organized in April 1961 to keep in touch with the radio congregation. A *News Letter*, Vol. I. No. I, dated June 1961, was prepared for their benefit and to keep the membership informed. This effort soon gave way to Dr. Birtch's more modest *Pastoral Newsletter*. His exceptional preaching brought larger congregations. When the radio ministry continued on CFGM, it was estimated that 8,500 families were being reached every week.

Noon-day Lenten services, conducted by the well-known evangelist, Stanley Jones, and the Reverend John Wilkie, proved to be so successful that the Session decided to continue them on a year-round basis. The Women's Federation undertook to serve lunches every Wednesday. Rowland Pack, the noted cellist who had been appointed as the interim organist, conducted the choir in *Messiah* at Eastertime and in June arranged a Festival of Music with the Senior, Junior and Intermediate choirs and with the choirs of several other churches as well as the Rowland Pack Chamber Singers. A member of the choir was heard to say: 'We have never enjoyed singing so much.'

The new organist, Paul Murray, arrived from St. John, New Brunswick, at the end of August, in time for the first radio broadcast and the induction of the Reverend James M. Finlay as the Pastoral Assistant. Mr. Murray, who had earned a Bachelor of Music degree at the University of Toronto, had studied under Dr. Drummond Wolff, becoming a Fellow of the Royal College of Organists in 1954. His qualifications were in order since the Official Board, through the efforts of the church solicitor, John B. Allen, was able to have the stipulations of the 1915 bequest of the late Mrs. Lillian Massey Treble changed to include, as well, graduates of Canadian Universities granting degrees in music and Fellows of the Royal Canadian College of Organists. The 'Metropolitan United Church of Toronto Act, 1961-62' received Royal Assent early in 1962.

A fire in the Church House caused considerable damage to the chapel and to Mr. and Mrs. McCready's apartment. The chapel was restored in

1961, a memorial window, the gift of the Barclay family, was installed and the Misses Hanna presented an electric organ in memory of their parents. Communion services took place there at ten o'clock on the first Sunday of every month.

On 1 January 1962, the United Church Women (U.C.W.) was inaugurated with Mrs. Ruby Allen as the first President. The Women's Council, which had been active for twenty years, ceased to exist. The new organization boasted a membership of one hundred and fifty women in six groups: the Mission and Study Unit (formerly the Evening Auxiliary of the W.M.S.), the Morning Sewing Group, the Noon Hour Unit, the Fidelis Unit, the Fourth Monday Evening Unit and the Mothers' Club. The Guild members elected to retain their independence.

Staff changes occurred in 1962. Miss Margery Stelck, the Deaconess 'beloved by many' left the Metropolitan for study abroad. She was succeeded by Miss Vera Moore who came from Newfoundland to become the 'Community and Family Life Worker'. She, too, soon won the hearts of the congregation. Mr. James Slater was appointed the Carillonneur. He had studied since 1954 under Stanley James who had played the carillon twice on Sundays for twenty-one years. Their roles were reversed and Stanley James became the assistant carillonneur.

Mrs. Jickells became Mrs. Temple and retired from her position as Church Hostess. She was a person of many talents. As well as supervising the kitchen, she played the carillon before the Wednesday noon-hour services and the chapel organ for the 'Roses' weekly worship services and the monthly communion services. She taught a Ladies' Bible Class and arranged the chancel flowers for the Sunday services. Miss Constance Mortson succeeded her. The kitchen responsibilities were taken over by a new Kitchen Committee chaired by Mrs. Gilbert Storey and organized as a sub-committee of the joint Church House Board and Property Committee. Mr. Herbert Matheson, the Building Superintendent for more than thirty years, died in office. Always kind and obliging, he was known as 'Mr. Metropolitan' to generations of children. He was succeeded by his assistant, George Angove, who served until his death in 1965.

The Metropolitan Church entered into an agreement with the Parks Department to take over the care and upkeep of the grounds in 1962. Ownership was retained by the church. The fence surrounding the property was taken down. The parking lot was relocated, paved and fenced at the City's expense. That year the interior of the Sanctuary was cleaned and painted. The entire cost was borne by the contributions to the Restoration Fund, fully subscribed by the membership and the radio congregation. Improved illumination of the chancel window was made possible by a gift for that purpose.

Mr. Lloyd Perry, the Chairman of the Christian Education Council, reported in 1961 that the morning School had one hundred and forty-five scholars and a staff of twenty; the afternoon School had an enrollment of one hundred and twenty-five with fourteen teachers and officers. The next year, the Metropolitan Sunday Schools were chosen to test the first draft of the new United Church Curriculum for Christian Education. To assist with the programme, Miss Ada McKenzie was appointed as Christian Education Adviser on a part-time basis. It was observed that some children were attending both schools. At the Session meeting of 16 January 1963, Dr. McIntosh's motion that the afternoon Sunday School should be amalgamated with the morning School was approved.

The Metropolitan Optimist Boys' Club, sponsored jointly by the Metropolitan Church and the Optimist Club of Toronto, was officially opened on 30 November 1962. All the boys' work of the church came under the supervision of the Club staffed by two full-time leaders and several volunteers. The Metropolitan supplied nine Board members including Ben Geisbrecht whose Metro Boys' Club, after five successful years, was merged with the Optimist Club, open on five afternoons and four evenings a week and on Saturday mornings.

After twenty-seven years during which the Band had played seven hundred concerts, the P.S.A. meetings were discontinued, for all kinds of entertainment were now available on Sunday afternoons. The Band decided to play at two Sunday evening services a month and at the Acquaintance Hour after the second service. The Metropolitan Clothing Cupboard was closed when the United Church opened the Downtown Clothing Centre, a more efficient service. The first Coffee Hour took place in the Morley Punshon Room after the morning service on 15 October 1962 with the U.C.W. in charge. The next year a group of girls, who became known as the Punshon Girls, took over the duties of making and serving coffee.

❂

Three special Missions were conducted during Dr. Birtch's pastorate. Planning Committees, working months in advance, sent out invitations to the other United Churches in the city. Dr. Howard Thurman, the Professor of Spiritual Resources and Disciplines at the Boston University School of Theology was the Anniversary preacher in November 1961. Noon-hour services were held from Monday to Friday and evening services from Monday to Thursday during the following week. The Mission was so well attended and appreciated that a similar event was planned for 1962, when the Reverend Dr. George McLeod of Glasgow, a former Moderator of the Church of Scotland and founder of the Iona Community, preached at the Sunday and week-day services. His dynamic and inspiring messages deepened and strengthened the faith of the large numbers who heard him. A third successful Mission took place in February 1964 when Dr. Elton Trueblood came from Richmond, Virginia, to carry out similar services during Lent.

The Christmas Eve service was televised from coast to coast and a service was included in the C.B.C. Church of the Air series. The choir united with the choir of St. George's United Church for a performance of Vivaldi's *Gloria*, accompanied by musicians from the Toronto Symphony Orchestra. On Passion Sunday, the Metropolitan Choir gave its first performance of Brahms' *Requiem*. The Junior and Intermediate Choir had a waiting list of children seeking membership. Games followed the practices that the conductor, Mr. Paul Murray, filled with fun. He gratefully acknowledged the efforts of Mr. and Mrs. Carl Shard 'who gave of their time almost ceaselessly week after week.' Their gallant son, Jimmy, who suffered from muscular dystrophy, was the choir's treasurer for eight years.

Despite the efforts of Ron Bolt and other faithful young people, the Young Adults group eventually disbanded. In the autumn of 1963, 'Talk Back' was inaugurated and younger people met with Dr. Birch after the evening service. He also initiated 'The Companions in Discipline' that met monthly in the homes of the members for study, worship and discussion led by the theological student, Robert Ross, who was an elder of the church.

A Prayer Fellowship came into existence in November 1963 when Miss Moore sent a letter to twelve members of the congregation who had expressed willingness to engage in daily prayer for the people in distress who had requested special prayers. In June a meeting was called and twenty-four people agreed to meet in the chapel on three Sunday mornings of the month from ten to ten-thirty to pray 'one for another'. By the end of

December monthly letters were sent to forty people. The Fellowship continued to meet as long as Miss Moore was at the Metropolitan.

Changes in staff occurred again in June. Dr. Finlay and Miss Ada McKenzie left in June 1964. Miss Beatrice Maclean came as the Director of Christian Education in September. She began planning for a Mission Festival in 1965 and she introduced the first Family Christmas Workshop which became an annual event. David Nelson, a member of WoodGreen Church, became the Executive Director of the Metropolitan Optimist Boys' Club for both boys and girls, now open five afternoons and evenings a week. He and his assistant supervised the twenty-four 'valuable volunteers' and planned educational and recreational programmes to encourage boys and girls 'to grow into useful and responsible citizens regardless of race, creed or condition'. The Atkinson Charitable Foundation provided a generous grant which was used for equipment, sports, and crafts.

Although most of the activities for the young were taken over by the Optimist Boys' Club, the Metropolitan Community Centre continued to provide leaders for the Summer Fun Club, the Explorers, the C.G.I.T. and Teens Club and to give financial support for the Junior Band which had a membership of forty boys. The Play Hour for little girls only was closed in 1965.

The Session held a stimulating all-day Conference on Policy Direction at the Guild Inn in October 1964. The next month, a successful week-end of four seminars took place at Victoria College under the auspices of the Metropolitan, planned by the Committee on Mission, chaired by Don Weir, including Mrs. Helen Bray, secretary, R. McKinlay, treasurer, J.C. Carson, Ben Geisbrecht, Lloyd Perry, Fred Stinson and Dr. John McIntosh. The registration fee of $8.00 per person, or $15.00 for a married couple included a study booklet and lunch at the Park Plaza Hotel on Saturday. Notices were sent city-wide but registration was limited to two hundred and fifty people. Arnold Edinborough, the Editor of *Saturday Night*, was the Moderator. He introduced the panels and the four seminars: 'The Christian in the Market Place' on Friday evening, 'The Christian in Politics' on Saturday morning, 'The Christian and the Arts' on Saturday afternoon, and 'The Christian and his Social Set' on Sunday afternoon. Four clergymen, the Reverends George Morrison, Clarke MacDonald, Gene Young and Stewart Crysdale were 'Research Editors'. Group discussions followed each panel presentation.

The Session discussed ways and means of reaching the tenants in the new Moss Park Housing Project through ecumenical endeavours which failed to take place. Instead, letters of welcome and a brochure were sent to the newcomers to the area. Dr. Birtch was invited to take part in the civic dedication ceremonies.

The Toronto Institute of Family Relations, sponsored jointly by the congregations of the Metropolitan, Rosedale, St. Andrew's, and Saint Luke's Churches, with financial assistance from the National Marriage Guidance Council and the Board of Evangelism and Social Services, was located at the Metropolitan in October 1964 and officially inaugurated in March 1965 with the Reverend Kenneth R. Allen as Director. Two years later, after amalgamation with the Pastoral Counselling Service, the name was changed to the Toronto Institute of Human Relations. It continues to the present day to be part of the Metropolitan Family.

The Welfare Advisory Committee which Mrs. Kay Stockwell had chaired for more than ten years was disbanded in 1965. Two new committees were formed: the Committee for Community Service and Christian Action, and the Family Life Committee. With the approval of the Home Missions Council of the United Church and the staff of St. Michael's Hospital, Miss Constance Mortson, the Church Hostess, took on, instead, the duties of Official Church Visitor on 1 May, visiting all the United Church patients in the Hospital.

The bequest of the late Mrs. C.B. Sharpe made it possible for the Property Committee to have the two new tiled washrooms installed in the narthex. The Youth Worship Centre was completely renovated, the tryptych was stored and the room was dedicated as the Chancel Room on 12 September 1965. On the next Sunday, the Coffee Hour was transferred there from the Morley Punshon Room. Mr. Arnold Edinborough was the Anniversary preacher on Sunday 21 November. By the next Sunday, Dr. Birtch's ministry at the Metropolitan had come to an abrupt end. Mr. W.A. Haddow, the Clerk of Session, wrote in his annual report:

> We are grateful for the blessings both personal and congregational which his five years with us brought. He did much to deepen and vivify our congregational life. His pastorate at the Metropolitan will be remembered as a very distinguished one.

Mr. McCready, with unselfish consideration, carried on the ministerial duties, ably assisted by Vera Moore and Beatrice Maclean. At the beginning of the New Year, the Acquaintance Hour was discontinued and the Committee was discharged by the Session. The Pastoral Relations Committee, chaired by Mr. Austin Thompson, began their search for a new minister. In April 1966, at the request of the Session, the Personnel Committee made plans to revise the church records and to develop a new card system to reflect the needs, interests, and capabilities of members and adherents. This effort was named Personnel Resource Information Service at Metropolitan and became known as PRISM. During the first two weeks of May, seventy-seven people visited the rest of the congregation, filling in a questionnaire designed to discover the experiences and potential of the membership. At the end of the year, seventy names were tentatively withdrawn from the roll, leaving six hundred and seventy-four.

In August, Mr. McCready retired from the ministry to pursue a career as an authority on Canadian Art. For twelve years, with the staunch support of Mrs. McCready, he had exerted an influence for good, especially among the young people of the community. They are remembered with gratitude.

The Metropolitan Church choir, 1960, with John Sidgwick, the organist and choirmaster, in centre.

CHAPTER 13

The Metropolitan United Church

1966 - 1975

Two new ministers arrived in September 1966: the Reverend Dr. Clifford A.S. Elliott (soon to be known by many as 'Cliff') and the Reverend Keith Whitney. They were both inducted at a service on 7 September 1966. Dr. Elliott, who was born and educated in Saskatchewan, was ordained in 1942. Two years later he enrolled at Union Theological Seminary in New York City, receiving a master's degree in 1945 and a doctorate from Columbia University in 1950. His wife, Patricia, was an accomplished pianist. Cliff, a bass soloist, took vocal lessons while studying in New York. They served at pastorates in North Battleford, Saskatchewan, St. Giles in Hamilton, and in Robertson United Church in Edmonton before coming to the Metropolitan. Keith Whitney was called as the Associate Minister to be chiefly responsible for Outreach. He had been engaged in industry before returning to university. He was ordained in 1963 and came to the Metropolitan from his first charge in Bideford, Prince Edward Island. To equip themselves for our special ministry, Mr. Whitney took a six-week course at the newly formed Canadian Urban Training Programme, and Dr. Elliott spent two weeks visiting downtown churches in large American centres observing new developments.

At the Metropolitan he soon became involved in Session reform. Through the years many subcommittees had been formed to carry out its responsibilities. Dr. Elliott added a new one: the Reconstruction of Session Committee. In 1967, all standing committees were dissolved and the Session, made up of sixty men and women, was divided into four new committees 'to embrace the functions and responsibilities of eldership':

Congregational Life and Work (chaired by Ruth Tillman)

Outreach (chaired by Dr. John McIntosh)

Membership and Worship (chaired by George McLeish)

Membership Role and Visitation (chaired by Isabel Uren)

Soon the Session was meeting bi-monthly, the committees once a month.

The Metropolitan carillon rang out at midnight to welcome 1967, Canada's Centennial Year. Mrs. Jackman opened her home for a Centennial Tea and the U.C.W. provided money for Muriel Cairns to take six C.G.I.T. girls to Expo '67 in Montreal. The United Church Women by 1967 was composed of only two units. The highlight of the year was an ecumenical meeting during Holy Week when women from other churches in the area were invited to hear the Reverend Sister Charbanal, who was in charge of Religious Education for Roman Catholic Youth, speak on the 'Generation Gap'. She drew an unexpectedly large audience of about two hundred and fifty women representing thirteen churches in six denominations. Refreshments followed tours of the Sanctuary.

In September 1967, Dr. Melville Cook succeeded the popular Paul Murray who returned to the Maritimes. For more than thirty years Dr. Cook had served as organist and choir leader at Leeds Parish Church and at Hereford Cathedral in England. He began a long and successful association of nineteen years at the Metropolitan. He soon initiated midweek organ recitals and monthly 'Musical Hours', renamed the Chancel Concerts. Mrs. Cook took over the Junior and Intermediate Choirs for a few months.

Plans to celebrate the 150th Anniversary began in January 1967 when Austin Thompson was appointed Coordinator of Centennial Projects and Chairman of the Anniversary Committee which included Mrs. Harvey Good, the President of the U.C.W., Mrs. Gilbert Storey, Chairman of the Kitchen Committee, Miss Margaret Martin, John Bryce, and Dr. Cook. Before the festivities began, Miss Vera Moore resigned after six years of faithful service as the Social Worker. Mr. George Bruce was welcomed in September as the Ministers' Assistant. He had had a rich and varied experience as a missionary teacher in Korea, as the Director of the Correspondence Branch of Alberta's Department of Education and as the Director of the United Church Program for Certified Employed Churchmen. Mr. Bruce found many ways of serving the Metropolitan by visiting the elderly, sick, and shut-in members and by looking after the Membership Roll and the books of the visiting elders. Mrs. Bruce became identified with the U.C.W. and soon they were beloved and respected by a grateful congregation. Mr. Harold Young, who had joined the church from Edmonton in May, was appointed Clerk of Session in September. Many new members accepted responsibility as elders, stewards and Sunday School teachers.

The sesquicentennial celebrations which took place from September 1968 to April 1969 began with a series of five organ recitals. On Reunion Sunday in October, ninety-three former members of Dr. McIntosh's IHS Class and the Couples Club enjoyed a buffet supper at the Church House with Miss Ruby Brown as guest speaker. The United Church Women assumed responsibility for the Egerton Ryerson Retrospective Exhibition, mounted in the Morley Punshon Room with the assistance of Ron Bolt. At the opening on 30 October, the members of the U.C.W., in period costumes, acted as guides and served coffee and birthday cake. Guest preachers were invited for three Sunday services in November. Dr. Elliott preached at the service attended by the Governor-General, Roland Michener, and Mrs. Michener. Dr. Cook's Festival Choir, including the choirs of Bloor Street and Eastminster United Churches, performed on two Sunday evenings, *Two Psalms* by Holst with Benjamin Britton's *Saint Nicolas*, and Handel's *Messiah* with the choir of Bishop Strachan School. The Metropolitan Choir gave a programme of music by Bach. The choirs were accompanied by the Metropolitan Festival Orchestra.

In March 1969, the *Digby Play of Mary Magdalena*, produced for the Anniversary by the Centre of Study for Drama of the University of Toronto, was presented by the Centre for Mediæval Studies. Dances by the Toronto Dance Theatre were included with music augmented by the organ, band, and carillon. The final event was an Open House on Sunday afternoon 27 April which was concluded by a five o'clock vesper service.

❂

Despite the Anniversary celebrations, the attendance at church services and the givings continued to decline. In June 1969, Miss Beatrice Maclean, the Deaconess for Christian Education, resigned to continue further studies. The next year two therapy groups from St. Michael's Hospital and two groups from Alcoholics Anonymous began to meet in the Church House. Mr. and Mrs. Morris Yates formed the 'Yakity Yak Club' for hardof-hearing teenagers of which their son, Jim, was a member.

The Junior Choir was reorganized in September 1968 under the direction of Mrs. Louise Pritchard who was hired on a part-time basis to act, as well, as the Superintendent of the Sunday School. Faithful young choir members were awarded the Chorister's Guild Pin provided by the generous women of the Guild. Heather Spry succeeded Mrs. Pritchard in 1971. After three successful seasons, the choir ceased to function in 1974.

The Junior Band was disbanded after twenty-five years in 1970. That year, the Board of the Metropolitan Optimist Boys' Club, renamed the Metropolitan Downtown Boys' Club, decided that the Club should be moved to Regent Park where most of the children lived. In 1969, the Summer Fun Club had carried on as usual with Bryone Lehman as Camp Director, assisted by Cheryl Ko, Evie Gilmour, and George Stinson, although the grant of $2,000 from the City of Toronto was not forthcoming. The Stewards continued to finance the Club in 1970 and again in 1971 under the direction of Evie Gilmour, when eighty-seven children from five to fourteen years of age were enrolled in the daily programmes during July and August. In her enthusiastic report of 1971, Evie recommended that the Metropolitan should continue a year-round programme for these children. However, as other agencies were conducting programmes, the Metropolitan abolished the Summer Fun Club after providing summer activities for children for thirty-two years. The C.G.I.T. and the Explorers also ceased to exist. The Church School of the Fred Victor Mission united with the Metropolitan Church School in September 1971. The next year, with the help of the artist, Ron Bolt, the children designed and painted a mural of the Christmas Story as if it had happened in 1972. The children presented it to the church on Christmas Sunday. Elizabeth St. John, at the request of Ruth Tillman, undertook to send birthday, Easter and Christmas cards to all the baptized children until they were eight years old. This minor ministry has continued to the present day.

The Long-Range Planning Committee of ten people, chaired by Harold Young, had been set up in 1968 to consider the future fate of the Metropolitan. A feasibility study, authorized by the Committee, recommended the sale of the whole property and advised against saving the church. At the Sunday morning service on 25 January 1970, a debate took place between Jean Lee, a member of the Committee, with the Reverend Glynn Firth, associated with CUT (Canadian Urban Training Centre), and Professor Ted Mann, with Susan Rees, co-chairmen of RAN (Responsible Action Now) who argued that the property should be sold. The newspapers gave the debate full coverage. Dr. Elliott was quoted as saying that he thought that most of the people who attended the service 'were "open" to

RAN's ideas . . . but there are a few quite hostile'. Mrs. Gilbert Storey, a member of the Committee, thought the 'RAN people quite sensible'. Seven congregational meetings followed the service. In November, five 'Options' were presented. Four involved the sale or development of the property. The fifth option, 'to try to continue and expand our present kind of work' was approved by an overwhelming majority of members who were determined that the church and her ministry should be maintained. At the last meeting of the series, in December, the congregation decided to retain the present property for two years, making money available from capital funds for the implementation of new programmes. It was agreed that Dr. Elliott should continue his one-minute radio spots that had replaced the broadcasts of Sunday morning worship services, that experimentation should continue, and that alternate uses of the property should be studied.

By 1970, the United Church Women had only one Unit which met at noon on the first Wednesday of the month. Mrs. Nellie Bruce was the President of this group of about fifty women who generously supported the work of the Church through free-will offerings. Molly Bryce was elected as Treasurer and continued in office for seventeen years.

Keith Whitney left to take up new duties as Superintendent of the Fred Victor Mission at the end of December. In January 1971, the Reverend Noble Hatton, who had retired from his position with the Canadian Council of Christians and Jews, became once again the Assistant Minister. Mr. and Mrs. Hatton had been worshipping at the Metropolitan since 1963. The Brisbin family had returned to the church in 1968 when Dr. Brisbin assumed the post of Secretary of the Division of Communication for the United Church. Mr. Bruce relinquished his position of Ministers' Assistant but continued to serve as a dedicated member until his death in 1986. The Reverend George Morrison and his wife, Bindy, were also active members at this time.

Innovative forms of worship were introduced from the beginning of Dr. Elliott's ministry. He encouraged active participation by the congregation: providing petitions for corporate prayer; baking Communion bread; making audible responses in the liturgy. The laity began to take part in the services. The first Lay Sunday service took place on 20 October 1968. Dance interpretations by the Toronto Dance Theatre were introduced in 1969. Occasional 'Coffee-House-Worship', at eight o'clock in the Chancel Room, began to be substituted in 1970 for the regular seven o'clock worship services which terminated in 1972.

Six experimental morning services were prepared in 1971 by the newly formed Committee, named by Mrs. Marjorie Wood, CREDO (I believe) with the letters standing for Celebration, Renewal, Experimentation, Dialogue or Drama, Others. It had begun in 1968 as the Arts Committee, a sub-committee of the Worship Committee. Soon CREDO, chaired by Mrs. Beth Robinson, had its own sub-committee, Contemporary Services Committee, chaired by Mrs. Eleanor Skelton. In his 'Message' to the congregation, written at the end of 1971, Dr. Elliott wrote:

> In trying to find new ways of worshipping, we are bound to have differences of opinion in the congregation. Some of these differences became painfully apparent during the past year. We must find ways to express our differences in constructive ways.

Lenten services were withdrawn in 1971 in favour of the ecumenical services taking place in the Toronto-Dominion Centre. At the Anniversary in November, the new red *Hymn Book of the Anglican Church of Canada and the United Church of Canada* was introduced, replacing the *Hymnary*. During 1971, eight meetings were held with officials of Saint Luke's United Church to consider and finally reject the idea of merging the two congregations.

Through the generosity of the Massey Foundation (the last gift with a Massey connection) nineteen bells were added to the Carillon, making a total of fifty-four bells. Ranging in weight from twelve to fifty-seven pounds, they were cast in France by the firm of Georges Passard et Fils. A new console was designed by Richard M. Watson of Ohio. The bells were dedicated on 28 March 1971, soon after their arrival and before their installation which was not completed until October. The official dedicatory recital by Richard M. Watson took place on 18 June 1972 to celebrate the fiftieth anniversary of Chester Massey's original gift. It served, as well, as the opening recital for the Congress of the Guild of Carillonneurs in North America. At the morning service, a plaque was unveiled by Mrs. Stanley James, assisted by Percival Price, to mark the event, to serve as a memorial to the late Stanley James who had died in September 1971, and to recognize the half-century career of Percival Price, the Metropolitan's first carillonneur.

The Session was dissolved in 1972. The elders were dismissed and a new Official Board was constituted, made up of the Committee of Stewards; the Worship, Congregational Life and Work, Outreach and Membership Committees; the Music Committee, and representatives of the United Church Women. The Committee chairmen became the Executive Committee, meeting monthly.

The Outreach Committee cooperated with the Fred Victor Mission and St. Bartholomew Anglican Church in opening, in January 1972, the Non-Profit Temporary Work Centre '4U' on Dundas Street East to provide work for the unemployed. It was financed, in part, by a government LIP grant (Local Initiatives Project). The next year the Metropolitan, with the Fred Victor Mission, opened a Drop-In Centre for transient men who had to leave the hostels at an early hour. It was housed in the Church House gymnasium, open from 7:00 a.m. until noon, six days a week and later, for seven. The grant of $10,000 made it possible to pay the church a rent of $150 a month. This venture continued until it was moved in 1978 to the Friendship Centre at All Saints Church. Early in 1973, the Canadian Urban Training Centre moved its offices to the Metropolitan.

The CREDO Committee mounted a modest but 'very successful Festival of Creation' in May 1972, named 'dayspring' by Marjorie Wood whose husband, Roy, still sings in the choir. 'dayspring '73' was an enlarged 'festival of the arts to open the senses to a new awareness'. The Annual Report of Mrs. Eleanor Sanderson, the Convenor, reads in part:

> . . .You will remember that our festivals were to be festive in a truly spiritual sense and because people's spiritual needs are many-faceted and urgent, we believed that we must use the rich language of many arts as media; that we must speak of contemporary needs with contemporary voices; that we should use only the best of these. . . . As you will recall, we opened the festival on a high note of joyousness with Cathedral Brass—a band and organ concert—and climaxed the six-day event with Nick Kaethler and four choirs and orchestras in R. Murray Schafer's 'In Search of Zoroaster', an intense experience of joy and pain, light and dark. . . . The unique report of dayspring '72, in kit form, was sent by Mission in Canada of the United Church across the entire country and to our festival came fourteen delegates from six provinces.

Mary Sanderson, the administrative co-ordinator, was responsible for publicity, hospitality, property and finance. Grants from the United Church of Canada and the Ontario Arts Council, the Metropolitan Church and special donations paid the cost of 'dayspring '73' which amounted to $11,607.77. Dr. and Mrs. Elliott, with their creative talents and expertise, provided supportive advice which was essential to these undertakings.

An abbreviated 'dayspring' took place in 1974. Brad Cumings reported for the Committee:

> For the first time we commissioned an original work: 'The Experiences of Eden' by Jane Beecroft. This forceful long poem was translated into an event of dance, song and music, presented on Friday and Saturday nights, May 11 and 12, 1974. Also, and equally important, we opened on Saturday the rooms of the church and the Church House for a variety of experiences including an organic cooking session, a quilt making . . . a stained glass window session . . . and an attempt at sensory perception.

Out of this celebration came the appointment in July 1974 of Bill Bartram, 'trained in arts, education and theology', for a pilot project in Religion and the Arts, co-sponsored by the Division of Mission of the United Church of Canada which provided half his salary.

Two weeks after the celebration of 'dayspring '74', Mrs. Marjorie Wood died suddenly. The congregation was deeply saddened for she had been vitally involved in many areas. To celebrate her creative life and spirit, the CREDO Committee conceived the idea of making wall-hangings with the theme, 'the Incarnation as revealed in the life of Jesus and as expressed in many ways in the life of Marjorie Wood.' About forty people volunteered to work on this project under the direction of the artist, Doris McCarthy, who had been Marjorie's close friend. One banner depicts episodes in the life of Christ, the other, the interests of Marjorie Wood with words from the poem by e.e. cummings beginning: 'i thank you God for most this amazing day.' The materials were supplied by a memorial gift of money from the National Committee of Ministry and Personnel of which Marjorie was a member. The banners were dedicated to the Glory of God on 16 March 1975 as a thank-offering for the life of Anne Marjorie Wood, 1903-1974. Measuring twenty-three feet by four feet, they hang on each side of the chancel arch.

❂

The Reverend Noble Hatton retired in June 1974. He was succeeded by the Reverend James Norquay who, with his family, had been attending the Metropolitan while Jim was spending a year of study in Clinical Pastoral Education. Ordained in 1944, he had served for nine years on the mission fields of rural Alberta, and for seven years in suburban Edmonton. After attending the Toronto School of Social Work, he became the minister of Earlscourt United Church in 1962. His warmth and loving-kindness endeared him to the Metropolitan congregation and his effective ministry continued until his sudden death in 1980. Mr. Norquay was inducted and William Bartram was installed on 29 September 1974.

That month, Mrs. Ruth Cathcart, the Chairman of the CREDO Committee, assumed the post of Public Relations Officer, working one day a week on a trial basis. She handled publicity for major events, including 'dayspring '75', she conducted tours and with Joyce Anne Cumings began producing a monthly newsletter. The *Metropolitan Newsletter*, Vol. I, No. I, was published in October 1974. The December issue, under the revised title, *Newsletter, Metropolitan United Church* used the Metropolitan logo designed that month by John Hansplant. The newsletter has appeared regularly in the same format to the present day, edited since 1978 by Joyce Anne Cumings, alone. Eight issues a year supply accurate and readable accounts of church activities and items of interest to the congregation.

The future policy of the church was again debated in 1974 when new schemes for selling or redeveloping the property were discussed. Once again, the congregation voted to remain for another two years. The House Church, meeting weekly in the homes of members, was organized in the Spring of that year. In March, the Band, under the new leader, Alan Moody, celebrated its fortieth anniversary and released a record, 'Memories of Met'. About forty people participated in a week-end seminar conducted by Dr. James Gustafson, Professor of Ethics at the University of Chicago. In addition to the annual performance of the *St. Matthew Passion*, the choir gave the Canadian première of Monteverdi's *Vespers of the Blessed Virgin*. The Congregational Life and Work Committee, chaired by Mrs. Norma Moodie, organized the annual October Fellowship Weekend at Friendly Acres led that year, by 'our beloved minister, Clifford Elliott'. The organization, Canadian Pensioners Concerned, opened an office at the Metropolitan.

'Dayspring '75' took place for three days in May with workshops, a dinner, and a theatrical presentation. The theme was 'Citytree', a coined word which 'indicates a relationship between men, technology and nature in an uneven environment'. The Festival was made possible by personal contributions and grants from the Ontario Arts Council, International

Business Machines, Imperial Oil, the *Toronto Star* and the Metropolitan Toronto Grants Committee. Bill Bartram resigned at the end of June.

The fiftieth anniversary of Church Union was celebrated Sunday 8 June 1975 by the publication of *The "Fifty Years" at Metropolitan*, a booklet of twenty pages written by Mary Jackman and J. Bascom St. John, with the cover design by John Hansplant. A plaque commemorating six historic gatherings from 1873 to 1925 was placed in the vestibule. The U.C.W. mounted a display of photographs and memorabilia in the west transept. The Guild celebrated its sixty-fifth anniversary for it had been organized by Mrs. W.G. Watson in Elm Street Methodist Church in 1910. Dr. Elliott concluded his ministry at the Metropolitan on Sunday 22 June at a special innovative communion service, incorporating dancing and poetry, arranged by the Worship Committee. A tribute in the June *Newsletter* read in part:

> He has been our leader, our teacher, our enabler. He has brought us moments of illumination, beauty, emotion. . . . His approach to his work is deeply serious—but leavened with an irrepressible wit.

Dr. Elliott became the minister of Bloor Street United church.

The Reverend Ernest E. Long assumed the post of Interim Minister in September. For more than twenty years he had been the Secretary of the General Council and his work took him to all parts of the world. During his time at the Metropolitan, he widened the horizons of the congregation. In September, the Kitchen Committee made up of Mrs. Harvey Good, Mrs. Beatrice Maxwell, Miss Ruth Carruthers and Mrs. Storey, the Chairman, realizing that an era had ended, resigned in a body.

To celebrate the 157th anniversary on 2 November 1975, an historical plaque was placed at the Queen Street entrance to the grounds by the Ontario Heritage Foundation, an agency of the Ministry of Culture and Recreation. The year before, the City of Toronto had identified the church as an historic building to be preserved. After the morning service, while the carillon rang out, the people gathered for the service of dedication conducted by Dr. Long. The band led in the hymn 'Rejoice, the Lord is King'. Dr. Donald Hambleton introduced Miss Irene Carrick who was the oldest member. She had been baptized at the Metropolitan by the Reverend LeRoy Hooker and was an active member all of her long life. Her father, John Carrick, had been a leading layman, her grandparents belonged to the Adelaide Street Church and her great-grandparents attended the King Street Chapel after emigrating from Northern Ireland in the late 1820s. The plaque was unveiled by Master Allan Payne, and dedicated by Mr. Norquay, who also pronounced the benediction. The ceremony took place in the presence of representatives of local, provincial, and federal governments, the Ontario Heritage Foundation, the Toronto Historical Board, the Toronto Conference and Presbytery and the archivist of the United Church, the Reverend Dr. C. Glenn Lucas. A luncheon for invited guests took place in the Church House.

During Advent, 1975, the CREDO Committee sponsored, for the first time, carol singing in the narthex while the people gathered for morning worship. Mrs. Margaret Norquay conducted the singers and the talented members who had brought their instruments to form a small orchestra. This custom has continued to the present day. As another project of the CREDO Committee, Ron Bolt interviewed members of 'Roses in December' about their Christmas memories. He designed a composite picture made up of line-drawings to illustrate their memories, and then invited the 'Roses' to paint the picture, working with them on three occasions. It was presented at the service on Christmas Sunday. The lighting of candles on an Advent Wreath was also introduced that year.

The Advent Ensemble plays for the annual Christmas Party in the Church House.

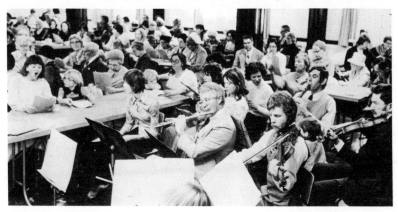

In November 1975 the Ontario Heritage Foundation unveiled a plaque. At the ceremony, from left to right: the Reverend Glenn Lucas, Archivist-Historian of the United Church of Canada; Mrs. E. Vickers, Toronto Historical Board; William Kilbourn, Toronto Alderman; Professor J.M.S. Careless, a Director of the Ontario Heritage Foundation; Mrs. Margaret Campbell, M.P.P.; the Reverend Ernest E. Long; the Reverend A. James Norquay; Master Allan Payne; Dr. Donald Hambleton, chairman of the Official Board of the Metropolitan; and the Honourable Margaret Scrivener, Minister of Government Services.

METROPOLITAN UNITED CHURCH

This "Cathedral of Methodism" was designed by Henry Langley in the High Victorian Gothic style. The cornerstone was laid by the Rev. Egerton Ryerson, D.D., in 1870 and the church was dedicated in 1872. It replaced an earlier structure at the southeast corner of Adelaide and Toronto Streets. The first missionaries from Canada to Japan were commissioned in this church on May 7, 1873. The inaugural service of the Methodist Church of Canada was held here September 16, 1874. The World Ecumenical Methodist Conference meetings in 1911 and the first General Council of the United Church in 1925 met here. The church was badly damaged by fire in 1928 and rebuilt, incorporating most of the original walls, tower, narthex, and much of the stained glass.

Erected by the Ontario Heritage Foundation,
Ministry of Culture and Recreation

Top, Muriel Cairns entertains children at a picnic. Centre, the Reverend Cliff Elliott assists in a tree planting at 'dayspring '72'. Bottom, artist-in-residence Leo Del Pasqua encouraged others to share his love of painting.

The Reverend Dr. Clifford Elliott serving communion to a group who reveal something of the diversity of people for whom the Metropolitan has become 'our church'.

CHAPTER 14
The Metropolitan United Church

1976 - 1984

The Reverend Dr. Douglas C. Lapp was called from the Stoney Creek charge near Hamilton to begin his ministry at the end of March 1976. He had graduated from Victoria University in 1948. For two years before entering Emmanuel College, he served as Boys' Work Secretary for the British Columbia Conference. During his theological training, he was assigned to Cliffcrest, a new United Church in suburban Scarborough. He was ordained in 1953. On graduation from Emmanuel, he was awarded a Travelling Fellowship which took him with his wife, Ethel, and their two young children, to England for a year of post-graduate study at Chestnut College, Cambridge. On his return, he was appointed Boys' Work Secretary for the Ontario Council of Christian Education, an inter-demoninational post. After two years, he became Field Secretary for Christian Education for the Hamilton Conference. He pursued doctoral studies at the University of Ottawa while serving at pastorates in Quebec and Ottawa before going to Stoney Creek United Church in 1970. Dr. Lapp was inducted on 28 March 1976 when the Moderator, the Right Reverend Wilbur Howard, was the preacher. At the reception afterwards, Joe Franklin, the 'ever-cheerful and obliging' Property Superintendent, presented the keys of the church to Dr. Lapp. Mr. Norquay gave him a Toronto street-guide and offered him a 'strong shoulder to lean on'.

The Beavers, formerly members of the Couples' Club, spent fifteen hundred hours refurbishing the manse for Dr. and Mrs. Lapp and their younger daughter, Valerie. They arrived in time to experience the annual performance of the *St. Matthew Passion*, the Maundy Thursday service with Saint Luke's, the joint Good Friday service and the service on Easter

Day when the Silver Band joined with the choir and organ in triumphant praise. Valerie soon asked Dr. Cook for an audition and joined the choir.

The new Kitchen Committee was organized in May under the chairmanship of Mrs. Phyllis St. John with Mrs. Kay Penman, Mrs. Ellen Turner, Miss Doris Moss, Mrs. Cecilia Slater, Miss Amye Love and later, Mrs. Annie Sheehan. The June *Newsletter* recorded the death in New York City of the generous benefactor, Thayer Lindsley, who had continued to contribute $12,000 a year until he set up a charitable foundation in memory of his father. It provided the Metropolitan with substantial blocks of mining shares, and its income, according to Mr. Jackman, 'largely made possible the continuance in recent years of our work at Metropolitan.'

With assistance from the Ontario Arts Council, the CREDO Committee engaged Leo Del Pasqua as an artist-in-residence from January to June 1976. For four days a week he worked in his studio (the former Junior Choir Room) on a series of paintings based on *The Revelation of John*. He participated in meetings held every second week to study the *Revelation*. Twelve enthusiastic adults enjoyed his weekly art classes. Two Saturday morning classes were arranged for children of the Church School.

The CREDO Committee, at the suggestion of the Chairman, Mrs. Margaret Norquay, launched a new and novel programme, 'August-in-the-Park', with the cooperation of the Outreach Committee. Funded by the Metropolitan Church and a grant from the Ontario Arts Council, a two-week programme of activities took place from noon until two o'clock in an effort to make the church an actual Presence to the adults who came to the park. Twenty volunteers assisted Keith Alford in arranging the games, carillon concerts, and entertainments by a mime, a gymnast, and a 'balloon man'. August-in-the-Park was so acceptable that it was decided to hold June-in-the-Park in the summer of 1977 for three weeks.

In October, Dr. Lapp visited downtown churches in Montreal and New York. He returned convinced that the Metropolitan's vital need was an 'enthused, dedicated and attending membership'. Since June a Campaign Steering Committee, under the chairmanship of Mr. Hatton, had been making plans for an every-member canvass in November. At the 157th anniversary, when Dr. Brisbin was the special preacher, Dr. Lapp commissioned the Visitors who were embarking on the canvass that afternoon.

At the Annual Meeting held on 7 February 1977, the Chairman of the Committee of Stewards, Thomas F. Shaffer, reported on the successful canvass, observing that the visits 'resulted not only in a re-awakening of

Christian love within the congregation but in an increase of thirty percent in the pledged offerings for 1977'. Heavy capital expenditures had resulted in the largest deficit that the Trustees had been asked to meet. 'A quick calculation,' he continued, 'shows that at the present rate of the sale of our endowment securities, these funds will be exhausted in less than six years!' Mr. David Walker, a Trustee, made the chilling suggestion that 'serious consideration should be given to razing the Church House'. A Task Force on the Mission of the Metropolitan Church was organized in March, chaired by Ruth Tillman, ten years after the Long-Range Planning Committee had been formed.

Dr. Lapp's vision of restoring the Metropolitan to its unofficial status of a cathedral for the United Church and all people was reflected in the meetings of the Moderator's Consultation on Churches in the Inner Core, a unique event called by the Right Reverend Wilbur Howard and hosted by the Metropolitan. Delegates came from every Conference of the United Church. The Metropolitan was represented by Mr. and Mrs. Norquay, Jean Lee and Evie Gilmour. The energetic Kitchen Committee, assisted by fifty volunteers, served three lunches, two dinners and at five coffee hours. Jim Norquay presided at a Communion Service, assisted by Keith Whitney, whose untimely death occurred six months later after a brief illness.

Dr. Cook's tenth anniversary as organist was recognized at the Sunday service on 17 June 1977 when Bascom St. John, the Chairman of the Music Committee, read the citation and invited Dr. Cook to unveil the photographic portrait that had been commissioned by the Official Board. The picture hangs today in the west stairwell of the narthex. Earlier that year, an anonymous donor had presented the church with a magnificent Steinway Grand piano to honour the musicianship of Dr. Cook and to enhance the chancel concerts of chamber music.

Midweek services were held during the weeks of Advent 1976 and Lent 1977 at 12:30 p.m. The Tuesday services were conducted by the laity; Mr. Norquay conducted a Communion service on Wednesdays; Dr. Lapp took the Thursday services. Douglas Hallman, a theological student and a trained pianist, was appointed from May to August in an experimental ministry, spending half his time at the Metropolitan, and half at the Fred Victor Mission. He conducted noon-hour services five days a week using various forms: prayer litanies, biblical expositions, free-form acts of devotion and some outdoor services in connection with 'June-in-the-Park' which proved to be so popular that Douglas and his wife continued programmes until the end of August. The next year, 'Summer-in-the-Park' was inaugurated from June until the end of August, and it has continued to the present day.

Mr. Norquay continued the midweek Communion services until November when, regretfully, they came to an end because of the heavy burden of ministerial responsibilities not only connected with the church and its membership but also with the troubled, the defeated, and the hungry who turned to the church in their need for succour and advice.

The Public Relations Support Committee, which included Dr. Brisbin, Donald Hambleton, and Mary Stewart, produced three brochures in the autumn of 1977. Mrs. Ruth Cathcart wrote the text for the *Tour Guide* and *Welcome* brochures for the pews. Dr. Lapp prepared the text for the brochure on programmes and membership.

The worship services, traditional in form but with liturgical variety, were attracting larger congregations. Young people appreciated the 'substance' of Dr. Lapp's teaching ministry which illuminated the Bible, explained Christian doctrine, addressed social issues and gave a message of Christian hope for those bowed down by adversity or perplexity. The services had a unity of purpose in prayers, Scripture and music. Weekly consultations with Dr. Cook, who had been given the forthcoming themes well in advance, prompted him to write in his report of 1983 that their association was 'unique in my long career as a church musician'.

The 160th Anniversary was celebrated for fifteen weeks with a series of Sunday services beginning on 10 September 1978 with 'Our Moderator', when the Right Reverend George Tuttle was the preacher. The celebrations concluded with 'Our Family' on 17 December when the children of the Church School lighted the Advent candles, read from Scripture, received the offering, and after the Congregational Christmas Luncheon, presented a simple but moving Nativity pageant. At the service, 'Our City', the flag of the City of Toronto was received from the Acting Mayor, Fred Beavis, and dedicated by Dr. Lapp. The theme for Anniversary Sunday on 5 November was 'Our Church' when the Reverend Dr. Howard Pentland, Deputy-Secretary of the General Council, preached the sermon. Scripture was read and greetings were expressed by Bishop Hugh Stiff, the Dean of Toronto, representing St. James' Cathedral; by Monsignor Pearce Lacey from St. Michael's Cathedral; and by the Reverend Dr. Eoin Mackay who represented St. Andrew's Presbyterian Church. At the congregational luncheon which followed the service, 'Our Congregation', the

Task Force on the future of Metropolitan informed the gathering that a new site was being considered for the National Headquarters of the United Church. It was agreed that a letter should be sent proposing the north end of the Metropolitan property as a convenient location. The Task Force hoped that such a building might resolve the deep financial problems faced by the congregation.

During the weeks of celebration, the Congregational Life and Work Committee arranged the first 'At Home', designed to give new members an opportunity to become acquainted with the congregation. It was so successful that 'At Homes' became a regular part of the church's programme, twice a year. The Festival Choir presented Handel's *Stabat Mater*, the Silver Band gave a Remembrance Day as well as a Christmas concert. A reunion of Dr. McIntosh's IHS Class and the Couples' Club, the first since the 150th Anniversary, took place in October when eighty-five people gathered for a Thanksgiving dinner prepared by the Kitchen Committee. Charlie Matthews was the Master of Ceremonies at this jolly affair. Their beloved leader, Dr. McIntosh, died six months later on 4 April 1979.

In an article, 'Visions of Faith', Dr. Lapp wrote in the January *Newsletter:* 'Our series of services commemorating the 160th Anniversary *affirmed* us in our place and *confirmed* us in our mission.' At the Annual Meeting in January, a new harmonious spirit was evident after a decade of acrimonious debates. Dr. Lapp's wise admonitions to the Task Force, the Stewards, the Official Board, and, by request, to the congregation through the *Newsletter*, had been fruitful. Another three-year period of deficit financing was authorized by the members who were determined to pursue 'a programme of membership recruitment and financial stabilization'. The CLAW Committee printed a brochure, *Invitation to the Metropolitan Church*. A careful membership analysis, begun in 1976 with the Every Member Canvass, had revealed that about three hundred people had moved away, died, or become inactive. These names were put on a reserve list leaving three hundred and seventy members and one hundred and twenty adherents to carry on the work of the church and the upkeep of the property. A Stewardship Campaign, under the leadership of John Bryce, had gratifying results.

In response to a request from a group in the congregation, the Metropolitan Study Class began its informal meetings in the Morley Punshon Room in January 1979 with a study of Paul's *Epistle to the Philippians* led by Dr. Lapp, an excellent teacher who translated his wide theological and biblical knowledge into understandable terms as he skilfully and patiently led the discussions. Adults of all ages, from young people in their twenties to those in their eighties, took advantage of this opportunity to study the Word of God. This class continued until March 1984.

The historic bond between the Metropolitan and Victoria University was rekindled on 28 March 1979 when the Baccalaureate Service took place in our 'cathedral' beginning a custom that has continued to the present day. The next month, the church was filled to capacity for the Ordination Service of the fifty-fifth annual Toronto Conference. The members of the U.C.W. baked one hundred and forty-four dozen cookies for the receptions that were held after these services.

The Worship Committee planned in detail the Sunday morning service held in October to commemorate the International Year of the Child. Lloyd Perry, the Official Guardian for the Province of Ontario, returned to the Metropolitan that Sunday as the special preacher. Representatives from government, from the judiciary, the consular service, and the United Church of Canada, were invited to attend. Children were represented by the Church School, the Junior Choir of St. Michael's Choir School, and by Scouts and Guides from central Toronto. Mrs. Yvonne Frazer and Mrs. Ann Shaffer were the Co-ordinators of the Metropolitan Church School, which though small in numbers, was praised by Dr. Lapp as an 'attractive, spiritually sound, Christ-centred experience for boys and girls on a Sunday morning'. They were succeeded by Mrs. Cynthia Lash.

The fiftieth anniversary of the rebuilt church was celebrated on 16 December 1979, with the band that had been affiliated with the church for forty-five years in attendance. The Very Reverend A.B.B. Moore was the guest preacher. Dr. Lapp dedicated the seven-branched candelabra, the gift of the Guild, and the new hymn boards presented by Mrs. H.R. Jackman in memory of her mother, Mrs. N.W. Rowell.

The funeral of Henry Rutherford Jackman had taken place on 26 November 1979 in the church he had served with devotion for almost fifty years. In an obituary, David Walker, the Secretary of the Board of Trustees wrote: 'A strong case could be made that without his inspired stewardship, the Metropolitan would have closed its doors.' A memorial tablet was placed in the church by his family on 7 December 1980.

On Sunday afternoon, 20 January 1980, eighty people from downtown churches met at St. James' Cathedral for instruction before visiting the apartments of the new St. Lawrence Neighbourhood. Twenty visitors were from the Metropolitan. Going in pairs, they distributed folders bearing the word 'Welcome' in twenty languages and a list of all the churches in the area. Encouraged by the City Council, thousands of people who had grown tired of suburban living, were returning to the downtown area where houses were being restored and new apartments were being built. Many people, new to the community, were finding their way to the Metropolitan where they were warmly welcomed.

Mr. Norquay submitted his resignation in March 1980 to take effect at the end of June when he planned to assume less arduous duties as a hospital chaplain. His sudden death on 9 May, while on holiday, shocked and saddened the congregation he had served faithfully and well. Because Dr. Lapp had taken no study leave for two years, he continued with his plans to study in Wales and to visit the Holy Land for the first time. Mr. Hatton was appointed the Assistant Minister for the third time while a Pastoral Relations Committee searched for a new Associate Minister.

The Executive of the World Methodist Council convened in Toronto in September 1980, almost seventy years after the memorable meetings held in 1911. Methodists from all over the world gathered for three services in the Metropolitan sanctuary. The Kitchen Committee catered for two luncheons and a banquet, assisted by volunteers from the congregation. After the dinner, the Metropolitan Silver Band gave a short concert in the church, closing their programme with 'Mine Eyes Have Seen the Glory of the Coming of the Lord' which they played with such deep religious fervour that the audience spontaneously rose in appreciation when it ended. The Band, taken aback, rose with the audience in homage to the Glory of the Lord.

The Queen's York Rangers (First American Regiment) that had attended the Remembrance Day service in 1978, decided to become formally affiliated with the Metropolitan Church in October 1980. The York Rangers had come to York in 1793 at the request of John Graves Simcoe who wanted a corps to help build the new community and to serve as a military presence as well. (John McGill, who arrived with the Regiment, became the first owner of McGill Square.) It was to these men that Elijah Woolsey, the Methodist circuit-rider, probably preached in 1795. The regiment disbanded in 1802 and was not reactivated until the Rebellion of 1837. The York Militia was organized before the War of 1812. After serving in the 1837 Rebellion and the Fenian raids, the regiment was renamed the York Rangers in 1872. Both regiments served in the First World War and were amalgamated in 1936 as the Queen's York Rangers. A document of affiliation with the Metropolitan Church was signed on 7 October 1980 by Ian F. Rankin, Fred T. Stinson and Dr. Lapp, when it was agreed that the church would become 'the safe repository for the Regimental Colours'. Sunday 19 October was designated 'Affiliation Sunday'.

In 1981 the United Church decided not to move its Headquarters to the Metropolitan site. As by this time encroachments from the Trust Funds had become alarming, the Trustees forged ahead with other measures to stabilize the finances and to replenish the Trust Funds. Steps were taken to inaugurate the Metropolitan Heritage Fund, which was officially established in January 1982 to receive capital gifts and bequests. The response of the congregation and friends to an appeal to provide such capital donations was most encouraging. In addition, the Trustees explored the possibility of selling the church's Commercial Density Rights (known popularly as Air Rights), which sale would not affect the buildings on the property in any way. While the 'air rights' were not sold, an option agreement for their sale was negotiated, which proved to be of substantial financial benefit to the Church. John Bryce, the Chairman of the Trustees, was able to report:

> In the light of these events, your Trustees are very optimistic about the future financial well-being of our church.

The Reverend Orville P. Hossie was appointed the Pastoral Assistant in January 1981. He and his talented wife, Greta, soon earned a firm place in the life of the church. He assisted the Roll Committee and prepared the Congregational Directory, in addition to pastoral responsibilities.

Following the service on Sunday 31 May, a congregational meeting unanimously voted that Mr. Hatton should be named Pastor Emeritus, to honour his long association with the Metropolitan. A reception followed the meeting which gave the congregation the opportunity of expressing to Mr. and Mrs. Hatton their affectionate gratitude.

The Reverend Patricia Ann Howes was inducted on 5 July and on that day began her happy association with the Metropolitan. She came well qualified for the work of the church. After graduation from Queen's University with a master's degree in Divinity, she took a nine-month course in Clinical Pastoral Counselling. She served as a chaplain at Kingston Pennitentiary for Women and at the Hamilton Psychiatric Hospital. She came to us from the Trinity-Elfreda Charge in the Hamilton Presbytery and remained at the Metropolitan until February 1986. The Very Reverend Wilbur Howard became affiliated with the Church as an Honorary Associate in September 1981, joining what Dr. Lapp playfully referred to as his '4 H Club' (Howes, Hatton, Hossie, Howard).

In June 1981 Dr. Lapp was inducted as the Chairman of the Toronto Area Presbytery for a two-year term. In September, Mr. Frank Lehman, who had recently retired, became a voluntary Business Manager, a post that removed administrative duties from the clergy staff and has continued to be a most important service. Frank and Audrey Lehman came to the Metropolitan in Dr. Bryce's time. Frank served as Chairman of the Property Committee for nine arduous years from 1962 to 1971. He continued on the Committee, served as a Steward and became the Church Treasurer in 1977.

With the additional staff, it was possible to hold midweek Lenten services again in 1982 on Wednesdays at 12:30 and 5:00 p.m. The Worship Committee decided to continue them through the summer months. In September they became a regular part of the devotional life of the church until Easter, 1984. For the first time in fifteen years, regular evening services, named 'Worship at Seven' by Dr. Howard, began on an experimental basis on 24 October 1982. The *Newsletter* reported:

> This has been a long-standing objective of many members of our congregation and we thank the Worship Committee and our ministers for bringing it to fulfillment.

These quiet services were held in the West transept with Lloyd Frazer and Michael Hart as the pianists, leading in the singing of familiar hymns. The Band played occasionally. People from the community came regularly to these simple and helpful services which continued until September 1984.

In May 1982, Dr. Lapp and the Reverend John Murray, minister of St. Andrew's-on-the-Terrace Presbyterian Church in Wellington, New Zealand, exchanged pulpits, manses and cars. This invitation came as an honour and an opportunity for Dr. Lapp and as an enriching experience for the Metropolitan. In writing to an official in New Zealand, Tom Shaffer wrote: 'Both our ministers will return to us with new ideas and a fresh outlook that can only benefit both our churches.'

Soon after Dr. Lapp's return, the Outreach Committee commenced an emergency programme of 'Food for Families' after discussions with other churches in the area and with government officials. The economic recession, the scarcity of affordable housing and the rising costs of commodities, had brought severe hardship to people living on unemployment insurance, on pensions or welfare, or insufficient income. A special congregational meeting authorized the distribution of Emergency Food Parcels 'over our long cold winter'. Money and food were solicited from the congregation. Assistance came from sources outside the church. Gordon Redford acted as the purchaser of food which was packed and carefully distributed by a staff of volunteer members. Thousands of men, women and children took advantage of this service until it was discontinued in May 1984.

The year 1982 abounded in celebrations. It marked the forty-fifth anniversary of the Bond Street Nursery School and the twentieth anniversary of Mrs. Irene Mather's connection with it. Mrs. Jean Faber, the Minister's Secretary since 1972, read the Scripture Lesson and was honoured at a reception following the service on 28 March. The carillonneur, James Slater, celebrated his twentieth anniversary in conjunction with the sixtieth anniversary of the carillon. Summer-in-the-Park planned to have sixty carillon recitals to celebrate the sixty years. The choir arranged a testimonial dinner to honour Dr. Cook on his seventieth birthday which coincided with his fifteenth anniversary as organist. That summer an anonymous donor provided money for the first series of James Norquay Memorial Concerts of classical music which have continued as a weekly attraction of Summer-in-the-Park.

During the summer of 1981, the narthex was manned by volunteers who welcomed the people who came inside the church for prayer, meditation or to admire the beautiful sanctuary. This service was found to be not only rewarding but necessary and it has continued year round, seven days a week, as the Narthex Circle of Volunteers. A brief history was prepared in 1982 to be given to interested visitors who came from all parts of the city, Canada, and the world. That summer a visitor from England took the pamphlet to the Reverend James Gattrick, the minister of Punshon Memorial Methodist Church in Bournemouth. He wrote to Dr. Lapp expressing his interest in reading of our connection with Morley Punshon who had been responsible for building the Bournemouth church. A correspondence resulted in a summer exchange of pulpits in 1983.

Mr. Ray Potten paid tribute to the clergy at the Annual Meeting of 31 January 1983:

> Dr. Douglas Lapp, our spiritual leader and mentor is, I am sure, justly proud of his colleagues as he co-ordinates the ever-growing activities at Metropolitan. In his capable, resourceful and dedicated hands, our ancient heritage is secure and its future assured....In our congregation there is a new sense of direction of which we are all a part.

Because of the number of memorial gifts received by the Heritage Fund, John Bryce, the Chairman of the Trustees, brought to the Official Board in June 1983 the suggestion that a Memorial Book Committee be appointed to make sure that these gifts would be permanently and suitably recorded. Mrs. Phyllis St. John chaired the Committee made up of William and Evelyn Goddard, Enid Schulze, Isabel Uren and Dr. Hossie.

Summer-in-the-Park reached its potential that year as an extension of the outreach ministry of the church. Under the direction of Barbara Bouck, the park achieved a spirit of community. She has been able to give a sense of purpose to the discouraged, through programmes and informal contacts.

In October 1983, Dr. Cooke conducted the Festival Choir and Orchestra in the presentation of Elgar's *Dream of Gerontius* which was acclaimed a triumph. The church was again filled to capacity for Bach's *St. Matthew Passion* which Dr. Cook had conducted every Easter since 1972. The members of the Band published a history, *Metropolitan Silver Band Celebration 50,* for their fiftieth anniversary in 1984.

Dr. Lapp accepted an invitation from Westdale United Church in Hamilton. He left at the end of April 1984 leaving Ann Howes in charge of all ministerial duties until the induction of Dr. Bruce McLeod the following October. During the eight years of Dr. Lapp's pastorate, the people of the Metropolitan were led through the deep waters of discouragement to the threshold of a future of promise and opportunity. May Almighty God continue, as the old hymn affirms, to 'strengthen them, help them, and cause them to stand, upheld by His righteous, omnipotent hand'. Amen.

In 1976, Lord Donald Soper of England, internationally famous for his open-air sermons on Hyde Park Corner in London, visited the Metropolitan and led an outdoor service.

One of the two huge banners hung on either side of the chancel in memory of Marjorie Wood.

LIST OF PHOTOGRAPHIC PLATES

INDEX